Borges, between History and Eternity

Borges, between History and Eternity

Hernán Díaz

continuum

Continuum International Publishing Group
A Bloomsbury company

50 Bedford Square	80 Maiden Lane
London	New York
WC1B 3DP	NY 10038

www.continuumbooks.com

Library of Congress Cataloging-in-Publication Data
A catalog record for this book is available at the Library of Congress.

ISBN: HB: 978-1-4411-8811-3
PB: 978-1-4411-9779-5

Typeset by Deanta Global Publishing Services, Chennai, India

Para mis padres, Ana y Pablo

CONTENTS

PREFACE

South, north, beyond

Two circumstances mitigate the somewhat grandiose title of this book. The first is that it is not fully mine, but a paraphrase of one of Borges's own titles, that of his 1936 collection of essays, *History of Eternity*. The paradox condensed in those three words highlights the fundamental distinction that inspires my own book: the opposite of eternity is not ephemerality or brevity—after all, as Borges has shown repeatedly through Zeno's parable, even the shortest segment of time or space can be subjected to infinite subdivisions. The opposite of eternity is history: if eternity is an abstraction, history is material; if eternity is universal, history is particular; if eternity is a smooth, unmarked continuum, history is nothing but notches. This leads to the second justification of my title: it identifies the extremes between which Borges seems to be trapped. On the one hand, the Latin American writer with his political contradictions; his profoundly Argentine language, topics, and characters (yet skirting, miraculously, becoming a folkloric curiosity); his old *criollo* lineage, his gaucho fetishes, and his knife-fighting obsession; his profoundly revolutionary views of literary history; and his subversive conception of the canon. On the other hand, the cosmic mystic, the labyrinth-maker, with his incorporeal enigmas; his passion for obscure metaphysical conundrums; his esoteric and apocryphal references; his universal approach to literature; his theological thought experiments; and his nesting realities that ultimately show there is no reality. In brief, the "historical" vision of Borges is context-saturated, while the "eternal" view is context-deprived.

This tension between history and eternity is not always clear-cut or irreconcilable, and in Borges's own texts these lines often intertwine. However, among Borges scholars there tends to be an opposition between the "institutional" and "transcendental" approaches. The first position could be best illustrated by Borges's own "The Argentine Writer and Tradition." In this 1951 lecture, Borges reflects on the definition of "national literature," analyzes how it relates to history, and finally overturns basic hierarchies by arguing that the periphery is a far more productive territory for a writer than the center. Although the following passage has been quoted countless times, it is worth reproducing it here once again: "What is Argentine tradition? I believe that this question poses no problem and can easily be answered. I believe that our tradition is the whole Western culture, and I also believe that we have a right to this tradition, a greater right than that which the inhabitants of one Western nation or another may have" (SF 425–26) ["¿Cuál es la tradición argentina? Creo que podemos contestar fácilmente y que no hay problema en esta pregunta. Creo que nuestra tradición es toda la cultura occidental, y creo también que tenemos derecho a esta tradición, mayor que el que pueden tener los habitantes de una u otra nación occidental" (OC 272)]. Borges then quotes Veblen, who "says that Jews are prominent in Western culture because they act within that culture and at the same time do not feel bound to it by any special devotion" (SF 426) ["dice que [los judíos] sobresalen en la cultura occidental, porque actúan dentro de esa cultura y al mismo tiempo no se sienten atados a ella por una devoción especial" (OC 272)]. This sets the stage for Borges's main point: "I believe that Argentines, and South Americans in general, are in an analogous situation; we can take on all the European subjects, take them on without superstition and with an irreverence that can have, and already has had, fortunate consequences" (SF 426) ["Creo que los argentinos, los sudamericanos en general, estamos en una situación análoga; podemos manejar todos los temas europeos, manejarlos sin supersticiones, con una irreverencia que puede tener, y ya tiene, consecuencias afortunadas" (OC 273)]. Expanding the premises and consequences of this hypothesis occupies a great number of Borges scholars who investigate his ideas on tradition and innovation, his provocatively "minor" literature, and his appropriation of the "margins." These contextual readings are concerned with Borges's interventions in history—in both a political and literary sense. How (and why) does Borges connect, say, Evaristo Carriego and Heinrich Heine or Ralph Waldo Emerson and Justo José de Urquiza? How does his fascination with Argentine popular myths coexist with his rabid anti-Peronism, or his obsession with an archetypal Argentina with his cosmopolitan approach to literature? How did his avant-garde writings break with Latin American *modernismo*, and how are these early experiments related to the classical style of his later period? How does he splice "high" and "popular" literature? How did he manage to turn a physical space (the *orillas*, the outskirts of Buenos Aires, a margin that is neither urban nor rural) into a literary territory that revised the contrast between the modern lettered city and the romanticized, rustic *pampas*? How did he turn these *orillas* into a synecdoche of Argentina as a whole? These are a few of the important questions that have been asked from the historical perspective over the years.

On the other hand, there is the transcendental approach, according to which Borges is an almost inexplicable celestial body orbiting in ether, a blind sage detached from tradition—*any* tradition. As with the contextual approach, Borges himself was to a large extent responsible for this kind of reception. Many of his stories seem to take place out of time and in an untraceable space, like "The Library of Babel" or "The Circular Ruins." His essays too are hard to pin down to a particular period or country: where does one place the author of "A Defense of the Kabbalah," *Nine Dantesque Essays*; "On *Gauchesca* Poetry," "The Translators of *The Thousand and One Nights*," "The Kenningar," "Nathaniel Hawthorne," and "Paul Valéry as a Symbol"? The span of these (randomly chosen) titles certainly makes it difficult to ascribe Borges to one single geographical and chronological domain—a difficulty that is often resolved by not associating him with any tradition at all. The grotesquely ignorant opening sentence of a review published by *Time* magazine in 1967 sums this up: "Argentina has no national literature, but it has produced a literary mind that is as mysterious and elusive as the fretted shadows on the moonlit grass." This nonsense condenses, with the eloquence of a caricature, the "universalist" approach: Borges is a magical occurrence, springing from the void ("Argentina has no national literature"), to present us with enigmatic, cosmic riddles (note, also, the reviewer's lyrically cryptic tone). Many academics have indulged in this kind of talk as well. A professor from the University of Texas declares, in his introduction to *Dreamtigers*, that Borges's is "the work of a spirit so withdrawn that solitude has enlarged it and made him now see in that solitude the secret of the whole universe, now tremble before its undecipherable mysteries" (12). These farcical snippets are a *reductio ad absurdum* of an approach that has of course also asked valid questions. What are the philosophical implications of the nesting worlds so recurrent in Borges's fiction, those *mises en abyme* where each new layer questions the authenticity of the preceding one? What does Borges's questioning of authorship and originality tell us about the crisis of the notion of subjectivity? How do his vast metaphysical conspiracies affect the definition of "reality" and the ways in which it is represented? How do his elusive erudition and his distortion of literary genres (mainly by blurring the boundary between essay and fiction) shift the location and even challenge the presence of truth in writing? How do his essays and stories about imaginary (or outrageous) literatures and linguistic systems show the limitations of our own natural languages? These are only some of the important issues raised by the "transcendental" angle.

Both perspectives are, that is to say, equally limiting and productive, and *Borges, between History and Eternity* aims to intervene into one approach from the other. Nothing represents better the opposition between history and eternity than politics and metaphysics, which is the subject of "Political Theology," the first half of this book. My general thesis is that there is a chiasmic relationship between these interests in Borges's literature. Put differently, it is in Borges's more "metaphysical" texts where we find his most daring political interventions—and vice versa. If, for instance, all things are (according to Plato) a degraded copy of their archetype, then there is a "more real" reality behind reality. If the world requires (as Berkeley believed) a permanent perceiver in order to be, our own existence depends on being observed by a higher instance. Philosophical problems like these, dealt with in the first chapter of this book, obsessed Borges, and they provide a blueprint for a political theory. Following (and slightly bending) the Platonic premise, everyday life is a fiction, an ideological fabrication imposed on us; and extending (and slightly distorting) the Berkeleian principle, we live under continuous surveillance, constantly scrutinized. In this sense, many of Borges's classic allegories, like the map of an empire whose size is that of the empire, or the chessman moved by a hand moved by god moved by a god behind god, are not mere abstractions but rather reflections on how power may manipulate our perception of the world and condition our interaction with it.

Conversely, his more overtly political texts tend to be sustained by a particular take on metaphysics. A good example (analyzed in detail in this book) is his political poetry. Borges wrote many poems commemorating historical figures with clear ideological connotations and has several odes to the *patria* (not an easy term to translate; neither "homeland" nor "fatherland" do it justice). He even wrote poems celebrating contemporary events, such as the *Revolución Libertadora*, the military uprising that overthrew Perón in 1955. In each of these cases, when Borges needs to define the "patria" and the emotions it stirs, he invariably turns to metaphysics: it is an idea, an archetype; it depends on a transcendental perceiver; etc. In brief, if Borges's take on Plato and Berkeley (to continue with the same examples) is susceptible to a political reading, it is also true that his political texts are susceptible to a metaphysical reading. Idealism supports his view of material history in the same way material determinations inform his view of idealism. However, Borges's particular articulation between politics and metaphysics outlined in the first half of the book may have been impossible without his peculiar appropriation of a couple of North American writers.

North American literature is the foreign tradition that influenced Borges the most—although he would probably claim that the English canon made the greatest impact. Nevertheless, as I will show, Whitman's presence alone in Borges's literature justifies my assertion. In addition to Whitman, North American literature in general pervades Borges's entire work. He wrote about Emerson, Hawthorne, Melville, William and Henry James, Twain, Bret Harte, Bierce, and Lovecraft, among others; he reviewed numerous American films; he was obsessed with American criminals and hoodlums, from Billy the Kid to Al Capone; he translated Faulkner's *The Wild Palms*; he helped promote detective fiction as a serious literary genre, and made significant contributions to it. In fact, as I will argue, Poe was as important to Borges as Whitman. "The United States of America," the second half of this book, explores how these two quintessential North American authors constitute the historical determinations that make some of Borges's seemingly context-deprived, "eternal" texts possible.

The first section of this second part, "Edgar Allan Poe (On Murder Considered as Metaphysics)," shows how Borges's more "universal" and "metaphysical" stories are, in fact, grounded in a particular take on North American history and its literature—though these, of course, are not their sole sources. Rather than viewing, as most of his forerunners and contemporaries did, the United States as the culmination of instrumental reason (for better or for worse), Borges unorthodoxly focuses on its barbaric side. This is the case with his North American stories in *A Universal History of Infamy*, all of which deal with hoodlums, gangsters, and killers in what seems to be a lawless state of nature or a "war of all against all." All this, however, changes with Poe, the creator of a figure that rationalizes violence— the detective. Even the most brutal crimes (the murderer in the first detective story ever written is, in fact, literally, a brute) can be subjected to and understood through reason. And thanks to the detective, who is capable of *making sense* of what does not even register as a sign at all to the ordinary eye. By looking for clues and deciphering them, the detective turns the entire world into a legible surface. This is, then, a historical component of many of Borges's "transcendental" stories: the idea of the entire universe as something readable ("The Library of Babel"), the notion that the solution to the most transcendental enigmas are encrypted in some ordinary object ("The Writing of the God"), or the perception of reality as a vast conspiracy ("The Lottery in Babylon" or "Tlön, Uqbar, Orbis Tertius") can, in fact, be traced back to Borges's fascination with different American criminals—a fascination later filtered through Poe.

"Walt Whitman, an American, a Kosmos," the second part of the North American section,[1] follows Borges's lifelong fascination with Whitman. No other foreign author is so visible in his work, from his first book (1923) to his last (1985). Not only did he write *about* Whitman profusely (and translate an abridged version of *Leaves of Grass*) but he also wrote *like* Whitman. This formal influence, I claim, is evident in most of his books of poetry, but I also show how Whitman is present in Borges's prose. No one else (not even his most beloved authors, such as Shakespeare, Johnson, De Quincey, and Stevenson) affected Borges's style as profoundly and as consistently over time. In his relationship with Whitman, Borges,

---

[1] The title paraphrases a verse in "Song of Myself": "Walt Whitman, an American, one of the roughs, a kosmos . . ." (50).

once again, reexamines the articulation of historical determinations and transcendental ambitions. Borges sees in Whitman the first politically "engaged" writer. It is the desire to represent the experience of American democracy that leads Whitman to question the notion of a central subject (the epic hero but also the figure of the author himself) in favor of a plural protagonist, and to include in his poem every single aspect, person and action of the world in equal terms, abolishing hierarchical boundaries. However, what is a material determination in Whitman becomes, in Borges, a purely intellectual "game with infinitude" (paraphrasing "Borges and I"), removed from its historical and political sources. There is, again, a chiasmus: Poe, the "decadent" writer, designing puzzles of ratiocination, is the prime source of Borges's political fiction—the one dealing with conspiracies, paranoia, and the administration of reality. On the other hand, Whitman, the "engaged" writer, singing to America and its novel political configuration, becomes the inspiration for fundamental aspects of Borges's aesthetic program (such as a literature freed from the tyranny of a central subject—the author) and the source of many of his experiments with eternity and totality, such as "The Aleph." In other words, Poe and Whitman, each in his own fashion, provided Borges with a way to articulate America and the "kosmos," the historical and the eternal.

The confluence of the universal and the historical is not, therefore, an accidental detail in Borges's literature. It is one of its defining traits and one of its driving forces from the very beginning. Indeed, one of Borges's first essays contains a passage that, in retrospect, reads like a manifesto. In "El tamaño de mi esperanza," published in 1926, Borges considers the problems inherent in the opposition between progressiveness (which he views as too Europeanizing and even North Americanizing) and *criollismo* (which has become a mere nostalgic longing for Argentine fetishes and clichés) and resolves that the solution is to widen ("enanchar") the definition of *criollismo*. Borges concludes with a statement that can be taken as the program guiding great part of his future work: "Let it be *criollismo*, then, but a *criollismo* able to address the world and the self, God and death. I hope someone helps me find it." ["Criollismo, pues, pero un criollismo que sea conversador del mundo y del yo, de Dios y de la muerte. A ver si alguien me ayuda a buscarlo" (TE 14)]. To a large extent, this book can be considered a tentative response to this call.

PART ONE

Political Theology

Introduction

If Borges is often perceived as a writer utterly detached from reality, dealing in abstractions, literary puzzles, and unsolvable philosophical riddles, it is mostly because of his own doing. He cultivated this myth in his texts ("Borges," the shy bibliophile, is a character in several of his stories and poems), and in the all too numerous interviews he indiscriminately granted toward the end of this life, where he played the part of the blind sage, slightly confused by the world, surprised to find himself, somehow, in the present, turning every earthly matter into a literary one. To his credit, he famously denounced his own affectations and how they had become "attributes of an actor" ["atributos de un actor"] in "Borges and I" (SF 324) ["Borges y yo" (OC 808)]. In that same text, he admits that his "games with time and infinitude" ["juegos con el tiempo y con lo infinito"] have also become clichés of his public act.[1] It is these "games with time and infinitude," supposedly removed from reality and concerned only with speculative, esoteric matters, that most readers (and dictionaries) quickly identify with the adjective "Borgesian"—how reality can be perforated

---

[1] Ironically enough, denouncing his own tics became Borges's most notorious tic. Over the years, Borges kept belittling himself for having turned into his own epigone. In the foreword to *In Praise of Darkness* (*Elogio de la sombra* [1969]), he deplores his own gimmicks and refers to "the mirrors, labyrinths, and swords that my resigned reader expects" (SP 265) ["los espejos, laberintos y espadas que ya prevé mi resignado lector" (OC 975)]. A similar self-deprecating objection can be found in "The Watcher" ["El centinela"], a poem in *The Gold of the Tigers* (*El oro de los tigres* [1972]) (SP 326; OC 1115). And yet again in "The Other" ["El otro"], a late short story included in *The Book of Sand* [*El libro de arena* (1975)]. Bioy Casares criticizes the stereotypical self-portrait that Borges draws in this last text in a 1972 entry of his journal: "Borges dines at home. He tells me the plot of his new story ["The Other"]. Admirable, with the sole flaw of being 'The Other Borges' or 'Borges and I' *once again* [English and italics in original]" ["Come en casa Borges. Me cuenta su cuento ["El otro"]: admirable, con el defecto de ser 'El otro Borges' o 'Borges y yo' *once again*" (1430)]. For the historical and literary resonances of this calculated shyness, see Alan Pauls's brilliant analysis of what he aptly calls Borges's "politics of modesty" ["política del pudor"] (47–56).

by fiction, how our waking life may be someone else's dream, how memory may completely overtake the present, how actuality can turn out to be a representation staged for our benefit, and how infinitude lurks everywhere, in the imploding subdivisions of the most insignificant segments of time and matter. All these are clearly "Borgesian" commonplaces. Yet, all these supposedly abstract brainteasers question the stability of our place in the world and expose the precariousness of the categories that rule our perception of it. In this, oddly enough, they reveal themselves to be profoundly terrestrial, inasmuch as they examine how our reality is administered, rather than merely "given." And this issue can quickly become a political one—political power is always concerned with the imposition of a reality.[2] Borges's obsession with dreams, his often outrageously skeptical arguments, his solipsistic plots, and his theological conundrums can therefore be read as the juncture where literature, metaphysics, and a general reflection on power (and the institutions that embody it) come together.

In 1933, in the magazine *Contra*, Borges wrote: "It is an insipid and notorious truth that art must not serve politics. To speak about social art is like speaking about vegetarian geometry or liberal artillery or hendecasyllabic pastry making" ["Es una insípida y notoria verdad que el arte no debe estar al servicio de la política. Hablar de arte social es como hablar de geometría vegetariana o de artillería liberal o de repostería endecasílaba" (TR II: 343)]. He considered this statement to be true enough to reproduce it verbatim in 1964 in another magazine, *La Rosa Blindada*. Even though this passage targets different opponents in each context,[3] the main point is the same—literature constitutes an autonomous sphere that must not be subordinated ("estar al servicio") to anything beyond itself.

---

[2] Sarlo eloquently summarizes this relationship between fantastical literature and politics in the introduction to the last chapter of her book (177–78).

[3] In 1933, the jab is aimed at the heirs of "Boedo," Argentina's openly "social" (to use Borges's term) literary group in the 1920s. The Boedo group (named after a working-class neighborhood in Buenos Aires) was opposed to that of Florida (in reference to the posh downtown section). Borges downplayed the rivalry between the politically engaged faction and the decadent one and even claimed that the whole affair was a hoax (see "La inútil discusión de Boedo y Florida" in TR I: 365 and "'Florida' y 'Boedo'" in TR III: 325). In its 1964 incarnation, the provocation is directed against the new generation of "engaged" writers inspired by Sartre.

There are, however, ways in which literature can be political without being in an ancillary position, and Borges's own work offers many examples of this.

Borges was, perhaps despite himself, an overtly political writer, and there are a vast number of his own texts to prove it, from a few forgotten poems to the Russian Revolution written in his youth in Switzerland to his last book of verse, *Los conjurados* (1985), whose title poem is, coincidentally, an ode to Swiss cosmopolitanism and neutrality. Several of his first essays, published in the 1920s, are strong manifestos, almost populist harangues (which he later regretted and refused to reprint), where he articulates clear cultural programs for Argentina (Borges even intended to "instigate a politics of language" ["instigar una política del idioma" (TE 39)] in these texts, some of which are written following an "Argentinean" orthography).[4] Borges also wrote several historical poems, which are, given their subject matter, necessarily political ("Rosas," "General Quiroga Rides to His Death in a Carriage" ["El general Quiroga va en coche al muere"], "Conjectural Poem" ["Poema conjetural"], "Sarmiento," "La tentación," and "Juan López y John Ward" are just a few and random examples of many). During World War II, while Argentina remained neutral (and notwithstanding a widespread philo-Nazi atmosphere), he produced essays denouncing the Nazi regime (such as "Two Books" ["Dos libros"], "An Essay on Neutrality" ["Ensayo de imparcialidad"], "A Comment on 23 August 1944" ["Anotación al 23 de agosto de 1944"], "Definition of a Germanophile" ["Definición de germanófilo"], his review of Watherhouse's *A Short History of German Literature*, and "1941"). He also wrote politically outspoken fiction: "*Deutsches Requiem*" (the soliloquy of a Nazi officer the night before his execution), "The Secret Miracle" ["El milagro secreto"] (about the execution of a Jewish scholar and playwright during the Czech occupation), "The Simulacrum" ["El simulacro"] (narrating the staging of Evita's fictitious funeral in a small town), or "La fiesta del monstruo" (an anti-Peronist, and, to an enormous extent, classist and xenophobic satire written together with Bioy Casares) are a few of the stories of this nature.

---

[4] "Queja de todo criollo" (in *Inquisiciones* [1925]), "La pampa y el suburbio son dioses," and "Las coplas acriolladas" (in *El tamaño de mi esperanza* [1926]) are some examples of these exalted essays.

Finally, Borges's tightest connection with politics comes from the fact that he had an extremely personal relationship with Argentine history. In a 1967 interview published by *The Paris Review*, Borges offered a succinct account of his lineage:

> I come from military stock. My grandfather, Colonel Borges, fought in the border warfare with the Indians and he died in a revolution; my great grandfather, Colonel Suárez, led a Peruvian cavalry charge in one of the last great battles against the Spaniards; another great uncle of mine led the vanguard of San Martín's army—that kind of thing. And I had, well, one of my great-great-grandmothers was a sister of Rosas—I'm not especially proud of that relationship, because I think of Rosas as being a kind of Perón in his day; but still all those things link me with Argentine history and also with the idea of a man's having to be brave, no? (122)[5]

Given his lineage, Borges often sees the national past in a romantic light, as an extension of his own family romance. He writes of himself (in the third person), at the end of his *Obras completas*, in an entry of an imaginary future encyclopedia, supposedly published in 2074: "He [Borges] was of military lineage, and felt nostalgic about the epic destiny of his ancestors" ["Era de estirpe militar y sintió la nostalgia del destino épico de sus mayores" (OC 1144)]. This is also why, according to Borges himself, he felt attracted to knife fights, gangsters, hoodlums, and other violent figures—he believed this fascination was a degraded, distorted (even secular)

---

[5] Edmund Williamson gives a more detailed chronicle of Borges's ancestry: "On his mother's side, Fancisco de Laprida was president of the congress that declared the independence of the 'United Provinces of South America.' General Miguel Estanislao Soler commanded a division in the patriot army that the great Argentine liberator, San Martín, lead across the Andes to free Chile and then Peru from the Spanish yoke. On his father's side, Juan Crisóstomo Lafinur was one of the first poets of Argentina and a friend of Manuel Belgrano, a founding father of the nation. . . . Isidoro Suárez, a great-grandfather on his mother side . . . , at the age of twenty-four, . . . led the cavalry charge that turned the tide of the battle at Junín, the second-last engagement in the liberation of South America" (3). And in 1870, "Borges's grandfather, Colonel Francisco Borges . . . commanded the troops sent by President Sarmiento to suppress the gaucho rebellion in [the province of] Entre Ríos" (9). Borges elaborates on his ancestors in AN 41–42.

embodiment of the epic, and quasireligious exaltation of his elders: "He thought," Borges continues in the apocryphal encyclopedia, "that courage was one of the few virtues men are capable of, but idolizing it led him, as it did many others, to the clumsy veneration of criminals" ["Pensaba que el valor es una de las pocas virtudes de que son capaces los hombres, pero su culto lo llevó, como a tantos otros, a la veneración atolondrada de los hombres del hampa" (OC 1144)]. Ancestry, history, and literature intersect in many of his texts, for instance the second of his *Two English Poems*, included in *The Other, the Same* [*El otro, el mismo*, 1964], a collection of poetry published in 1964 (sometimes translated, mysteriously, as *The Self and the Other*):

> I offer you my ancestors, my dead men, the ghosts that living men have honoured in marble: my father's father killed in the frontier of Buenos Aires, two bullets through his lungs, bearded and dead, wrapped by his soldiers in the hide of a cow; my mother's grandfather—just twentyfour—heading a charge of three hundred men in Peru, now ghosts on vanished horses. (OC 862)

Borges made sure to keep these heroic myths alive by conjuring up the ghosts of his forefathers in numerous poems—"Inscripción sepulcral," "*Dulcia linquimus arva*," "Alusión a la muerte del coronel Francisco Borges (1833–74)," "Página para recordar al coronel Suárez, vencedor en Junín," "Cosas," "Una mañana," "1972," "Coronel Suárez," and "La suerte de la espada" are a few of the poems where Borges engages in "the hero worship of dead soldiers" (SP 325) ["el culto idolátrico de militares muertos" (OC 1115)], as he writes in "The Watcher" ["El centinela"].

The purpose of the following chapter is not to determine Borges's political consistency, or lack thereof—as said, he wrote poems for the Russian Revolution,[6] though he repeatedly declared

---

[6] "Rusia," published in *Grecia* on January 9, 1920 (TR I: 56–57). Later, in a 1972 interview, Borges would say that he "saw the Russian Revolution as the beginning of peace for all men, as something that has nothing to do with current Soviet imperialism" ["a la Revolución Rusa yo la veía como un principio de paz entre todos los hombres, como algo que no tiene nada que ver con el actual imperialismo soviético"] (S 16).

to be an Anarchist,[7] flirted with Rosas and rebuffed Sarmiento in his youth,[8] later became an extreme anti-Peronist,[9] joined the conservative party,[10] and declared overtly to be antidemocratic[11]. Neither do the following pages aim to establish how progressive or reactionary he was on the ideological dial. I do not intend to show how, secretly, Borges was an "engaged" writer—"The notion of art as engagement," he wrote, "is naive, for no one knows entirely what

---

[7] "At the moment, I would define myself as a harmless anarchist, this is, as a man who wants a minimum of government and a maximum of individual rights" ["Actualmente yo me definiría como un inofensivo anarquista; es decir, un hombre que quiere un mínimo de gobierno y un máximo de individuo"] (D I 59). Borges's conception of anarchism, which he claimed to have inherited from his father, who, in turn, was influenced by Spencer's *The Man versus the State* (cf. S 15–16), is probably closer to what today we would call "libertarianism." In "Our Poor individualism," he writes: "Nationalism seeks to captivate us with the vision of an infinitely tiresome State; this utopia, once established on earth, would have the providential virtue of making everyone yearn for, and finally build, its antithesis" (SNF 310) ["El nacionalismo quiere embelesarnos con una visión de un Estado infinitamente molesto; esa utopía, una vez lograda en la tierra, tendría la virtud providencial de hacer que todos anhelaran, y finalmente construyeran, su antítesis" (OC 659)]. Borges's utopia, then, was a stateless (but, of course, orderly) world: "I believe that in time we will deserve to be free of government" (CF 345) ["Creo que con el tiempo mereceremos no haya gobiernos" (OC 1021].

[8] The most conspicuous example is the title essay in *El tamaño de mi esperanza*, where he states that Sarmiento, a "Norteamericanized untamed Indian, big hater and non-understander of the *criollo*[,] europeanized us with the faith of someone who is a newcomer to culture and expects miracles from it" ["norteamericanizado indio bravo, gran odiador y desentendedor de lo criollo[,] nos europeizó con su fe de recién venido a la cultura y que espera milagros de ella" (12)]. On the other hand, "our greatest champion is still don Juan Manuel [de Rosas]: a great paragon of the fortitude of the individual, a great certainty of knowing how to live" [the phrase is almost as awkward in Spanish] ["nuestro mayor varón sigue siendo don Juan Manuel: gran ejemplar de la fortaleza del individuo, gran certidumbre de saberse vivir"] (13). See also "Queja de todo criollo" (I 140).

[9] The number of references is overwhelming. Some of his fiction dealing with Peronism has been quoted above. Ideological motives aside, Borges had personal reasons for his relentless anti-Peronism—mainly the imprisonment of both his mother and sister in 1948 after their partaking in protests against the regime (see C 136 for Borges's own account of these facts). During Perón's administration, Borges was famously "promoted" from his modest position at a small public library branch to inspector of poultry and rabbits at the municipal market. The coup that overthrew Perón in 1955 then named him the director of the National Library.

he is doing" (SP 343) ["El concepto de arte comprometido es una ingenuidad, porque nadie sabe del todo lo que ejecuta" (OC III: 75)]. Finally, I will not try to "deduce" similarities between Borges and different political philosophies—how, for instance, Borges is (without even suspecting so himself) related to Mikhail Bakunin, or secretly indebted to Max Weber, or tacitly addressing Walter Benjamin or Louis Althusser, or following Menard's "technique of deliberate anachronism" (CF 95) ["la técnica del anacronismo deliberado" (OC 450)], engaging in dialogue with Robert Nozick or Giorgio Agamben. Instead, the main purpose of the following two sections is to reveal how certain basic political concepts present *in* Borges's texts (such as his ideas of nation, power, and representation) relate to the view of metaphysics present *in* his texts (such as his concern about idealism and his syncretic approach to theology). I will show how Borges's metaphysical discussions have, to a large extent, political connotations and, conversely, how his idea of the nation, its history, and its institutions is supported and informed by metaphysics.

The purpose of the following two sections ("God and Country" and "When Fiction Lives in Fiction") is to explore the dissonance between what could hastily be called the "metaphysical" and the "political" sides of Borges's literature. I claim that both these sides coexist simultaneously and inform each other. Borges's view

---

[10] In the foreword to *Brodie's Report* [El informe de Brodie (1970)], Borges writes: "I have joined the Conservative Party, an act that is a form of skepticism" (CF 346) ["Me he afiliado al partido conservador, lo cual es una forma de escepticismo" (OC 1021)]. Later, in the apocryphal entry to the nonexistent encyclopedia that Borges wrote for the 1974 edition of his complete works, he says of himself: "Toward 1960 he joined the Conservative Party because (he used to say) 'it is doubtlessly the only one that could never stir any form of fanaticism'" ["Hacia 1960 se afilió al Partido Conservador, porque (decía) 'es indudablemente el único que no puede suscitar fanatismos'" (OC 1144)].

[11] In the foreword to *The Iron Coin* [La moneda de hierro, 1976], Borges wrote: "I am well aware that I am unworthy of uttering opinions on political matters, but perhaps I might be forgiven for doing so by adding that I have doubts about democracy, that curious abuse of statistics" (SP 371) ["Me sé del todo indigno de opinar en materia política, pero tal vez me sea perdonado añadir que descreo de la democracia, ese curioso abuso de la estadística" (OC III: 121–2)]. The text is dated 27 July 1976—four months and three days after the bloodiest military coup in Argentinean history.

of metaphysics ultimately becomes a political philosophy—the question of god, for instance, is the question of power taken to its highest instance. Conversely, beyond Borges's take on certain historical or present events (be it Rosas, Hitler, or the Malvinas War), his overtly political texts tend to slide toward metaphysics and theology.

1

God and country

"Ode Composed in 1960," a poem included in *The Maker* [*El hacedor* (1960)],[12] is a good place to begin unfolding the relationship between Borges's conception of the nation and his idea of metaphysics. It is a text that clearly engages both with Argentina's history and contemporary political events. These issues, however, are articulated in philosophical and even theological terms. The second stanza begins:

> Fatherland, I have felt you in the ruinous
> Sunsets of the vast suburbs . . .
> And in the vague, pleased memory
> Of patios with slaves bearing
> The name of their masters and in the poor
> Pages of those books for the blind
> Dispersed by fire and in the downpour
> Of the epic rains of September
> That no one will forget, but these things
> Are merely your modes and your symbols.
>
> You are more than your extended territory
> And than the days of your extended time,
> You are more than the inconceivable sum
> Of your generations. We do not know
> How you are for God in the living
> Bosom of the eternal archetypes,

---

[12] This poem was not included in Penguin's *Selected Poems*. There is a translation by Harold Morland in *Dreamtigers*. The translation offered here, however, is my own.

But for that barely glimpsed face
We live and die and yearn,
Oh inseparable and mysterious fatherland.

[Patria, yo te he sentido en los ruinosos
Ocasos de los vastos arrabales . . .
Y en la vaga memoria complacida
De patios con esclavos que llevaban
El nombre de sus amos y en las pobres
Hojas de aquellos libros para ciegos
Que el fuego dispersó y en la caída
De las épicas lluvias de setiembre
Que nadie olvidará, pero estas cosas
Son apenas tus modos y tus símbolos.

Eres más que tu largo territorio
Y que los días de tu largo tiempo,
Eres más que la suma inconcebible
De tus generaciones. No sabemos
Cómo eres para Dios en el viviente
Seno de los eternos arquetipos,
Pero por ese rostro vislumbrado
Vivimos y morimos y anhelamos,
Oh inseparable y misteriosa patria (OC 834)].

The poem, substantially abbreviated here, sings about the
landscape and riches of the homeland, extols its myths and icons,
revisits its history, and praises its heroic (for Borges) present—the
"epic rains of September" clearly remit to the *Revolución Libertadora*,
the military coup that overthrew Perón five years before the poem
was written. In a few verses, then, Borges condenses several of the
qualities that define Argentina, from its geography to its mythology,
from its colonial past to the political turmoil of the present day.
However, neither its territory nor its history suffices to define the
homeland: "You are more than your extended territory/And than
the days of your extended time." The "patria," the poem claims,
transcends these earthly determinations and even goes beyond space
and time. It can only be defined in terms of Platonic archetypes,
pure forms, and an inaccessible idea that ultimately remits to god.
Thus, the poem makes a leap from extreme historical attributes and

accidents (slaves, battles, the flag, the *Revolución Libertadora*) to a completely transcendental, metaphysical notion of the nation that can only be understood within the tradition of idealism.

If behind Borges's notion of "patria" there is a discussion with idealism, the reverse is also true. His engagement with this philosophical tradition is tinted with strong political connotations. In Borges's literature, idealism—from the Platonic notion that our immediate reality is just corrupted projection to the Berkeleian requirement of a perceiver to guarantee the being of all things—is reread in a conspiratorial key: we are trapped in a lie, which is also a Benthamic hell. The political consequences of thinking that our reality is, indeed, a deceit or a hallucination framed within a larger (and truer) world are clear: we live in some sort of a lie engineered by a higher power. Taken to the extreme, this premise reveals that theology is the continuation of politics by other means.[13] But this fractal structure of nesting realities (which will be considered at length in the next section) is not merely one of Borges's topics. It is, above all, one of his main and most recurrent formal traits: his framed stories, as we will see, are the node where politics, philosophy, and metaphysics coincide in a reciprocally mimetic fashion. In other words, fractals are not just the pattern defining Borges's fearfully symmetric ideas of time and space but rather a figure drawn by the intersection of metaphysics and politics.

The Other, the Same contains a poem that takes these issues further. "Ode Written in 1966" ["Oda escrita en 1966"], a text that has never really caught the attention of scholars and critics, resembles the one written in 1960, both in title and spirit.[14] However, the later ode is highly illustrative of the issues considered above: the most interesting political reflection takes place in the

---

[13] This paraphrase of Clausewitz demands the mention of Carl Schmitt. "Sovereignty is the highest, legally independent, underived power," writes Schmitt in his *Political Theology* (17). The representation of politics in many of Borges's texts has to do, precisely, with a literal rendition of part of this quote—the "highest" and "underived power" (but has not much to do with the legal conclusion Schmitt deduces from this definition). However, this is where, for my purposes, the relationship between both authors end. Despite the fact that the title of this chapter echoes that of Schmitt's 1922 book, I will not consider or follow his particular articulation of politics and theology, although his thoughts on the relationship between the miracle in theology and the state of exception in politics could be highly productive to read some of Borges's texts, such as, for instance, "The Secret Miracle" or "The Other Death."

poem's seemingly most apolitical moment. Paradoxically, as the text removes itself from concrete contextual events, its political stance becomes stronger; the deeper it delves into metaphysical and theological problems, the closer it gets to being a reflection on power and sovereignty. The poem, in its entirety, reads:

> No one is the homeland. Not even the rider
> High in the dawn in the empty square,
> Who guides a bronze steed through time,
> Nor those others who look out from marble,
> Nor those who squandered their martial ash
> Over the plains of America
> Or left a verse or an exploit
> Or the memory of a life fulfilled
> In the careful exercise of their duties.
> No one is the homeland. Nor are the symbols.
>
> No one is the homeland. Not even time
> Laden with battles, swords, exile after exile,
> And with the slow peopling of regions
> Stretching into the dawn and the sunset,
> And with faces growing older
> In the darkening mirrors,
> And with anonymous agonies endured
> All night until daybreak,
> And with the cobweb of rain
> Over black gardens.
>
> The homeland, friends, is a continuous act
> As the world is continuous. (If the Eternal
> Spectator were to cease for one instant
> To dream us, the white sudden lightning
> Of his oblivion would burn us up.)
> No one is the homeland, but we should all
> Be worthy of that ancient oath
> Which those gentlemen swore—

---

[14] The first edition of *El otro, el mismo* (1964) did not include "Oda escrita en 1966." The poem was originally published in the newspaper *La Nación* on 9 July (Independence Day), 1966. It was included in the sixth edition of *El otro, el mismo*.

To be something they didn't know, to be Argentines;
To be what they would be by virtue
Of the oath taken in that old house.
We are the future of those men,
The justification of those dead.
Our duty is the glorious burden
Bequeathed to our shadow by those shadows;
It is ours to save.
No one is the homeland—it is all of us.
May that clear, mysterious fire burn
Without ceasing, in my breast and yours. (SP 237)

[Nadie es la patria. Ni siquiera el jinete
Que, alto en el alba de una plaza desierta,
Rige un corcel de bronce por el tiempo,
Ni los otros que miran desde el mármol,
Ni los que prodigaron su bélica ceniza
Por los campos de América
O dejaron un verso o una hazaña
O la memoria de una vida cabal
En el justo ejercicio de los días.
Nadie es la patria. Ni siquiera los símbolos.

Nadie es la patria. Ni siquiera el tiempo
Cargado de batallas, de espadas y de éxodos
Y de la lenta población de regiones
Que lindan con la aurora y el ocaso,
Y de rostros que van envejeciendo
En los espejos que se empañan
Y de sufridas agonías anónimas
Que duran hasta el alba
Y de la telaraña de la lluvia
Sobre negros jardines.

La patria, amigos, es un acto perpetuo
Como el perpetuo mundo. (Si el Eterno
Espectador dejara de soñarnos
Un solo instante, nos fulminaría,
Blanco y brusco relámpago, Su olvido.)
Nadie es la patria, pero todos debemos

Ser dignos del antiguo juramento
Que prestaron aquellos caballeros
De ser lo que ignoraban, argentinos,
De ser lo que serían por el hecho
De haber jurado en esa vieja casa.
Somos el porvenir de esos varones,
La justificación de aquellos muertos;
Nuestro deber es la gloriosa carga
Que a nuestra sombra legan esas sombras
Que debemos salvar.
Nadie es la patria, pero todos lo somos.
Arda en mi pecho y en el vuestro, incesante,
Ese límpido fuego misterioso. (OC 938)]

Many of Borges's classic topics and verbal fetishes can be found
in this poem: his obsession with manly courage before the advent
of gunpowder (Borges's heroes brandish swords and daggers, rarely
guns), his fascination with the liminal, ambiguous space between
country and city ("The slow peopling of regions/Stretching[15] into the
dawn and the sunset"), his perennial mirrors, and the questions about
eternity and god. Shakespeare, a constant presence throughout his
work, is alluded to in the first stanza: the fatherland is "Not marble,
not the gilded monuments," as the first verse of sonnet 55 reads.
The presence of Whitman, one of Borges's most decisive influences,
is also apparent in this ode: as opposed to the 1960 ode, written
in hendecasyllables, many verses in this poem are unmetered. The
enumerations, the simultaneous negation and affirmation of the self
through the multitude, and the tone of what could hastily be call
an "American fervor" are all reminiscent of the North American
poet.[16] But particularly interesting is that in this poem Borges
overtly bridges politics and metaphysics. It is an unusual poem in
that it is very close to a nationalistic harangue, not only in tone but
also in form: the direct appeal to a mass of readers through the use
of the second person plural vocative— "friends" in the first verse

---

[15] "Bordering" is a closer translation of "lindan," a word that relates to the paradigm
of the margin and the edge ("orilla"), crucial in Borges's invention of the "suburbio"
or "arrabal" a territory that is, precisely, a "linde."

[16] The relationship between Whitman and Borges is analyzed extensively in "Walt
Whitman, an American, a Kosmos," in the second part of this book.

of the last stanza and the oddly Castilian "vuestro" (as opposed to the American "suyo," the choice one would expect in Borges) in the next-to-last verse, reminiscent, in its pomp, of loud anthems, ceremonious school performances, and inaugural speeches. The reticence to translate "patria" into its literal, etymologically obvious counterpart, "fatherland," is quite meaningful—it is precisely the loudness and objectionable overtones that resound in "fatherland" that echo in Borges's poem. Although Borges has a number of poems glorifying the nation and its heroes, his nationalism rarely is as boisterous as here.

The ode gravitates around a refrain, "nadie es la patria." No one is the fatherland. Not our founding fathers, not our literature, not our symbols, not our battles, not our territory, not our population. In this, the poem much resembles the "Oda compuesta en 1960," where Borges also lists the attributes of the nation (its land, its history, its flag, his own private fetishes) only to conclude: "but these things/Are merely your modes and your symbols." Toward the end of "Oda escrita en 1966," however, in the third line from the end, this string of negative moments finally becomes an affirmation: "No one is the fatherland—it is all of us" ["Nadie es la patria, pero todos lo somos"]. This tension between everyone and no one is one of Borges's favorite aporias (a paradox he took, as we will see, from Whitman). It deeply informs his idea of literature—a literature without authors, written by everyone and no one, and it appears, in different guises, in many of his short stories.[17] Throughout his poems, essays, and fictions, Borges explores this oscillation from nothingness to totality and back. In fact, this tension can already be found in what could be considered his second short story—a review of a nonexistent book included in a collection of essays published in 1936. Buried in a footnote at the end of the text is a gloss of a poem by Attar of Nishapur. In it, a flock of birds look indefatigably for their king, the Simurg, which in Persian means "thirty birds." After endless travails, only 30 birds remain. They finally arrive to the Simurg's mountain, "and look upon their king at last: they see that they are the Simurg and that the Simurg is each, and all, of them" (CF 87) ["Lo contemplan al fin: perciben que ellos son el Simurg

---

[17] Most famously, "Pierre Menard, Author of the *Quixote*," but also "A Survey of the Works of Herbert Quain," and "The Library of Babel."

y que el Simurg es cada uno de ellos y todos" (OC 418)].[18] Here, in a more abstract fashion, is the same notion that will reemerge, 30 years later, in the "Ode Written in 1966"—sovereignty as a metaphysical allegory that simultaneously affirms and denies the possibility of a center: "no one is the fatherland [or the Simurg], but all of us are."[19] If this paradox were to be represented geometrically, it would probably take the shape of the equally paradoxical sphere of Pascal. In his 1951 essay "Pascal's sphere," Borges writes a history of the sphere from the pre-Socratics to modernity (in three pages) to conclude with the following quote by Pascal: "Nature is an infinite sphere, the center of which is everywhere, and the circumference nowhere" (SNF 353) ["La naturaleza es una esfera infinita, cuyo centro está en todas partes y la circunferencia en ninguna" (OC 638)]. By being everywhere, the center (or the site where political power concentrates) is annulled as such—and yet emphatically affirmed in every single point of the circumference, and yet, because of its omnipresence, denied. . . .

This paradox runs through many of Borges's texts and almost always has a political connotation. Consider "The Sect of the Phoenix," a story published in 1944, about a timeless secret society (named after a bird). "There is no group of human beings that does

---

[18] The bird of birds was a permanent presence in Borges's work. Four years before, it can be found in his essay on Walt Whitman (OC 251) and, oddly enough, in his scathing review of Victor Fleming's film adaptation of *Dr. Jekyll and Mr. Hyde* (OC 286), both included in *Discusión* (1932). Borges returns to it about 50 years later, in "El Simurg y el águila," one of his *Nine Dantesque Essays* (OC III: 166–68), and it is also alluded to in "La larga busca" ("The Long Search"), an untranslated poem included in *Los conjurados*, his last book.

[19] It is rather curious that Borges did not show an interest in Thomas Hobbes. One of the few mentions of his work (the most conspicuous one being the second epigraph to "The Aleph") can be found in Borges's piece on the Simurg in his *Nine Dantesque Essays*. The resemblance between the bird composed of birds and the graphic representation of the sovereign in Hobbes's *Leviathan* is apparent, and Borges takes notes of this, comparing the Simurg with "that strange king made of men who occupies the frontispiece of *Leviathan*, armed with sword and staff" (SNF 294) ["aquel extraño rey hecho de hombres que llena el frontispicio del *Leviatán*, armado con la espada y el báculo" (OC III: 366)]. Another mention can be found in a 1975 article published by the magazine *Crisis*, where Borges, once again, refers to the illustration rather than to the text—"the famous frontispiece of *Leviathan* . . . is a plural figure . . . made up by a multitude of beings" ["el famoso gigante del frontispicio de *Leviathan* . . . es una figura plural . . . integrada por una multitud de seres" (TR III: 38)]. As I will show in the second part of this book, Borges briefly links this image to Whitman's idea of democracy.

not include adherents of the Sect of the Phoenix" (CF 172) ["No hay grupo humano en el que no figuren partidarios del Fénix" (OC 523)], and they "are indistinguishable from other men" (CF 171) ["Se confunden con los demás" (OC 522)]. The members of the Sect "like Hazlitt's infinite Shakespeare,[20] resemble every man in the world. They are all things for everyone" (CF 172) ["se parecen, como el infinito Shakespeare de Hazlitt, a todos los hombres del mundo. Son todo para todos" (OC 522)]. Furthermore, it is believed that their initiation ritual is by now instinctive—in other words, by becoming a universal natural determination, the ritual ceases being a particular cultural practice. Because the Sect is everywhere, it loses its definition as such. It is nowhere.[21]

Another clear example of an omnipresent and therefore totally absent organization can be found in "The Congress," a late short story (included in *The Book of Sand*) in which a wealthy Uruguayan landowner starts a secret society (the Congress of the World), only to realize, at the end of the story, that "The task [they had] undertaken is so vast that it embraces . . . the entire world. . . . The Congress of the World began the instant the world itself began, and it will go on when we are dust. There is no place it is not" (CF 434) ["La empresa que [han] acometido es tan vasta que abarca . . . el mundo entero. . . . El Congreso del Mundo comenzó con el primer instante del mundo y proseguirá cuando seamos polvo. No hay un lugar en que no esté" (OC III: 31)]. In both these stories a subset (the Sect or the Congress), becomes the superset: the Congress disappears *because* it is total. As Borges himself writes in the afterword, "'The Congress' is perhaps the most ambitious of this book's fables; its subject is an enterprise so vast that it merges [*se confunde con*] at

---

[20] Cf. "From Someone to Nobody" ["De alguien a nadie"] a title that is a variation on that other Borgesian juxtaposition — everything and nothing), included in Other Inquisitions [*Otras inquisiciones* (1952)]: "Hazlitt corroborated or confirmed . . . : '[Shakespeare] was just like any other man, but that he was unlike other men. He was nothing in himself, but he was all that other were, or could become'" (SNF 342) ["Hazlitt corrobora o confirma: 'Shakespeare se parecía a todos los hombres, salvo en lo de parecerse a todos los hombres. Intimamente no era nada, pero era todo lo que son los demás, o lo que pueden ser.'" (OC 738)].

[21] Many critics insist on the fact that this story is an allegory of masturbation or homosexuality—unanimous consensus on the exact nature of the activity has not been reached. Some provide more or less plausible or absurd keys to decipher the genital references supposedly scattered through the text. Others even quote conversations with Borges that would confirm this onanistic interpretation.

last into the cosmos itself and into the sum of days" (CF 484) ["*El Congreso* es quizá la más ambiciosa de las fábulas de este libro; su tema es una empresa tan vasta que se confunde al fin con el cosmos y con la suma de los días" (OC III: 72)].[22] This pan-determinism is beautifully summarized in one of Borges's *Seven Nights*: "there is no chance; what we call chance is our ignorance of the complex machinery of causality" (SN 8) ["no hay azar, salvo que lo que llamamos azar es nuestra ignorancia de la compleja maquinaria de la causalidad" (OC III: 208)].

This is also true for "The Lottery in Babylon," where the "Company" that administers the lottery expands to such an extent that it becomes a synonym of every form of causality, including what seemingly is blind chance. If the Company, at first, only is in charge of regular lottery draws, eventually, the people of Babylon "made the Company accept all public power. . . . Second, it made the lottery secret, free or charge, and open. . . . Every free man automatically took part in the sacred drawings" (CF 103) ["logró que la compañía aceptara la suma del poder público. . . . En segundo término, logró que la lotería fuera secreta, gratuita y general. . . . Todo hombre libre automáticamente participaba en los sorteos sagrados" (OC 458)]. The Company, clearly a subsection of Babylonian society, takes over the entirety of public and private life. What was once, in a strict sense, partial (some people bought lottery tickets, others did not) becomes universal ("every free man automatically participated in the sacred drawings"). An edict issued by the government, a crime of passion, or even the cry of a bird—the Company rules it all through its strictly managed chaos. There is, then, once again, an utter affirmation of the institution through its dissolution, or, put differently, the maximum of expansion coincides with a minimum of determination.

It is not a coincidence that politics is an overt presence in all these essays, poems, and stories: they all deal with institutions—kings, secret societies, a congress, a Kafkaesque "company."[23] However, most of these stories strive to blur all historical and contextual

---

[22] In the foreword to a 1982 European edition of this story, Borges wrote: "The central idea is an enterprise that expands until it embraces the history of the world" ["La idea central es la de una empresa que se dilata hasta abarcar la historia del mundo" (TR III: 208)].

[23] Kafka, in fact, is hidden in "The Lottery in Babylon": "There were certain stone lions, a sacred latrine called Qaphqa, some cracks in a dusty aqueduct" (CF 104) ["Había ciertos leones de piedra, había una letrina sagrada llamada Qaphqa" (OC 458)].

reference, either by being set in archaic, premodern times, or by playing with the notion of an almost divine timelessness.[24] As he turns away from (or distorts) direct statements on immediate historical phenomena, Borges addresses rather fundamental questions about the definition of power, its relationship to the notion of representation, and how it conditions our perception of reality. And it is precisely because Borges takes the question of power to its highest conceivable instance that it eventually becomes a theological issue. This triangulation of politics, theology, and metaphysics appears explicitly in "The Lottery in Babylon." The narrator discusses the origin of the "company's *omnipotence*—its *ecclesiastical, metaphysical* value" (CF 102; my emphasis) ["el *todopoder* de la Compañía: su valor *eclesiástico, metafísico*" (OC 457)]. Power becomes transcendental (ecclesiastical, metaphysical, as opposed to merely terrestrial, institutional) when it is absolute.

Returning to the "Ode Written in 1966" will help clarify Borges's metaphysical take on politics. As said, the first two negative stanzas ("no one is the fatherland") conclude with an affirmative moment toward the end of the poem ("we all are the fatherland"). And it is the beginning of the last stanza that clearly illustrates Borges's philosophical approach to politics: "The fatherland, friends, is a perpetual act/As the world is perpetual" ["La patria, amigos, es un acto perpetuo/Como perpetuo es el mundo"]. Borges turns an obviously historical construct (the nation, the "patria") into a timeless, "perpetual" entity. The contradiction is evident: if there is something that is emphatically *not* perpetual, that is a nation. A nation can only be the result of concrete historical processes and is at odds with the abstract, smooth continuum that is eternity.

Following this affirmative moment, where the fatherland is defined as a perpetual act, comes a parenthesis: "(If the Eternal/Spectator were to cease for one instant/To dream us, the white sudden lightning/Of his oblivion would burn us up)." If the first

---

[24] Thus, "The Lottery in Babylon" takes place in an almost mythical past and the conception of time *within* the story itself goes against the basic notions of succession and progress, on which chronologies depend: "In reality, *the number of draws is infinite*.... The ignorant assume that infinite drawings require infinite time; actually, all that is required is that time be infinitely subdivisible, as in the famous parable of the Race with the Tortoise" (CF 105) ["En la realidad *el número de sorteos es infinito. . . .* Los ignorantes suponen que infinitos sorteos requieren un tiempo infinito; en realidad basta que el tiempo sea infinitamente subdivisible, como lo enseña la famosa parábola del Certamen con la Tortuga" (OC 459)].

two verses dehistoricized the nation by rendering it eternal, this is very obviously a leap further into this metaphysical conception of the fatherland. This parenthesis is of course indebted to Berkeley's subjective idealism, according to which the existence of objects and ideas depends on their being perceived by our senses and minds. As Berkeley's too-often quoted dictum would have it, *esse est percipi*, or "to be is to be perceived." "Esse est percipi" is also, incidentally, the name of a hysterically funny short story Borges wrote together with Bioy Casares, which helps illustrate Berkeley's doctrine. In a way, this story, included in *Chronicles of Bustos Domecq* [*Crónicas de Bustos Domecq* (1967)], is a jocular take on many of the issues in "Tlön, Uqbar, Orbis Tertius." In a nutshell, the story postulates that there are no "real" public events anymore—in a literal sense, football games, public openings, state ceremonies, even the landing on the moon are only scripted fictions broadcasted on the radio and the television. They are reported, narrated, televised but they have never actually taken place. None of these events happened (soccer, for instance, has not been played in years and stadiums have been reduced to ruins, but soccer is very much alive—on the radio), but the fact that they are *perceived* by large masses means that they *are*. This link between Berkeley and the media reappears in one "A Weary Man's Utopia" ["Utopía de un hombre que está cansado"], in *The Book of Sand*. Portraying the absurdity of modern society, the harm and mediocrity brought about by mechanical reproduction, the ridiculous pomp surrounding politicians, the obsession with money, and the omnipresence of advertisement, the narrator with bitter humor mistranslates Berkeley's famous sentence: "*Esse est percipi* (to be is to be *portrayed*) became the principle, means and end of our singular conception of the world" (CF 462; my emphasis) ["*Esse est percipi* (ser es ser *retratado*) era el principio, el medio y el fin de nuestro singular concepto del mundo" (OC III: 54)].

In a 1944 essay, "A New Refutation of Time" ["Nueva refutación del tiempo"], Borges quotes Berkeley profusely, and transcribes the relevant paragraph from the *Principles of Human Knowledge*. "For as to what is said of the absolute existence of unthinking things without any relation to their being perceived, that seems perfectly unintelligible. Their *esse* is *percipi*, nor is it possible they should have any existence, out of the minds or thinking things which perceive them" (Berkeley 25; Borges SNF 319; OC 759).

And in this essay, Borges writes, in a parenthetic sentence that very much resembles the one in the "Ode Written in 1966": "(Berkeley's god is a ubiquitous spectator whose purpose is to give coherence to the world)" (SNF 328) ["(El dios de Berkeley es un ubicuo espectador cuyo fin es dar coherencia al mundo)" (OC 767)]. A similar use of Berkeley's doctrine will resurface about 30 years later, also in a poem, "Things" ["Cosas"], where Borges reflects on "The things/which no one sees, except for Berkeley's God" (SP 319) ["Las cosas/Que nadie mira, salvo el Dios de Berkeley" (OC 1106)]. Borges's argument seems to unfold thus: if, according to Berkeley, things *are* only as long as they are perceived, the world as a whole can only be if someone is permanently perceiving it— and this can only be god. "Berkeley affirmed the continuous existence of objects, inasmuch as when no individual perceives them, God does" (SNF 320) ["Berkeley afirmó la existencia continua de los objetos, ya que cuando algún individuo no los percibe, Dios los percibe" (OC 760)]. In "A New Refutation of Time," Borges quotes Berkeley once again:

> Some truths there are so near and obvious to the mind, that a man need only open his eyes to see them. Such I take this important one to be, to wit, that all the choir of heaven and furniture of the earth, in a word all those bodies which compose the mighty frame of the world, have not any subsistence without a mind, that *their being is to be perceived or known; that consequently so long as they are not actually perceived by me, or do not exist in my mind or that of any other created spirit, they must either have no existence at all, or else subsist in the mind of some eternal spirit.* (Berkeley 26; Borges SNF 319; OC 759–60; my emphasis)

The conclusion is, then, returning to the parenthesis in the ode, that "(If the Eternal/Spectator were to cease for one instant/To dream us, his oblivion, white and sudden lightning, would blast us)." It should be added that the parenthetical segment in the poem is an almost literal transcription of a passage from the title essay of his 1936 book *History of Eternity*: "The universe requires eternity. Theologicians are not unaware that if the Lord's attention were to waver for a single second from my right hand as it writes this, it would instantly lapse into nothingness as if blasted by a lightless

fire" (SNF 134) ["El universo requiere la eternidad. Los teólogos no ignoran que si la atención del Señor se desviara un solo segundo de mi derecha mano que escribe, ésta recaería en la nada, como si la fulminara un fuego sin luz" (OC 363)].[25]
As the metaphysical and theological arguments thicken, it may not be futile to pause and remember that "Ode Written in 1966" is about a specific nation, about Argentina. However, by now it should be clear that the *patria* is conceived not in terms of transient institutions or historical processes. Even if there is a reference, in the third stanza to the declaration of independence in 1816 ("the oath taken in that old house"), the nation cannot be anchored to specific events or their protagonists: "no one is the fatherland," "not even time laden with battles," or its heroes, or its monuments, or its writers. The *patria* is not conceived in terms of traditions or political configurations but of a timeless, higher power—the "Eternal Spectator." There is then, in this poem, a passage from history to eternity or rather an attempted reconciliation between them.

This link between religion and nation can become quite explicit in Borges: ". . . all religion is an act of faith. So too is patriotism an act of faith. I have often asked myself, what does it mean to be Argentine? To be Argentine is to feel that we are Argentines" (SNF 59) [". . . toda religión es un acto de fe. Así como la patria es un acto de fe. ¿Qué es, me he preguntado muchas veces, ser argentino? Ser argentino es sentir que somos argentinos" (OC III: 243)].

---

[25] Another philosophical antecedent of god as a spectator is Boethius, whose argument in *Consolation of Philosophy* Borges greatly distorts and embellishes: "Boethius the senator imagined a spectator at a horse race. The spectator is in the hippodrome, and he sees from his box, the horses at the starting gate, al the vicissitudes of the race itself, and the arrival of one of the horses at the finishing line. He sees it all in succession. Boethius then imagines another spectator. *This other spectator is the spectator of the spectator of the race*; he is, let us say, God. God sees the whole race; he sees in a single eternal instant the start, the race, the finish. He sees everything in a single glance; and in the same way he sees all of history" (SN 27; my emphasis) ["el senador Boecio . . . imagina un espectador de una carrera de caballos. El espectador está en el hipódromo y ve, desde su palco, los caballos y la partida, las vicisitudes de la carrera, la llegada de uno de los caballos a la meta, todo sucesivamente. Pero Boecio imagina otro espectador. *Ese otro espectador es espectador del espectador y espectador de la carrera*: es, previsiblemente, Dios. Dios ve toda la carrera, ve en un solo instante eterno, en su instantánea eternidad, la partida de los caballos, las vicisitudes, la llegada. Todo lo ve de un solo vistazo y de igual modo ve toda la historia universal" (OC III: 221–22)]. Cf. Boethius 433–35.

Also, in "1972," a highly political poem in *The Deep Rose* [*La rosa profunda* (1975), also translated as *The Unending Rose*]: "I begged my gods, whose names I ignore,/To send something or someone into my days./They did. It is the Fatherland" (SP 359) ["Rogué a mis dioses, cuyo nombre ignoro,/Que enviaran algo o alguien a mis días. Lo hicieron. Es la Patria" (OC III: 104]). The fatherland seems to require, for Borges a divine, ideal instance.

Borges rearticulates idealism, beginning with Plato, in political terms. It will become clear, momentarily, how Platonic formalism becomes a blueprint for Borges's political philosophy, but for the time being, suffice it to point out that Borges chooses to close (in a footnote) the rather lengthy refutation of Platonism offered in "A History of Eternity" with an example that revolves, precisely, around the fatherland:

> I do not wish to bid farewell to Platonism (which seems icily remote) without making the following observation, in the hope that others may pursue and justify it: *The generic can be more intense than the concrete.* There is no lack of examples to illustrate this. During the boyhood summers I spent in the north of the province of Buenos Aires, I was intrigued by the rounded plain and the men drinking mate in the kitchen, but terrible indeed was my delight when I learned that the circular space was the "pampa" and those men "gauchos".... The generic (the repeated name, the type, the fatherland [*patria*], the worshipped destiny invested in it) takes priority over individual features, *which are tolerated only because of their prior genre.* (SNF 129 fn.)

> [No quiero despedirme del platonismo (que parece glacial) sin comunicar esta observación, con esperanza de que la prosigan y justifiquen: *Lo genérico puede ser más intenso que lo concreto.* Casos ilustrativos no faltan. De chico, veraneando en el norte de la provincia, la llanura y los hombres que mateaban en la cocina me interesaron, pero mi felicidad fue terrible cuando supe que ese redondel era "pampa," y esos varones, "gauchos".... Lo genérico (el repetido nombre, el tipo, la patria, el destino adorable que se le atribuye) prima sobre los rasgos individuales, *que se toleran en gracia de lo anterior.* (OC 358 fn)]

The fatherland, once again, is thought of in ideal (i.e. generic) terms and *not* in terms of specific determinations ("which are tolerated only because of their prior genre").[26] It is, once more, the *idea* of the fatherland that is more than its "modes" and "symbols," more than the "extended territory/and the days of [its] extended time" (returning to the "Ode Composed in 1960"), and remits to the way it is "for God in the/living bosom of eternal archetypes." This archetypal nation[27] not only illustrates the Platonic idea but also provides the possibility of redeeming the very notion of archetype that Borges himself had elegantly rebutted during the preceding four pages of his essay. Although he produces solid philosophical reasons "for discrediting the Platonic doctrine" (SNF 128) ["descreer de la doctrina platónica" (OC 357)], he leaves it standing when it comes to the *patria*: the ideal, more general, intangible fatherland is "more intense" than its sensorial, concrete manifestations—which is, to a large extent, the driving principle of the "Ode Written in 1966." This is what Borges means when he refers to "that abstract thing, the fatherland" ["esa cosa abstracta, la patria"] in a poem about the gauchos (OC 1002). The openly political moment in the ode (and defining the fatherland is most surely that) coincides with a withdrawal from direct contextual references into a speculative, metaphysical realm.

There is, however, a crucial twist in Borges's idealist moment in the "Ode Written in 1966," a shift from "spectator" (which is in keeping with god's perception in all the other texts quoted here) to "dreamer." This turn is not specific to this poem, but can be found in both his verse and his prose throughout more or less four decades. With this displacement (which is, first and foremost, an intentionally distorted reading of the tradition of idealism), Borges's

---

[26] "Borges says that Plato's incredible ideas are real for everyone. For us, the Fatherland [*Patria*] is neither its inhabitants—our friends and enemies—nor the people that inhabited it in the past—the *Unitarios* and the *Rosistas*. It is that and something else" ["Borges comenta que las increíbles ideas de Platón son reales para todos; la Patria no es, para nosotros, las personas que ahora la habitan—nuestros amigos y nuestros enemigos—ni las personas que la habitaron en el pasado—los unitarios, los rosistas—: es eso y algo más" (Bioy 131)].

[27] Borges even links politics and Platonism in one of his most outrageously fictional ideas of the state—the Company in "The Lottery in Babylon." Even here, where the Company is clearly an ideal model (after all, the narrator claims the number of draws is infinite), there is a reference to "the Heavenly Archetype of the Lottery beloved of Platonists" ["el Arquetipo Celestial de la Lotería, que adoran los platónicos" (OC 459)].

entire conception of politics takes a new turn. To briefly sum up: first, the "Ode Written in 1966" decenters the idea of nation by saying it is no one and everyone. Then this displacement is taken further by turning the *patria*, a social, contingent construct into a transcendental, necessary essence. Later, Borges casts this idea of the fatherland in the mold of Berkeley's immaterialist god, thus utterly dissociating the nation from every historical determination. But there is a final turn: god is dreaming. This brings to mind such stories as "The Circular Ruins" where a reality is dreamed by a superior being (whose reality is dreamed by a superior being, and so on). The world is but a fantasy, a hallucination, an illusion dreamed up by a demiurge. Reality is one of the possibilities of the fantastic. This merger of philosophy and fiction seems to be in keeping with Borges's famous claim in "Tlön, Uqbar, Orbis Tertius" that "metaphysics is a branch of fantastic literature" (CF 76) ["la metafísica es una rama de la literatura fantástica" (OC 436)].[28] God is dreaming us. We (and our reality) are a dream, a fiction.[29]

---

[28] This claim also appears in a 1943 review of Weatherhead's *After Death*: "I have recently compiled an anthology of fantastic literature. While I admit that such a work is among the few a second Noah should rescue from a second deluge, I must confess my guilty omission of the unsuspected masters of the genre: Parmenides, Plato, John Scotus Erigena, Albertus Magnus, Spinoza, Leibniz, Kant, Francis Bradley. What, in fact, are the wonders of Wells or Edgar Allan Poe—a flower that visits us from the future, a dead man under hypnosis—in comparison to the invention of God . . . ? What are all the nights of Scheherazade next to an argument by Berkeley?" (SNF 254–55) ["Yo he compilado alguna vez una antología de la literatura fantástica. Admito que esa obra es de las poquísimas que un segundo Noé debería salvar de un segundo diluvio, pero delato la culpable omisión de los insospechados y mayores maestros del género: Parménides, Platón, Juan Escoto Erígena, Alberto Magno, Spinoza, Leibniz, Kant, Francis Bradley. En efecto, ¿qué son los prodigios de Wells o de Edgar Allan Poe—una flor que nos llega del porvenir, un muerto sometido a la hipnosis—confrontados con la invención de Dios . . . ? [Q]ué son todas las noches de Shahrazad junto a un argumento de Berkeley?" (OC 280–81)]. Almost 40 years later, Borges repeats this argument in the endnotes to one of his final books of poetry (*La cifra* [1981]), adding theology to philosophy: "La filosofía y la teología son, lo sospecho, dos especies de la literatura fantástica" (OC III: 340)—the examples he offers immediately after are almost a literal transcription of the 1943 article. In "A weary Man's Utopia," one of his late short stories, one of the characters declares "having read without displeasure . . . two tales of fantasy—the Travels of Captain Lemuel Gulliver, which many people believe to have really taken place, and the *Summa Theologica*" (CF 461) ["haber leído sin desagrado . . . dos cuentos fantásticos. Los viajes del Capitán Lemuel Gulliver, que muchos consideran verídicos, y la Suma Teológica" (OC III: 53)].

These questionings of the boundaries and the constitution of reality (and its ultimate dissolution into a dream) are, of course, to be expected in Borges's literature. What is noteworthy, however, is that these metaphysical puzzles are also present in those texts that supposedly are anchored in concrete contexts. Even in overtly political and historical poems, Borges resorts to a fractal logic and presents a reality included within another, a world devised by a higher power, dreamed up by a remote demiurge. "Sarmiento," an untranslated poem in *The Other, the Same*, offers a clear example. The poem, a panegyric to the essayist and Argentine president (1868–1874),[30] reads:

Marble and Glory do not overwhelm him . . .
It is he. He is the witness of the fatherland,
The one who sees our infamy and our glory . . .
I know that in those September dawns[31]
That no one will forget and that no one can
Recount, we have felt him . . .
. . . Abstracted
In his long vision as in a magic
Crystal that withholds at once the three faces
Of time, which is after, before, now,
Sarmiento, the dreamer, keeps on dreaming us.

[No lo abruman el mármol y la gloria . . .
Es él. Es el testigo de la patria,

---

[29] The fatal consequences of this premise do not escape Borges. Thinking that life is a dream "takes us certainly to solipsism, to the suspicion that there is only one dreamer and that dreamer is each one of us" (SN 29) ["nos lleva, desde luego, al solipsismo; a la sospecha de que sólo hay un soñador y ese soñador es cada uno de nosotros." (OC III: 223)]. However, Borges toyed with the metaphysics of dream over and again. The fractal argument (very much in the style of "The Circular Ruins") is applied to Flaubert (and other writers and philosophers): "the dreamer . . . notes that he is dreaming and that the forms of his dream are himself" (SNF 387) ["el soñador . . . nota que está soñándose" (OC 260)] until his very last book (see, for instance, "Someone Dreams" ["Alguien sueña"], an untranslated poem in *Los conjurados*).

[30] Borges wrote this poem in 1961, commissioned by Victoria Ocampo, director of *Sur* (cf. Bioy 748).

[31] This is, as in the "Oda compuesta en 1960," a reference to the Revolución Libertadora, the coup that put an end to Perón's second presidency. In this poem, abridged here, a clear line is drawn going from Rosas to Perón.

El que ve nuestra infamia y nuestra gloria . . .
Sé que en aquellas albas de setiembre
Que nadie olvidará y que nadie puede
Contar, lo hemos sentido . . .
. . . Abstraído
En su larga visión como en un mágico
Cristal que a un tiempo encierra las tres caras
Del tiempo que es después, antes, ahora,
Sarmiento el soñador sigue soñándonos (OC 899)].

Once again, a poem that is obviously about Argentine history
(spanning over a century, from *Facundo* to the *Revolución
Libertadora*); once again, as in the "Ode Written in 1966," the
impossibility of communicating an essence through signs ("marble");
and once again, in the closing verses, history turns into metaphysics.
Sarmiento appears not only as an observer but also as a Berkeleian
witness and warrantor of the fatherland ("Es el testigo de la patria"),
who sees Argentina from an Aleph of sorts: his "long vision" reaches
us as through a "magical crystal," which "at once" ("a un tiempo")
conjugates past, present, and future.[32] And then, as in both odes
(1960 and 1966), the shift to the idealist parable of the world as
a projection from a higher instance that perceives or dreams our
reality: "Sarmiento, the dreamer, keeps on dreaming us."

Oddly enough, now that we seem completely removed from
concrete historical determinations and contextual references, we
may have reached a crucial aspect of Borges's political thought.
By fictionalizing reality (by understanding it as a dream, as a
representation), Borges is making strong claims about politics
and power. It should be noticed that in most of the short stories
mentioned before ("The Cult of the Phoenix," "The Congress," and
"The Lottery in Babylon"), there are more or less secret institutions
superimposing their own order (their own fiction, their own dream)
onto reality, almost as in "On Rigor in Science," a short piece
about a kingdom where cartography has evolved to the point that
maps cover the territory they represent, and coincide inch by inch
with it. The dream is the condition of possibility of the world and

---

[32] In "The Aleph" Borges writes: "What my eyes saw was simultaneous; what I shall
write is successive, because such is the nature of language" (SF 283) ["Lo que vieron
mis ojos fue simultáneo; lo que transcribiré, sucesivo, porque el lenguaje lo es"
(OC 625)].

successive representations envelop reality—and one should listen to the political resonance of the word "representation": power always has to do with rights that, at some point, for some reason, were delegated, ceded, or snatched away, thereby establishing some form of representation.

Since the dawn of idealism there has been a well-established tradition of conceiving the world as a degraded reproduction of a transcendental original, or even as a complete deception. "Let us admit what all idealists admit: the *hallucinatory* nature of the world" ["Admitamos lo que todos los idealistas admiten: el carácter alucinatorio del mundo"] Borges writes in "Avatars of the Tortoise" ["Avatares de la tortuga"] (L 207–08; OC 258; my emphasis). This distorted hallucination goes back to the pre-Socratics and, according to Borges, reaches its peak with Berkeley. "From Parmenides of Elea to the present, idealism—the doctrine that declares that the universe (and even time and space, and perhaps we) is nothing but an illusion—has been professed in diverse forms by many thinkers. No one, perhaps, has articulated it with more clarity than the Bishop Berkeley" ["Desde Parménides de Elea hasta ahora, el idealismo—la doctrina que declara que el universo, incluso el tiempo y el espacio y quizá nosotros, no es otra cosa que una apariencia o un caos de apariencias—ha sido profesado en formas diversas por muchos pensadores. Nadie, tal vez, lo ha razonado con mayor claridad que el obispo Berkeley" (P 32)]. But it is, of course, with Plato that idealism becomes a system. We are trapped in a reality made up of imperfect reflections of ideas, just like the prisoners of his famous allegory of the cave, who, fettered in the dark, "deem reality to be nothing else than the shadows of the artificial objects" (*Republic* 123). Our reality is composed of flawed, contingent copies of perfect, necessary ideas (*Republic* 423, 427), and "those ideas are not relative to our world," but only to god's (*Parmenides* 227).[33] For over two millennia, this notion has

---

[33] However, Borges offers "specific arguments for discrediting the Platonic doctrine," the most delightful of which is the *regressus ad infinitum* lurking behind every Platonic idea: archetypes repeat "the very anomaly they seek to resolve. Lion-ness, let us say: how would it dispense with Pride and Tawny-ness, Mane-ness and Paw-ness. There is no answer to this question, nor can there be: we do not expect from the term *lion-ness* a virtue any greater than that of the word without the suffix" (SNF 128–29) ["repiten esas mismas anomalías que quieren resolver. La Leonidad,

persisted in different philosophical incarnations—the idea, the archetype, the form, the thing-in-itself, the noumenon that always remains inaccessible to our senses, which can merely grasp corrupted phenomenical reflections of this essence, degraded projections or appearances (in the double sense of emergence and semblance, but also as distinguished from *reality*). It is, in other words, impossible to reach "that supposed objectivity that Berkeley denied and Kant banished to the polar exile of the useless noumenon" ["esa objetividad supuesta que Berkeley negó y Kant envió al destierro polar de un noúmeno inservible" (TR I: 119)]. Underlying this entire principle is the belief that we live in a fiction made up of deceptive representations: "idealism affirms that the universe is an illusion" ["el idealismo afirma que el universo es una apariencia" (P 33)]. And not just any kind of illusion. It is a dream. In his essay on Nathaniel Hawthorne, Borges expands this notion. "The world is Someone's dream. . . . Someone is dreaming us up right now, and dreaming up the history of the Universe [according to] the doctrine of the idealist school" ["El mundo es el sueño de Alguien, . . . hay

---

digamos, ¿cómo prescindiría de la Soberbia y de la Rojez, de la Melenidad y la Zarpidad? A esa pregunta no hay contestación y no puede haberla: no esperamos del término *leonidad* una virtud muy superior a la que tiene esa palabra sin el sufijo" (OC 358)]. The beauty and elegance of this argument can hardly be underestimated. But Plato himself, in the *Parmenides*, offers a very Borgesian refutation, usually known as the "third man argument" (*Parmenides* 221). This same confutation is later picked up by Aristotle in his *Metaphysics* (I: 65, 335, 383; II: 197). Borges claims that Aristotle had Zeno's infinite subdivisions in mind and that "this recollection served as an inspiration for his famous *argument of the third man* against the Platonic doctrine. This doctrine tries to demonstrate that two individuals who have common attributes (for example, two men) are mere temporal appearances of an eternal archetype. Aristotle asks if the many men and the Man—the temporal individuals and the archetype—have attributes in common. It is obvious that they do: the general attributes of humanity. In that case, maintains Aristotle, one would have to postulate *another archetype* to include them all, and then a fourth . . . " (L 203) ["su recuerdo le inspira el famoso *argumento del tercer hombre* contra la doctrina platónica. Esa doctrina quiere demostrar que dos individuos que tienen atributos comunes (por ejemplo dos hombres) son meras apariencias temporales de un arquetipo eterno. Aristóteles interroga si los muchos hombres y el Hombre—los individuos temporales y el Arquetipo—tienen atributos comunes. Es notorio que sí; tienen los atributos generales de la humanidad. En ese caso, afirma Aristóteles, habrá que postular *otro arquetipo* que los abarque a todos y después un cuarto . . . " (OC 255)]. The fractal vertigo of the argument can be found in many of Borges's texts that will be discussed in the following section ("When Fiction Lives in Fiction").

Alguien que ahora está soñándonos y que sueña la historia del universo [según la] doctrina de la escuela idealista" (OC 679)]. Put differently, the "idealist doctrine has it that the verbs 'to live' and 'to dream' are at every point synonymous," Borges writes in "The Zahir" (CF 248) ["Según la doctrina idealista, los verbos *vivir* y *soñar* son rigurosamente sinónimos" (OC 595)]. This leads back to the "Eternal Spectator" who is dreaming us in the "Ode Written in 1966."

A contemporary of Plato, Buddha also affirmed the dreamlike or hallucinatory quality of reality. According to him, "we must reach the understanding that the world is an apparition, a dream; that life is a dream" (SN 71) ["debemos llegar a comprender que el mundo es una aparición, un sueño, que la vida es sueño" (OC III: 251)].[34]

However, not all gods are as benevolent as Plato's or Berkeley's. The idea of an overtly deceitful higher power enshrouding us all in his misleading rendering of the world is never as strong and overt as in Descartes's *Meditations*. Radical skepticism (the possibility that absolutely everything, including myself, is false and even nonexistent) is the beginning and the cornerstone of Descartes's philosophical edifice—I may doubt everything, but not the fact that I doubt, and if I doubt, I am. To arrive at this clear and distinct idea ("I am a thinking thing"), Descartes must first put *everything* into question and for this, in the first *Meditation*, he conjures up an evil genius. Someone, somewhere, hidden, but immensely powerful, is projecting a fictitious reality onto reality:

> I will suppose therefore that not God, who is supremely good and the source of truth, but rather some malicious demon of the utmost power and cunning has employed all his energies in order to deceive me. I shall think that the sky, the air, the earth, colors, shapes, sounds, and all external things are merely the delusions of dreams which he has devised to ensnare my judgment. I shall consider myself as not having hands or eyes, or flesh, or blood or senses, but as falsely believing that I have all these things. (Descartes 15)

---

[34] Borges draws a direct line between Buddha and Schopenhauer: "For Schopenhauer, the somber Schopenhauer, and for the Buddha, the world is a dream. We must stop dreaming it" (SN 71) ["Para Schopenhauer, para el sombrío Schopenhauer, y para el Buddha, el mundo es un sueño, debemos dejar de soñarlo" (OC III: 250)]. A few paragraphs down, he extends the link to David Hume and Macedonio Fernández.

In brief, as Borges has it in "Descartes," a poem in one of his last books, *The Cipher* (*La cifra*—translated as *The Limit* in SP): "I am the only man on earth, but perhaps there is neither earth nor man./ Perhaps a god is deceiving me" (SP 423) ["Soy el único hombre en la tierra y acaso no haya tierra ni hombre/Acaso un dios me engaña" (OC III: 295)].

At this point, the idea of reality being dreamed or devised by a higher power becomes political in a more direct, overt way: the "fantastic" plot of metaphysics can be read as the vastest of conspiracy theories. Paranoids and conspiracy theorists are always deeply religious—albeit in a secular way: according to them, there is an order, a plan, a higher power we have no immediate access to and that always remains invisible but whose work and influence on the world is palpable and indisputable, even if often its meaning is inscrutable. Manipulation, propaganda, and misinformation, are some of the names paranoids give these deceptive narratives and representations.

In many of Borges's stories, one character (or organization) weaves an alternate, false reality for one of the protagonists: "The Death and the Compass," "Theme of the Traitor and the Hero," "Ibn-Hakam al-Bokhari, Murdered in his Labyrinth," and "The Dead" are, perhaps, the most conspicuous examples. But the main point of this conspiratorial notion of representation has to do with the removal and inaccessibility of the source of power and the misled perception of the world it imposes on us. We take for valid a reality that is either false or merely derivative, a secondhand copy of a distant "more real" world (all of which remits, again, to Plato). Power, in brief, could be defined by the imposition of a representation as reality.

2

When fiction lives in fiction

I owe my first inkling of the problem of infinitude to a large biscuit tin that provided my childhood with mystery and vertigo. On the side of that abnormal object was a Japanese scene. I do not recall the children or the warriors who configured it, but I do remember that in a corner of the image the same biscuit tin reappeared with the same picture, and in it the same figure, and so (and least potentially) to the infinite. . . . (SNF 160)

[Debo mi primera noción del problema del infinito a una gran lata de bizcochos que dio misterio y vértigo a mi niñez. En el costado de ese objeto anormal había una escena japonesa; no recuerdo los niños o guerreros que la formaban, pero sí que en un ángulo de esa imagen la misma lata de bizcochos reaparecía con la misma figura y en ella la misma figura, y así (a lo menos, en potencia) infinitamente. . . . (TC 325)]

Thus begins "When Fiction Lives in Fiction" ["Cuando la ficción vive en la ficción"], published in *El Hogar* in 1939. The text is supposed to be a review of Flann O'Brien's *At Swim-Two-Birds*, but Borges devotes a mere dozen lines to the novel. Instead, he beautifully lists and describes cases of fractal vertigo—Josiah Royce's minute map of England, which contains a map of the map, and so on; *Las meninas*, the painting by Velázquez, and its famous mirror; Cervantes, with his nesting novels in *Don Quijote*; Apuleius and the embedded stories in *The Golden Ass*; night DCII in *The Arabian Nights* that turns the entire book into a loop; the third act of *Hamlet*; the shifting frames in Corneille's *L'illusion comique*; and the multilayered dreams in Meyerink's *Der Golem*. The fractal configuration the child saw in his cookie tin became decisive in Borges's articulation of politics and metaphysics and also turned out to be one of the decisive formal traits of his literature.

If power imposes a representation as reality, it follows that there ought to be another (vaster, truer) reality withholding the fictional one. The conspiratorial view of politics based on this particular take on idealism necessarily implies a model where worlds are nested within one another. Borges tends to multiply these layers of illusion or deception by an infinite number: "You have wakened not out of sleep, but into a prior dream, and that dream lies within another, and so on, to infinity, which is the number of the grains of sand. The path that you are to take is endless, and you will die before you have truly awakened" (CF 252) ["No has despertado a la vigilia, sino a un sueño anterior. Ese sueño está dentro de otro, y así hasta lo infinito, que es el número de los granos de arena. El camino que habrás de desandar es interminable y morirás antes de haber despertado realmente" (OC 598)]. The classical example of the premise of the dreamed dreamer is "The Circular Ruins" ["Las ruinas circulares"], a short story included in *Ficciones* (1944), and, as we shall see, examples of such structures abound in Borges's literature. These endless levels contained within one another raise an obvious question: is there a final frame, a source or an end? Borges's two-part sonnet on chess, included in *The Maker*, clearly plays with such a fractal structure and the power-related issues deriving from it. The first sonnet describes the chessmen and their fierce battle on the board, and even endows them with human traits. However, according to the second sonnet,

They do not know that the player's hand
Governs their destiny,
They do not know that an adamantine rigor
Holds their will and their day.

The player too is a prisoner
. . . of another board
Made of black nights and white days.

God moves the player, and he moves the piece.
What god behind God begins the round
Of dust and time and dream and agonies? (cf. SP 103)

[No saben que la mano señalada
Del jugador gobierna su destino,
No saben que un rigor adamantino
Sujeta su albedrío y su jornada.

También el jugador es prisionero
. . . de otro tablero
De negras noches y de blancos días.

Dios mueve al jugador, y éste, la pieza.
¿Qué dios detrás de Dios la trama empieza
De polvo y tiempo y sueño y agonías? (OC 813)]

The idea that there is a more real reality behind reality appears in many other texts, such as "The Writing of the God," where the narrator sees "the faceless god who is behind the gods" (CF 253) ["el dios sin cara que hay detrás de los dioses" (OC 599)], but in the chess sonnets Borges seems to have taken the paranoid's conspiratorial view of the world and made it literal: "we are being played."

In "The Sect of the Phoenix," Borges quotes an apocryphal adage, supposedly from Du Cange's *Glossary*, which reads: "*Orbis terrarum est speculum Ludi*" (OC 523; CF 173)—"The world is the mirror of the game." This proverb not only applies literally to the sonnets on chess but also to a brief scene narrated by Zimmermann, one of the two historians in "Guayaquil," a short story included in *Brodie's Report*:

In the Mabinogion, two kings are playing chess on the summit of a hill, while on the plain below, their armies clash in battle. One of the kings wins the game; at that instant, a horseman rides up with the news that the other king's army has been defeated. The battle on the battlefield below was the *reflection* of the battle on the chessboard. (CF 395; my emphasis)[35]

[En los Mabinogion, dos reyes juegan al ajedrez en lo alto de un cerro, mientras abajo sus guerreros combaten. Uno de los reyes

---

[35] Just like the chess game reflects the battle, the meeting of the two historians in the short story reflects that of San Martín and Bolivar in Guayaquil. The 1822 summit resulted in San Martín's withdrawal from political life and, shortly after, his retirement in France, and this situation mirrors the narrator's own: as San Martín, he too is forced into renouncing his rights in favor of his colleague and rival, fellow historian Zimmermann. It should be mentioned that the chess allegory also appears in Borges and Bioy's *Cuentos breves y extraordinarios*, where it is attributed to Edwin Morgan. Bioy Casares and Bioy translated the *Mabinogion* in 1953 (Bioy 80).

gana el partido; un jinete llega con la noticia de que el ejército del otro ha sido vencido. La batalla de los hombres era el reflejo de la batalla del tablero. (OC 1067)]

In the chess sonnets, the board was presented as a world within the world, which, in turn, was a board in a larger world. Here, however, the hierarchies are reversed, and what we thought was a representation (the board) is in fact the reality to which a secondary, derivative one (the battle) is subordinated. This is also the case in "The Game," a late (untranslated) poem included in *History of the Night*, where a man and a woman play a strange game involving silver and gold rings. "They proceeded with slow delicacy, as if afraid of making a mistake./They did not know that game was necessary so that a certain thing may happen, in the future, in a certain region" ["Procedían con lenta delicadeza, como si temieran equivocarse./No sabían que era necesario aquel juego para que determinada cosa ocurriera, en el porvenir, en determinada región" (OC III: 182)].

The paradox in these two last examples is that the smallest of the *matryoshkas* is, in fact, the outer frame that contains all the other dolls (or, that, following the adage, the world mirrors the game). But regardless of where the final frame is located, one common trait between all these texts remains: all these models are based upon a hierarchy of realities. The notion of a gradated reality—the idea that there is an inaccessible archetype behind the faulty representations we perceive—brings us back to idealism, and, more specifically, to Plato.

To illustrate the distance between the idea and its sensorial manifestation, Plato introduces a three-tiered comparison that has much in common with Borges's sonnets. Using a piece of furniture as example, Socrates explains: "We get . . . three couches, one, that in nature, which, I take it, we would say that God produces. . . . And then there was the one which the carpenter made. . . . And one which the painter. . . . The painter, then, the cabinet-maker, and God, there are these three presiding over three kinds of couches" (*Republic* 427). Borges paraphrases this argument in an (untranslated) essay on Pascal, when he refers to "that passage in the tenth book of the *Republic*, where we are told that God creates the Archetype of the table, the carpenter, a simulacrum of the archetype, and the painter, a simulacrum of the simulacrum" ["aquel pasaje del décimo libro de *La República*, donde se nos dice que Dios crea el arquetipo de la mesa, el carpintero, el simulacro del arquetipo, y el pintor, un simulacro del simulacro" (OC 705)].[36] Needless to say, the farther we get from god's piece of furniture, the more removed we are from the ideal one. Borges alludes to this passage in "History of Eternity": "Plato has . . . laborious universal forms to propose. For example Tableness, or the Intelligible Table that exists in the heavens; the four-legged archetype pursued by every cabinetmaker, all of them condemned to daydreams and frustration. (Yet I cannot entirely negate the concept: without an ideal table, we would never have achieved concrete tables)" (SNF 128) ["formas universales mucho más arduas nos propone Platón. Por ejemplo, la Mesidad, o Mesa Inteligible que está en los cielos: arquetipo cuadrúpedo que persiguen, condenados a ensueño y a frustración, todos los ebanistas del mundo. (No puedo negarla del todo: sin una mesa ideal, no hubiéramos llegado a mesas concretas)" (OC 357)].

Borges found different incarnations of this fractal model of the universe throughout the history of philosophy and religion. Plato is the main reference, but Zeno, with his endlessly subdivided space, is perhaps the earliest antecedent. And the same structure can be found in some images in Buddhism. Some texts narrating Buddha's enlightenment under the fig tree

> argue that nothing is real and that all knowledge is fictitious and that if there were as many Ganges as grains of sand there are in the Ganges and again as many Ganges as grains of sand in those new Ganges, the number of grains of sand would be smaller than the number of things that the Buddha *ignores*.[37]

> [razonan que nada es real y que todo conocimiento es ficticio y que si hubiera tantos Ganges como hay granos de arena en el Ganges y otra vez tantos Ganges como hay granos de arena en el Ganges y otra vez tantos Ganges como granos de arena en los nuevos Ganges, el número de granos de arena sería menor que el número de cosas que *ignora* el Buddha. (OC 738fn)]

---

[36] See also Borges's lecture on Nathaniel Hawthorne (OC 680).

[37] Mysteriously enough, the Penguin edition of the *Selected Non-Fictions* cut this entire footnote out.

Leibniz, a modern reference whose presence in Borges's work is only marginal, presents a similar image. In the *Monadology* "we read that the universe consists of inferior universes, which in turn contain the universe, and so on *ad infinitum*" (SNF 294fn) ["se lee que el universo está hecho de ínfimos universos, que a su vez contienen el universo, y así hasta el infinito" (OC III: 366fn)]. To quote Leibniz himself:

> Every portion of matter may be conceived as like a garden full of plants and like a pond full of fish. But each branch of the plant, each member of the animal, each drop of its bodily fluids, is also such a garden or such a pond. (228)

It seems unavoidable to compare this segment from the *Monadology* with a passage from "The Aleph," where the narrator tells he "saw the earth in the Aleph, and the Aleph once more in the earth and the earth in the Aleph" (CF 283–84) ["vi en el Aleph la tierra, y en la tierra otra vez el Aleph, y en el Aleph la tierra" (OC 626)].

But there are three references that antecede Leibniz's—and certainly occupy a more prominent place in Borges's literature. The first one is Zeno of Elea, one of Borges's lifelong obsessions:[38] if space is infinitely dividable, each single segment (regardless of its extension) will contain an infinite number of segments.[39] Zeno's paradox, it should be noted, is closely related to Cantor's "heroic theory of sets" (OC 386; SNF 116).

---

[38] In the foreword to *The Gold of the Tigers*, Borges goes as far as to say that the famous Eleatic paradox was his first contact with philosophy and recalls how his father introduced him to it—meaningfully, through chess: "My reader will notice, in some pages, a philosophical preoccupation. It has been with me since my childhood, when my father showed me, with the help of a chessboard . . . , the paradox of the race between Achilles and the tortoise" (SP 305) ["Mi lector notará en algunas páginas la preocupación filosófica. Fue mía desde niño, cuando mi padre me reveló con la ayuda del tablero de ajedrez . . . la carrera de Aquiles y la tortuga" (OC 1081)]. In an untranslated piece written in 1970, Borges adds Berkeley to this recollection: "with the help of an orange [my father also explained] Berkeley's doctrine. I was not even nine years old" ["con la ayuda de una naranja [mi padre también me explicó] la doctrina de Berkeley. Yo no había cumplido nueve años" (TR III: 160)].

[39] Cf. "The Perpetual Race of Achilles and the Tortoise" (SNF 43–48), and "Avatars of the Tortoise" (L 202–9), both included in *Discusión* (OC 244–58).

An infinite collection—for instance, the series of natural numbers—is a collection whose members can in turn be broken down into infinite series. The part, in these elevated latitudes of numeration, is no less copious than the whole: the precise quantity of points in the universe is the same as in a meter in the universe, or in a decimeter, or in the deepest trajectory of a star. (SNF 46)

[Una colección infinita—verbigracia, la serie de los números naturales—es una colección cuyos miembros pueden desdoblarse a su vez en series infinitas. La parte, en esas elevadas latitudes de la numeración, no es menos copiosa que el todo: la cantidad precisa de puntos que hay en el universo es la que hay en un metro de universo, o en un decímetro, o en la más honda trayectoria estelar. (OC 247)]

Each particle in the universe holds a universe, like Borges's Aleph, which is "one of the points in space that contains all points" (CF 280) ["uno de los puntos del espacio que contiene todos los puntos" (OC 623)]. Given the one-to-one correspondence of elements between sets, it is true that "there are as many multiples of 3018 as there are numbers" (SNF 46) ["hay tantos múltiplos de tres mil dieciocho como números hay" (OC 247)]. It is of course significant that Cantor named the infinite set of cardinals "Aleph."

The second source for this Chinese box universe comes from the Kabbalah. The final stanza of another of Borges's best-known poems, "The Golem," reproduces the same model found in the chess sonnets: the creature (the Golem) is being watched by his creator (the rabbi) who, in turn, is being watched by his creator (god):

In the hour of anguish and vague light,
Upon his Golem [the rabbi's] eyes would come to rest.
Who is to say what God must have felt,
Looking down and seeing his rabbi so distressed? (cf. SP 197)

[En la hora de angustia y luz vaga,
En su Golem [el rabino] los ojos detenía.
¿Quién nos dirá las cosas que sentía
Dios, al mirar a su rabino en Praga? (OC 887)]

In his foreword to The Other, the Same (SP 147; OC 857), Borges relates the gradually inclusive realities in "The Golem" to "The Circular Ruins." Even though the rabbi obviously has been initiated in the Kabbalah,[40] Borges does not go into this doctrine's conception of the creation, but in a later essay he does elaborate on its cosmogony, composed of nesting worlds. As Borges explains in a lecture on Kabbalah, according to this particular reading of the Torah

> in the beginning there is a Being analogous to the God of Spinoza . . . , the *en sof*. . . . Since the creation of the world is unfortunately necessary, we have ten emanations, the Sefirot, which emerge from Him but come after Him. . . . These ten emanations emanate one from the other. . . . The ten emanations form a man called Adam Kadmon, the Archetypal Man. That man is in heaven, and we are his reflection. Adam Kadmon, formed by the ten emanations, himself emanates a world, which emanates another, until there are four. The third is our material world. All of them are included in Adam Kadmon, who includes man and his microcosm: all things. (SN 100–01)

> [en el principio hay un Ser análogo al Dios de Spinoza . . . , el En Soph. . . . Ya que desdichadamente es necesaria la creación del mundo, tenemos diez emanaciones, las Sephiroth que surgen de Él, pero que no son posteriores a Él. . . . Esas diez emanaciones emanan una de otra. . . . Las diez emanaciones forman un hombre que se llama el Adam Kadmon, el Hombre Arquetipo. Ese hombre está en el cielo y nosotros somos su reflejo. Ese hombre, de esas diez emanaciones, emana un mundo, emana otro, hasta cuatro. El tercero es nuestro mundo material y el cuarto es el mundo infernal. Todos están incluidos en el Adam Kadmon, que comprende al hombre y su microcosmo: todas las cosas. (OC III: 271)

Once again, "The Aleph" comes to mind. After all, the Aleph is the ultimate example of these fractal worlds—the whole universe condensed in a minuscule point. "In the Kabbalah, that letter [Aleph] signifies the En Soph, the pure and unlimited godhead; it has also

---

[40] "Thirsty to know things only known to God,/Judá León shuffled letters endlessly,/Trying them out in subtle combinations/Till at last he uttered the Name that is the Key" (SP 193) ["Sediento de saber lo que Dios sabe,/Judá León se dio a permutaciones/de letras y a complejas variaciones/Y al fin pronunció el Nombre que es la Clave" (OC 885)].

been said that its shape is that of a man pointing to the sky and the earth, to indicate that *the lower world is the map and mirror of the higher*" (CF 285; my emphasis) ["Para la Cábala, esa letra significa el En Soph, la ilimitada y pura divinidad; también se dijo que tiene la forma de un hombre que señala el cielo y la tierra para indicar que *el mundo inferior es el espejo y es el mapa del superior*" (OC 627)]. Borges summarizes this fractal representation of the universe occurring in this lower emanation in "The Zahir": "The Kabbalists believed that man is a microcosm, a symbolic mirror of the universe" (CF 248) ["Los cabalistas entendieron que el hombre es un microcosmo, un simbólico espejo del universo" (OC 595)].

Finally, Borges finds a third source for this particular cosmogony in the Gnostics and their forerunners, like Plotinus. In his "Note on Walt Whitman," Borges notes that "Plotinus told his disciples of an inconceivable heaven, in which 'everything is everywhere, anything is everything, the sun is every star, and each star is every star and the sun'" ["Plotino describe a sus alumnos un cielo inconcebible, en el que 'todo está en todas partes, cualquier cosa es todas las cosas, el sol es todas las estrellas, y cada estrella es todas las estrellas y el sol'" (OC 251)]. This notion will later be picked up by the Gnostics. In "A Vindication of Basilides the False," published in *Discusión*, Borges writes:

> In the beginning of Basilides's cosmogony there is a God. . . . His medium is the *pleroma* or plenitude, the inconceivable museum of Platonic archetypes, intelligible essences, and universals. He is an immutable God, but from his repose emanated seven subordinate divinities who, condescending to action, created and presided over a first heaven. From this demiurgic crown came a second, also with angels, powers, and thrones, and these formed another, lower heaven, which was the symmetrical duplicate of the first. This second conclave saw itself reproduced in a third, and that in another below, and so on down to 365. The lord of the lowest heaven is the God of the Scriptures, and his fraction of divinity is nearly zero. He and his angels founded this visible sky, amassed the immaterial earth on which we are walking, and later apportioned it. (SNF 65–66)[41]

---

[41] A slightly different version of this account can also be found in the Kabbalah lecture in *Seven Nights* (SN 102; OC III: 271–72).

[En el principio de la cosmogonía de Basílides hay un Dios. . . . Su medio es el *pleroma* o la plenitud: el inconcebible museo de los arquetipos platónicos, de las esencias inteligibles, de los universales. Es un Dios inmutable, pero de su reposo emanaron siete divinidades subalternas que, condescendiendo a la acción, dotaron y presidieron el primer cielo. De esta primer corona demiúrgica procedió una segunda, también con ángeles, potestades y tronos, y éstos fundaron otro cielo más bajo, que era el duplicado simétrico del inicial. Este segundo cónclave se vio reproducido en uno terciario, y éste en otro inferior, y de este modo hasta 365. El señor del cielo del fondo es el de la Escritura, y su fracción de divinidad tiende a cero. Él y sus ángeles fundaron este cielo visible, amasaron la tierra inmaterial que estamos pisando y se la repartieron después. (OC 213–14)]

Despite their differences (and beyond the obvious thematic similarities), all these chess-driven allegories and theological *mise en abymes* have three aspects in common: truth is inaccessible, our will is subjected to someone else's, and our derivative reality is always a mere subset of a larger (more real) one—which, in turn, is also embedded in a larger, more real reality, and so on. In Basilides's argument, though, there is an added element: this gradual departure from the source (or god or the idea) by the multiplication of increasingly cheapened copies implies not only an ontological devaluation but also an *ethical* degradation. According to Borges, this model has the virtue of being "a quiet resolution of the problem of evil by means of a hypothetical insertion of a gradual series of divinities between the no less hypothetical God and reality" (SNF 67) ["resolver sin escándalo el problema del mal, mediante la hipotética inserción de una serie gradual de divinidades entre el no menos hipotético Dios y la realidad" (OC 215)]. The world is full of pain, sin, error, crime, and guilt because divine qualities have progressively decayed with each emanation until we arrive to this, our lower, fallible world. In the Kabbalah

we have the same mechanism in the creations of the ten Sefirot and the four worlds. Those ten emanations, as they move farther from the *en sof* . . . lose strength, until they reach the one that created this world, this world where we are, so exposed to misfortune, so fleetingly happy. It is not an absurd idea. *We are faced with and eternal problem, the problem of evil.* (SN 101–02; my emphasis)

[tenemos el mismo mecanismo en las diez Sephirot y en los cuatro mundos que va creando. Esas diez emanaciones, a medida que se alejan del En Soph . . . van perdiendo fuerza, hasta llegar a la que crea este mundo, este mundo en el que estamos nosotros, tan llenos de errores, tan expuestos a la desdicha, tan momentáneos en la dicha. No es una idea absurda; *estamos enfrentados con un problema eterno que es el problema del mal.* (OC III: 272)]

The Gnostic and the Kabbalistic explanation of evil is, according to Borges, the same:

The idea . . . refers to an essential problem, that of the existence of evil, which the Gnostics and the Kabbalists resolved in the same way. They resolved it by declaring that the universe is the work of a deficient Divinity, one whose fraction of Divinity approaches zero, of a God who is not *the* God. Of a God who is a distant descendant of God. (SN 103)

[La idea . . . se refiere a un problema esencial, el de la existencia del mal, que los gnósticos y los cabalistas resuelven del mismo modo. Lo resuelven diciendo que el universo es obra de una Divinidad deficiente, cuya fracción de divinidad tiende a cero. Es decir, de un Dios que no es *el* Dios. De un Dios que desciende lejanamente de Dios. (OC III: 273)]

The god behind the god in the chess sonnets (and all the related texts) is thus not a mere exercise in symmetry or just a set of nesting boxes: inasmuch as it implies a hierarchy, a power structure, and a gradation from good to evil, it is the blueprint for an ethical and political system.

Framed

In the Borgesian notion of politics, power is defined in terms of representation and verisimilitude: it can be measured by the degree to which the fiction it imposes is believable. A fiction that is *completely* believable, a fiction that is superimposed onto reality with absolute perfection (like the map on the empire), a fiction so credible that it even ceases to be perceived as a fiction implies total, boundless power. Needless to say, this would be a divine fiction, and it would coincide with our world. But in Borges's stories, national states, secret sects, sorcerers, and even gangsters also manage to impose their dream or their game on others.

In this context, one of Borges's most recurrent formal procedures, framing his narratives, becomes highly relevant. As said, Borges's conception of power derives mostly from considering reality an administered construct rather than a mere given. Truth tends to be layered, and can only be approached asymptotically, traversing endless fictional strata, representations of representations. However, this is not only a mere topic of his texts but also the formal premise on which they are organized. Thus, it is not surprising that a great deal of Borges's fiction depends on a contextual deferral, the interposition of mediations, and the succession of layers of realities. In framing, his conceptions of literature, metaphysics (or theology), and politics come together and reveal their tight interdependency.

This formal determination is already visible in what is considered to be his first piece of fiction, "Man on Pink Corner." At first glance, this story—a tale of knife fights in the semibarbaric, semirural, turn-of-the-century Buenos Aires—seems completely unrelated to the issues discussed here. Told in an oral tone,[42] it transcribes the peculiarities of the colloquial speech of the time: in the foreword to the 1954 edition, Borges declares that the story has been written in the "intonation of the slum" ("entonación orillera" [OC 291]), which almost turns it into an exercise in ethnography—and this is why, although being one of his most successful stories in Argentina,

---

[42] In fact, the whole story is the response to a previous (omitted) utterance in a dialogue, as seen from the first sentence: "Imagine you bringing up, after all this time, the late Francisco Real" ["A mí, tan luego, hablarme del finado Francisco Real" (OC 329; my translation. Also in CF 45)].

Borges often dismissed it as a gimmick.[43] The story is told from the perspective of an unnamed narrator, who witnesses the following events: an out-of-town thug, Francisco Real, shows up at a dance to provoke resident ruffian Rosendo Juárez, for no reason in particular—just for sport and to prove that he has no equal in courage and strength. Rosendo, apparently realizing the absurdity of it all,[44] refuses to fight. Everyone at the dance despises him for what they believe is a cowardly retreat.[45] Rosendo leaves, while Francisco Real remains as the new ruling *cuchillero*. Shortly after, Francisco Real slips out for a private moment with La Lujanera, Rosendo's girlfriend. Soon, however, La Lujanera rushes back into the bar, terrified, screaming that someone (a stranger) has stabbed Francisco. They drag the wounded man into the bar. He dies. Nobody knows the killer's identity, but they end up believing it

---

[43] In the 1954 foreword, Borges is surprised that the story "has achieved an unusual and somewhat mystifying success" ["ha logrado un éxito singular y un poco misterioso" (OC 291)]. Twenty years later, he still refers to this as "the most read of [my] stories" ["el más leído de [mis] cuentos"] in the afterword to his *Obras Completas* (1114). Borges also declared, more than once, that he "rather overdid the local color [in this story], and spoiled it" (*Conversations* 31).

[44] This will become a recurrent topic in Borges's later fiction: the true hero is the one that immolates himself *morally* and not merely physically. *Not* fighting and taking the scorn that comes with it is braver than fighting; being a traitor is harder than being a hero—Judas, and not Jesus, is the true martyr. About 40 years after the publication of "Man on Pink Corner" Borges wrote "The Story from Rosendo Juárez" ["La historia de Rosendo Juárez"], included in *Brodie's Report*. Now Rosendo himself tells the story from his perspective. The oral tone remains, but this new version does not read like a transcription (the orthography is normalized). Recalling that night's events, Rosendo describes Francisco Real trying to pick a fight with him: "In that bullying fool I saw myself, like in a mirror, and I felt ashamed" ["En ese botarate provocador me vi como en un espejo y me dio vergüenza" (OC 1037; my translation. Also in CF 363)]. This later version can be taken as a correction or a rectification of "Man on Pink Corner." In terms of form, Borges corrects the regionalist tone of the original story (which always bothered him). Content-wise, it is Rosendo's opportunity to correct Paredes's first, distorted version, and set the record straight.

[45] Once again, in "The Story from Rosendo Juárez," the second version of this story, Rosendo says: "I am not afraid of being taken for a coward" (["No tengo miedo de pasar por cobarde" (OC 1038; my translation. Also in CF 363)]. A similar logic can be found in the classical Borgesian inversion of the traitor/hero opposition: the true hero gives up heroism and bravely embraces betrayal. "Theme of the Traitor and the Hero" is the obvious reference, but other texts include "Three Versions of Judas" (Judas, rather than Jesus, is the true martyr: who could compare an afternoon of bodily agony on the cross to a continuous spiritual torment? [cf. OC 516; CF 165–66]) and "The Spy," an untranslated short poem in *The Cipher* (OC III: 328) that beautifully condenses this paradox.

was the spiteful Rosendo reclaiming his honor and finally showing
the courage everyone thought he had lost. They throw Francisco
Real's body into the river before the police arrive. Then, in the final
sentence, comes the revelation. The nameless narrator says: "And
then, Borges, for the second time I pulled out that short, sharp-
edged knife I always carried here, under my vest, under my left arm,
and gave it another long slow inspection—and it was just like new,
all innocent, and there was not the slightest trace of blood on it"
(CF 52) ["Entonces, Borges, volví a sacar el cuchillo corto y filoso
que yo sabía cargar aquí en el chaleco, junto al sobaco izquierdo, y
le pegué otra revisada despacio, y estaba como nuevo, inocente, y
no quedaba ni un rastrito de sangre" (OC 334)].[46]

This story inaugurates a crucial Borgesian procedure inasmuch
as it is *not* the narrative of certain events but rather the narrative
of someone listening to (or reading) the narrative of certain events,
very much like the *Quijote*, which is *not* the story of don Quijote,
but rather the story of someone reading a translation of a tale in
Arabic (by one Cide Hamete Benengeli) that narrates the story of
demented Alonso Quijano who believes he is Don Quijote. Borges
often referred to these multiple nesting's in the *Quijote*, as in the
following poem, where Alonso Quijano declares that Cervantes
dreamed him so that he, Alonso, could dream up don Quijote:

My brother and my father, Captain Cervantes,
Fought nobly on the waters of Lepanto,
Learned Latin and a little Arabic . . .
That I might be allowed to dream the other

---

[46] Once we learn that the nameless narrator is the killer, we also discover that he is
a cheat as a storyteller. When Francisco Real, bleeding to death, is brought into the
bar, the narrator (who had stabbed him minutes earlier) looks at him and says: "I
thought that, whoever had done him, had had a steady hand" ["Yo pensé que no
le había temblado el pulso al que lo arregló" (OC 333; my translation. Also in CF
51)]. The swindle consists in thinking of "whoever had done him" (in Spanish, that
vague "al que lo arregló"). The first person (the actual murder) invents a dissociated
third person (a hypothetical, mysterious murder with a steady hand). This breach
in narrative ethics (for this is what this break of point of view is) is, in a way,
acknowledged in the 1970 prequel, "The Story of Rosendo Juárez." There, Rosendo
refers to the narrator of "Man on Pink Corner" and bluntly calls him a liar: "*he
liked to lie*, not to deceive, but to amuse people" (CF 358; my emphasis) ["*le gustaba
mentir*, no para engañar, sino para divertir a la gente" (OC 1034)]. His conception
of lying as a form of entertainment (seemingly detached from malice) makes the
narrator of "Man on Pink Corner" a true literary man.

Whose fertile memory will be a part
Of all the days of man, I humbly pray:
My God, my dreamer, keep on dreaming me. (SP 399–401)

[Mi hermano y padre, el capitán Cervantes
Que militó en los mares de Lepanto,
Y supo unos latines y algo de árabe . . .
Para que yo pueda soñar al otro
Cuya verde memoria será parte
De los días del hombre, te suplico:
Mi Dios, mi soñador, sigue soñándome. (OC III: 178–79)]

Once again, reality appears as a dream dreamed by a god. Once again, worlds nested within one another—Cervantes dreams Quijano, Quijano dreams Quijote. And once again, the boundaries between these worlds are distorted—Cervantes is both Quijano's father (his creator) and his brother (since Quijano is, himself, also a creator—he dreamed up don Quijote). Furthermore, both in Borges and Cervantes, the outermost layer of the narrative is inhabited not by the heroes but by a listener or a reader—the nameless narrator who reads Benengeli's manuscript, and "Borges," the listener in "Man on Pink Corner."

It is worth noting that there are two frames in "Man on Pink Corner." First, the story within the story, the fake reality that the nameless narrator stages for the rest of the characters—the fiction he puts up for the people at the dance according to which it was courageous Rosendo who killed Francisco Real. The second frame is the conversation between the killer and the listener and transcriber of the whole story ("Borges"). This second frame creates and sustains the illusion that the narrative is not a piece of fiction but something that is part of *our* world. The transcription of oral speech is obviously an attempt at achieving this verisimilitude, but the key moment is the mention of "Borges," a proper name that creates the illusion that the outermost frame is actually the referential world. The second person plural ("ustedes") is used a few times in the text, thus justifying its oral tone (the story is being told to a group of listeners), but it is that vocative in the final sentence, "Borges," that conjures up a new, "more real" context. The true paradox is that the effect of immediacy ("you are listening in on a true story that is being told to me right now") is achieved through the exacerbation of mediations. What is notable about "Man on Pink Corner" is that it simultaneously reveals that there was a story, *within* the story (the narrator's ploy) and a story *outside* the story ("Borges" is transcribing the whole tale[47]). It is not less remarkable that this double expansion, inward and outward, occurs in one single sentence.

The similarities between the formal architecture of "Man on Pink Corner" and the metaphysical blueprint drawn out in, for instance, the chess sonnets or the Gnostic theory of emanations is apparent— there is a reality (the true account of the facts by the killer) within a reality (the distorted account of the facts the people at the dance are left with) within a reality (the hyper-real, hyper-referential context of "Borges's" account or transcription).

First published in 1927 as "Leyenda Policial" by the avant-garde magazine *Martín Fierro*, "Man of Pink Corner" was later included in *Universal History of Infamy* [*Historia universal de la infamia* (1935)], in a little appendix with miscellaneous texts bearing the modest title of "Etcétera." In its own way, the book as a whole is also a game with shifting frames. It is well known that none of the stories in the book was Borges's own: they were all adaptations from existing books (including Mark Twain's *Life on the Mississippi* and don Juan Manuel's *Tales of Count Lucanor*). At the end of Borges's book, there is even an "Index of Sources." The only original story in the book (Borges refers to it as the only "cuento directo") is "Man on Pink Corner"—and, as shown, even this narrative is presented as a retold, "indirect" story. In the context of *matryoshka*-like structures, derived universes, fictions embedded within fictions, and realities emanating from one another, it seems hard not to read the entire book as a structure

---

[47] In "The Story from Rosendo Juárez," Rosendo tells "Borges": "You, sir, have put what happened in a novel [referring to "Man on Pink Corner"], which I am not able to appreciate, but I want you to learn the truth about these lies" ["Usted, señor, ha puesto el sucedido en una novela, que yo no estoy capacitado para apreciar, pero quiero que sepa la verdad sobre esos infundios" (OC 1034; my translation. Also in CF 358)]. To continue with the parallels with Cervantes, this resembles the second part of the *Quijote*, where the hero comments on the first part of the book.

of multilayered encapsulations. Herbert Asbury, author of *The Gangs of New York*, is behind Monk Eastman; Borges is behind Herbert Asbury.

Beginning with *Historia universal de la infamia* and, in particular, with "Man on Pink Corner," framed narratives become a staple of Borges's fiction.[48] Some of these frames are presented in a very classical way. Two brief examples: "The Immortal" (a story included in *The Aleph*) begins with the princess of Lucinge buying a copy of Pope's translation of the *Iliad* from an antique dealer. After the dealer's death, "in the last volume of the *Iliad* she found this manuscript. It is written in an English that teams with Latinisms. This is a verbatim transcription of the document" (CF 183) ["en el último tomo de la Ilíada hallo este manuscrito. El original está redactado en inglés y abunda en latinismos. La versión que ofrecemos es literal" (OC 533)]. Only then, after establishing this frame, does the story proper begin. The second example is "Brodie's Report" (included in the 1970 book of the same name). The opening sentence reads: "Tucked inside a copy, bought for me by my dear friend Paulino Keins, of the first volume of Lane's translation of *The Thousand and One Nights* . . . , we discovered the manuscript that I will now translate into Spanish." And then, in the second paragraph: "I will faithfully translate the manuscript and its colorless language" (CF 402) ["En un ejemplar del primer volumen de las *Mil y Una Noches* . . . de Lane, que me consiguió mi querido amigo Paulino Kleins, descubrimos el manuscrito que ahora traduciré al castellano. . . . Traduciré fielmente el informe, compuesto en un inglés incoloro" (OC 1073)]. It also is highly significant that both manuscripts appear in translated books. Translation, a lifelong concern of Borges's (both in a theoretical and practical sense), is, in itself, a very clear example of this model of texts within texts and frames inside frames (as in the transposition from Arabic into Spanish in the exemplary case of *Don Quijote*).

It is hard to overestimate the pervasiveness and importance of this framing strategy in Borges's literature. Perhaps a brief survey of his fiction (some poems and essays, omitted in the following list, also are, in ways of their own, framed) will help give an idea of the extent to which this procedure is present in his stories and how the

---

[48] Pauls discusses this "ethics of subordination" (104) in the seventh chapter of his book, pertinently titled "Second Hand" (103–23). See also Molloy 211–12.

fractal structure of worlds including worlds constitute his literature formally.[49]

- In "The Shape of the Sword" ["La forma de la espada"], the narrator retells the story John Vincent Moon told him: "This is the story [Moon] told, his English interspersed with Spanish, and even with Portuguese:" (CF 139) ["Ésta es la historia que contó, alternando el inglés con el español, y aun con el portugués:"(OC 492)]. The framed structure is key to the story's unfolding: the final revelation—the "twist"— consists, precisely, in showing that the framing narrator and the framed character are one and the same. Furthermore, the narrator overtly explains that the mediation of framing is the form his story demands. After revealing his double identity, the narrator says: "I have told you the story this way so that you would hear it out" (CF 142) ["Le he narrado la historia de este modo para que usted la oyera hasta el fin" (OC 495)]. John Vincent Moon "frames" and cheats in both registers—he betrays his Irish comrades in the framed story and he betrays his listener in the framing one.

- "The Theme of the Traitor and the Hero" ["Tema del traidor y del héroe"] takes the framing procedure one step beyond: "I have conceived this plot that I will perhaps write.... There are areas of the story that have never been revealed to me. Today, 3 January 1944, I see it in the following way" (CF 143) ["He imaginado este argumento que escribiré tal vez.... Hay zonas de la historia que no me fueron reveladas aún; hoy, 3 de enero de 1944, la vislumbro así." (OC 496)] This is *not* the story (the narrator says he might write it one day) but the frame within which the story may be produced in the future.

- In "Story of the Warrior and the Captive Maiden" ["Historia del guerrero y de la cautiva"], the narrator first quotes Croce, quoting Paul the Deacon (OC 557; CF 208), then "a tale I had heard once from my English grandmother, who is now dead"

---

[49] For a brilliant commentary on Borges's framed narratives, see John Barth's "Frame-Tale," a micro story that gives the framing procedure a twist (literally: the reader is supposed to physically twist the framing text) and turns it into an infinite (literally: the text goes on forever) Möbius strip (*Lost in the Funhouse* 1).

(CF 210) ["un relato que le oí alguna vez a mi abuela inglesa, que ha muerto" (OC 558)].

- In "Ibn-Hakam al-Bokhari, Murdered in His Labyrinth" ["Abenjacán el Bojarí, muerto en su laberinto"], Dunraven tells his friend Unwin the story of Abenjacán, after which, the narrative returns to the present time (the frame), where Unwin provides the solution to the mystery.

- The framing structure of "The Man on the Threshold" ["El hombre en el umbral"] resembles that of "The Shape of the Sword." The relevant sentence in the first paragraph reads: "Among the stories that [Christopher Dewey, of the British Council] told us that night, I shall be so bold as to reconstruct the one that follows. My text will be a faithful one" (CF 269) ["De las historias que esa noche contó [Christopher Dewey, del Consejo Británico], me atrevo a reconstruir la que sigue. Mi texto será fiel" (OC 612)]. The framing paragraph is followed by an asterisk and only then does the framed story, entirely in quotes, begin.

- In "The Duel" ["El duelo"], there is, once again, a twist to the frame. Some frames are about reading (or hearing) a story, which is later retold, but in this case (as in, to certain extent, "Theme of the Traitor and the Hero"), the frame is about the act of writing it ("Dictating this story is for me a modest, sideline sort of adventure" (CF 381) ["Dictar este relato es para mí una modesta y lateral aventura" (OC 1053)]. Taking the framing and contextual games to the next level, the narrator directly addresses the reader in the next sentence: "I should prevent the reader that the episodes of the tale are less important than the situation that leads to them ... " (SF 381) ["Debo prevenir al lector que los episodios importan menos que la situación que los causa ... " (OC 1053)].

- "The Interloper" ["La intrusa"] begins: "They say (though it seems unlikely) that Eduardo, the younger of the Nelson brothers, told the story at the wake for Cristián. . . . The truth is that someone heard [the story] from someone . . . , and then retold it to Santiago Dabove, from whom I heard it. . . . I now commit it to writing ... and I will do so conscientiously, though I can foresee that I will yield to the literary temptation of accentuating or adding some occasional detail" (CF 348;

edited) ["Dicen (lo cual es improbable) que la historia fue referida por Eduardo, el menor del los Nelson, en el velorio de Cristián. . . . Lo cierto es que alguien la oyó [la historia] de alguien . . . y la repitió a Santiago Dabove, por quien la supe. . . . La escribo ahora. . . . Lo haré con probidad, pero ya preveo que cederé a la tentación literaria de acentuar o agregar algún pormenor" (OC 1025)].

- "Unworthy" ["El indigno"] is another framed story entirely in quotes. The narrative follows this framing paragraph: "One afternoon when the two of us were alone, [Fischbein] confided to me an episode of his life, and today I can tell it. I will change the occasional detail—as is only to be expected" (CF 352) ["Una tarde en que los dos estábamos solos [Fischbein] me confió un episodio de su vida, que hoy puedo referir. Cambiaré, como es de prever, algún pormenor" (OC 1029)].

- In "The Story from Rosendo Juárez," the protagonist approaches "Borges" and tells him his story: "He offered to buy me a drink. I sat down and we chatted. . . . The man said:" (CF 358; edited) ["Me invitó a que tomara algo con él. Me senté y charlamos. . . . El hombre me dijo:" (OC 1034)].

- In "Juan Muraña," Trápani tells "Borges" the story of his uncle, a famed *compadrito* (OC 1044; CF 370). The framed story is also in quotes and ends with the reinstatement of the frame.

- This oral frame can also be found in "The Other Duel" ["El otro duelo"], where the narrator tells a story he has heard from Carlos Reyles, who had heard it from his father who had heard it from his foreman, who, in turn, knew it because it was part of an "oral tradition" (OC 1058; CF 386).

- "*Undr*," a late story included in *The Book of Sand*, begins: "I must warn the reader that the pages I transpose and publish here will be sought in vain in the *Libellus* (1615) of Adam of Bremen. . . . Lappenberg found them within a manuscript in the Bodleian, at Oxford. . . . My Spanish version [once again, the story is a translation] is not literal, but it is faithful. Thus writes Adam of Bremen:" (CF 455; edited) ["Debo prevenir al lector que las páginas que traslado se buscarán en vano en el *Libellus* (1615) de Adán de Bemen. . . . Lappenberg las halló en un manuscrito de la Bodleiana de Oxford. . . . Mi versión española no es literal, pero es digna de fe. Escribe Adán de Bremen:" (OC III: 48)].

- "The Night of the Gifts" ["La noche de los dones"] begins by establishing a frame: "It was at the Old Café Águila . . . that we heard the story. . . . An elderly gentleman . . . decided to intervene. He spoke with slow assurance:" (CF 446) ["En la Antigua Confitería del Águila . . . oímos la historia. . . . Un señor de edad . . . se resolvió a tomar la palabra. Dijo con lenta seguridad:" (OC III: 41)].

- "The Sect of the Thirty" ["La secta de los treinta"], a story that resembles "The immortal" and "Brodie's Report" in many ways, begins thus: "The original manuscript may be consulted in the library at the University of Leyden; it is in Latin, but its occasional Hellenism justifies the conjecture that it may be a translation from the Greek [again, the issue of translation]. . . . These are the words of the anonymous author:" (CF 443) ["El manuscrito original puede consultarse en la Biblioteca de la universidad de Leiden; está en latín, pero algún helenismo justifica la conjetura de que fue vertido del griego. . . . Reza el autor anónimo:" (OC III: 38)].

The colon, with which many of the above quotes end, is the obvious graphic boundary between both planes. The frame tends to refer to the conditions that made the story contained within it possible—how the narrator came into its possession, or even how he managed to write it. In most cases, the desired effect of this artifice is to increase the narrative's verisimilitude. However, in some other instances the intention is, in fact, the diametrically opposite one: to stress the absolutely fictional quality of the story about to unfold. This is, for instance, the case with "The Duel." Instead of assuring the reader that the ensuing account is a true one (or a faithful transcription, or an accurate translation of a genuine testimony or document), the frame is there to emphasize the fact that what follows is a piece of literature. This is what "dictating this story" achieves. The paradoxical effect of this is that the more the narrator admits that his framed tale is a mere fiction, the more real the frame seems. In "El duelo" the reader feels she has had a glimpse into the blind man's study, where he is dictating, "now," the very words she is reading.

This is precisely what occurs in stories where the framing procedure is much subtler, such as in "Death and the Compass." In this detective story, Red Scharlach, the villain, famously weaves a fictional world for his archenemy, detective Eric Lönnrot: "I swore," the criminal tells Lönnrot toward the end of the story, "to weave a labyrinth around the man who had imprisoned my brother. I have woven it, and it has stood firm" (CF 154–55) ["yo juré . . . tejer un laberinto en torno del hombre que había encarcelado a mi hermano. Lo he tejido y es firme" (OC 506)]. At this point, the reader and the detective share the realization that the majority of the story (the murders, the motives behind them, the scattered clues, the Kabbalistic conspiracy) was a fabrication, an alternate reality (or an "emanation," as the Kabbalistic tradition would have it) created by Red Scharlach.[50] In this (loose) sense, this is a framed story. However, there is a god behind the god. When Lönnrot believes to have cracked the case and heads to prevent the last crime (thus falling into the labyrinthine trap devised by his rival), the text reads: "South of the city of *my* story flows a stream of muddy water" (CF 152; my emphasis) ["Al sur de la ciudad de *mi* cuento fluye un ciego riachuelo de aguas borrosas" (OC 504)]. This is the only use of a first person pronoun in a story otherwise narrated in a solid third person. As in "Man on Pink Corner," there is both an "inner" story (the fiction constructed by one of the characters—Scharlach and Nicolás Paredes) and an "outer" story (an exterior frame containing the entirety of the narrative). What the name "Borges" does in "Man on Pink Corner" here is achieved by the brief syntagm "mi cuento." Furthermore, this first person ("mi") is associated with the word "cuento," which, in Spanish, is an exclusively fictional narrative, something that the English word "story" does not fully convey. The whole story, which at first was presented as an unmediated, direct account of a reality (something that, at all events, had every intention to pass for a reality or, at least, never acknowledged its own imaginary status), now turns out to be a fiction, a *cuento*. As in "El duelo," declaring that the story is a mere invention has the effect of turning the one making the

---

[50] For an outstanding analysis of how these two stories intertwine, see Ricardo Piglia's "Tesis sobre el cuento" and "Nuevas tesis sobre el cuento" in *Formas breves* (103–37). Piglia cleverly calls the fiction Scharlach forces on Lönnrot an "imposed Bovarism" ["un bovarismo forzado"] in *El último lector* (35).

declaration (in this case, the one behind the possessive pronoun) seem real.

Borges takes this framing game even further in some of his other stories, like, for instance, "A Survey of the Works of Herbert Quain" ["Examen de la obra de Herbert Quain"]. At first sight, this seems to be a classic Borges story: it is a text in first person where different genres coexist in more or less equal terms—this is a piece of fiction, but it is also an essay, a biographical note and, like "Pierre Menard," an obituary and a panegyric. It is also highly typical in that it convincingly presents an apocryphal author together with a model for a new literature. It is, however, in the last sentence where, once again, in one single stroke, the entire story is framed. The narrator is examining Quain's last book and concludes by saying: "From [Quain's] third story, titled 'The Rose of Yesterday,' I was ingenuous enough to extract 'The Circular Ruins,' which is one of the stories in my book *Garden of Forking Paths*" (CF 111) ["Del tercer [relato], *The Rose of Yesterday*, yo cometí la ingenuidad de extraer *Las ruinas circulares*, que es una de las narraciones del libro *El jardín de los senderos que se bifurcan*" (OC 464)]. With this, the hitherto anonymous first person narrator suddenly acquires a new dimension—he becomes "Borges." Not only that, this declaration also affects "The Circular Ruins." The story, itself about successive framings (a man dreams a man, only to discover that he himself is another man's dream), now acquires another "more exterior" frame. This new dreamer is obviously "Borges" since he identifies himself as the author not only of "The Circular Ruins" but also of the book in which it, together with "A Survey of the Works of Herbert Quain," is included. Once again, the effect of the multiplicated mediations (or emanations or *matryoshkas*) is underscoring the fictive character of the "inner" realities and, by contrast, consolidating the verisimilitude of the "outer" frame.

Before proceeding, it may be helpful to recapitulate and emphasize the role of this framing structure within the general argument. The point of departure, in the previous section, was the relationship between politics and metaphysics in some of Borges's texts, starting with his idealistic conception of the homeland/fatherland ("patria") in the "Ode Written in 1966." It became clear in this poem that Borges's idea of nation was related to Berkeley's immaterialism: in order to be, it had to be perceived, and since the fatherland, according to Borges, is transhistorical, the perceiver can be no other than god. But in the poem, rather than being perceived, we are being dreamed. This turns the world into a fiction, or a second (and to some extent weaker) reality embedded within, derived from, and subordinated to a primordial (and therefore truer) reality. This is, in very broad strokes, the premise of idealism, in all its incarnations from Plato onward, which Borges extensively discusses throughout his work. This representation, as we saw, has political connotations: power consists in the ability of imposing these projections or fictions as "the real thing," and within this metaphysical context, the problem of power, taken to its ultimate source, necessarily ends up remitting to god. Some of Borges's sources for this model, aside from Plato and Berkeley, can be found in the Gnostics, in the Kabbalah, in Buddhism, and, to a lesser extent, in Leibniz and (through mostly negative references) Kant. In all these cases, albeit in radically different forms, our reality appears as a mere emanation or a degraded copy of a higher one. This is a frequent topic in Borges's literature: our world is a game where the players are, in fact, mere pawns—played by players who are, in fact, mere pawns. . . . However, and this crucial point brings us to our present discussion, this theological conspiracy is not simply a topic or a theme: for Borges, these emanations and multilayered games constitute a *formal* principle. A significant portion of his fiction, if not the majority of it, is shaped on the premise that there is another reality beyond (or nested within) reality. Fictions are encapsulated within fictions; hence, Borges's recurrent framing strategy of establishing a frame of reference containing the story proper (which, in turn, may contain yet a third reality, and so forth). The boundaries between these "emanations" sometimes are clearly drawn, but they can also be blurry and somewhat more sophisticated (as in "Death and the Compass" or "A Survey of the Works of Herbert Quain"), and one world may even filter through the dividing membrane and contaminate the other. This is the case with "Tlön, Uqbar, Orbis Tertius."

This is not an easy story to summarize, but a brief synopsis could help as a reminder of the general context of the discussion. In the first of the three parts of "Tlön, Uqbar, Orbis Tertius," an unnamed narrator is introduced, by his friend Bioy Casares, to Uqbar, a country only mentioned in one particular copy of a bootleg edition of the *Encyclopedia Britannica*. This entry contains general aspects of this strange country's geography and culture and states that its literature refers only to two imaginary worlds, one of which is called Tlön. All attempts to find more references to Uqbar prove fruitless. In the second part, the narrator comes across the eleventh volume of the *First Encyclopaedia of Tlön*. If Uqbar was just an entry about a country, this is a multivolume endeavor about a full planet, Tlön (which, it should be stressed, *is the fictional world where all the literature of Uqbar, a fictional country, takes place*). The narrator and his friends speculate that it must have taken decades, even centuries, and a legion of "Tlönists" to carry out a project of such magnitude. The narrator also offers a summary of Tlön's philosophy and conception of language: they are idealists to such a degree that their doctrine has ended up modifying the world itself. Intellectual objects become tangible ones (called "hrönir"), and those places and things that are no longer perceived disappear. These first two parts are followed by a postscript, dated seven years later. In it, the truth about Uqbar and Tlön is revealed. Uqbar was invented in the seventeenth century by a "secret and benevolent society" (CF 78) ["Una sociedad secreta y benévola" (OC 440)]. Ever since, the society had been constantly laboring on its imagined country. However, in 1824, one of the initiated in the Uqbar society befriends one Ezra Buckley, a millionaire from Memphis, Tennessee. Buckley finds the project laughable: "he told the man that in America it was nonsense to invent a country—what they ought to do was to invent a planet" (CF 79) ["le dice que en América es absurdo inventar un país y le propone la invención de un planeta" (OC 441)]. Buckley's vast wealth goes into the *First Encyclopaedia of Tlön*. *Orbis Tertius* is a revision (presumably still ongoing in the shadows) of the encyclopedia of Tlön written in one of Tlön's languages. During the seven-year hiatus that separates the two first parts from the postscript, Tlön has become public knowledge. With the dissemination of its existence, the alternate world grows stronger and floods and takes over our own. School curricula are rewritten to accommodate Tlön's reality. Our history is replaced by Tlön's fables. Our science, philosophy, and languages become, gradually, Tlönian. Hrönir even start to pop up here and there. Toward the end, the melancholy narrator deplores that eventually, "the world will be Tlön" (CF 81) ["el mundo será Tlön" (OC 443)].

In "Tlön, Uqbar, Orbis Tertius," then, most of the issues discussed so far come together in a constellation: the difficulty of tracing boundaries between worlds nested in one another, the problem of framing and how the layered worlds it creates relate to the idealist tradition, and finally, how all these matters acquire a political dimension—the conspiratorial figure of the secret society reemerges here, but more importantly, the entire world order is reorganized according to new metaphysical principles, thus showing the reciprocal determinations of politics and philosophy.

Unsurprisingly, this is a framed story, albeit in an unorthodox way: instead of preceding the narrative (as in most cases listed above), the frame follows it in the form of a postscript written seven years after the framed story: "I reproduce the article above exactly as it appeared in the *Anthology of Fantastic Literature*" (CF 78) ["Reproduzco el artículo anterior tal como apareció en la *Antología de la literatura fantástica* (OC 440)]," the narrator says after the first two parts. The first two parts are, then, texts quoted and embedded within another. This is the first manifestation of the series of inclusions and hierarchies around which the text is organized. Part of the complexity of "Tlön, Uqbar, Orbis Tertius" derives from the fact that the structure of the narrative does not follow the structure of these inclusions: the world of the narrator (postscript) contains the apocryphal country of Uqbar (part I), which, in turn, contains the fictional planet of Tlön (part II). However, in the end, it is Tlön, the innermost fiction, the one farthest removed from the referential world, that takes over reality.

It should be noted that the fictional status of Tlön is never disputed. As said, Tlön is one of the two imaginary planets where all of Uqbar's literature is set: "the literature of Uqbar was a literature of fantasy, and . . . its epics and legends never referred to reality but rather to the two imaginary realms of Mlejnas and Tlön" (CF 70) ["la literatura de Uqbar era de carácter fantástico y . . . sus epopeyas y sus leyendas no se referían jamás a la realidad, sino a las dos regiones imaginarias de Mlejnas y de Tlön" (OC 432)]. Succinctly put, the fictional planet of a fictional country in a compilation of fiction ends up inundating our own reality.

The dams between literature and reality start leaking at the very beginning of the story. Mentioned in passing, in the supposedly marginal details that set the scene in the first sentences, there is already a distortion of the boundaries between literature and life: "Bioy Casares had come to dinner that evening, and we had lost track of time in a vast debate over the way one might go about composing a first-person novel whose narrator would omit or distort things and engage in all sorts of contradictions, so that a few of the book's readers—a very few—might divine the horrifying or banal truth" (CF 68) ["Bioy Casares había cenado conmigo esa noche y nos demoró una vasta polémica sobre la ejecución de una novela en primera persona, cuyo narrador omitiera o desfigurara los hechos e incurriera en diversas contradicciones, que permitieran a unos pocos lectores—a muy pocos lectores—la adivinación de una realidad atroz o banal" (OC 431)]. This hypothetical text (which could easily be a book by Herbert Quain) is to be completed or corrected outside its own limits. In other words, the text extends itself *beyond* its own boundaries and into the reader's world. It requires this external intervention, not just as any text demands a reader: it needs to be rectified or concluded from the *outside* to work. This fiction that stretches into reality and that proposes new links between the textual and extratextual worlds foreshadows Tlön.[51]

The reverse current (from the real world to the literary one) is also at work in this text. The story is saturated with real and well-known names: Bioy Casares, Carlos Mastronardi, Néstor Ibarra, Ezequiel Martínez Estrada, Drieu La Rochelle, Xul Solar, and Alfonso Reyes are some of Borges's friends and colleagues roaming through the text. It may even be Borges's most overcrowded text in this sense. This is quite obviously a way to strengthen the verisimilitude of the narrative—and it is not a procedure new to Borges who, as seen, does not hesitate to use his own name as a device to render a story more credible. However, what makes this strategy noteworthy in this context is that it is an inversion of the whole premise of "Tlön, Uqbar, Orbis Tertius." The story is about fiction invading reality. But through this multitude of proper names, it is reality that pushes through and punctures fiction. And somehow, this makes the possibility of fiction invading reality more plausible, not merely because these proper names generate a "reality effect" but because the membrane separating both has been called into question, and now traffic between these two spheres is possible—regardless of the direction in which it flows.

Despite the numerous references to real people and places, once we reach the postscript (the frame), we learn that the first two

---

[51] Another premonition is the mention of Johannes Valentinus Andreae, "a German theologian who in the early seventeenth century described an imaginary community, the Rosy Cross—which other men later founded, in imitation of his foredescription" (CF 70) ["un teólogo alemán que a principios del siglo XVII describió la imaginaria comunidad de la Rosa-Cruz—y que otros luego fundaron, a imitación de lo prefigurado por él" (OC 433)], which clearly foretells what will later happen with Tlön: a fiction affects the real world to the point that the latter ends up being modeled after the former.

(framed) parts were, in fact, fiction: "I reproduce the article above exactly as it appeared in the *Anthology of Fantastic Literature*" (CF 78) ["Reproduzco el artículo anterior tal como apareció en la *Antología de literatura fantástica*" (OC 440)]. The postscript (the framing text) presents itself as the "real world," the referential universe the texts creates for itself, whose "reality" derives from the fact that it is the point of view from which fiction is identified as such—or, put differently, from being the site from which other texts, such as parts I and II, can be recognized as *fantastic* literature, as they are indeed in the *Antología*.[52] It is this real world that ends up being hijacked by the first (fantastic) one. The paradoxical effect of this is that the frame, supposedly the space where the text claims to be real, turns out to be the more fantastic part of the story: a secret society creating an encyclopedia about a nonexistent country or planet, as in the first two parts, is hardly fantastic compared to the invasion of our world by those fictions, as is the case in the postscript. Furthermore, the postscript/frame is dated 1947, even if the story was first published in 1940. In other words, Borges subverts the traditional hierarchies and procedures of framed stories by turning the frame into something more fantastic than what it frames. Thus, the story mimics formally its own content: if the tale is about a fictional world seeping into the real one, this is precisely what the text *does*—the fantastic story in parts I and II invades the real universe of the frame in the postscript.

The first sign of intrusion of the fictional planet can be found in a fleeting, almost marginal passage in section II: "Popular magazines have trumpeted, with pardonable excess, the zoology and topography of Tlön" (CF 72) ["Las revistas populares han divulgado, con perdonable exceso, la zoología y la topografía de Tlön" (OC 435)]. Tlön no longer is an esoteric project of a few illuminati: it has seeped into popular culture and has been widely disseminated by magazines with massive circulation. The second, more significant intrusion, appears in a footnote, also in section II: "Today, one of the churches of Tlön contends, Platonically, that a certain pain, a certain temperature, and a certain sound are the

---

[52] But the notion of "fantastic literature" itself is destabilized in the story. We are told that the previous two parts had been included in an anthology of fantastic literature. However, the narrator refers to these texts as an "article," which, of course, is a genre that does not belong (without some sort of explanation) in such an anthology.

only reality" (CF 76 fn.) ["En el día de hoy, una de las Iglesias de Tlön sostiene platónicamente que tal dolor, que tal matiz verdoso del amarillo, que tal temperatura, que tal sonido, son la única realidad" (OC 438 fn.)]. The alternate world of Tlön not only has been divulged through mass-circulation magazines but also has had a direct impact on reality—Tlönian institutions (in this case, a church) have taken root in the real world.[53] Later, the narrator recalls how the fictional world began leaking into his own. The first object from the other world is a compass, engraved with Tlönian characters: "That was the first intrusion of the fantastic world of Tlön into the real world" (CF 80) ["Tal fue la primera intrusión del mundo fantástico en el mundo real" (OC 441)]. This is followed by the finding of several hrönir (materialized ideas) around the globe. The narrator ventures the hypothesis that "disseminating Tlönian objects through various countries would complement [the] plan" (CF 81) ["La diseminación de objetos de Tlön en diversos países complementaría ese plan" (OC 442)] of the *Orbis Tertius* society to strengthen the verisimilitude of their world.[54]

The true cause of the collapse of the boundaries of reality, however, is textual. It is the dissemination of Tlönian texts that ends up fissuring our world: "Handbooks, anthologies, summaries, literal versions, authorized and pirated reprints of Mankind's Greatest Masterpiece filled the world, and still do. *Almost immediately, reality 'caved in'[55] at more than one point*" (CF 81; my

---

[53] Obviously, the footnote is, even if as a mere rhetorical artifice, removed (at least by one degree) from the fictional realm of the story—the footnote aims to identify the narrator, clearly a textual instance, with an extraliterary, empirical, "real" subject, such as an author or an editor, thus generating the illusion of the referential world intervening "from the outside." The adverbial phrase ("En el día de hoy") helps cementing the illusion that there is a church of Tlön in the real world.

[54] However, this last sentence is followed by a footnote: "There is still, of course, the problem of the *material* from which some objects are made" (CF 81) ["Queda, naturalmente, el problema del *material* de algunos objetos" (OC 442)]. At this point the text takes an eerie turn. Tlön is false, yes, and clearly, members of the secret society have planted the hrönir to later be "discovered." However, the problem of the material constitution of these objects remains—no known earthly matter has the uncanny density these small pieces of metal have.

[55] Andrew Hurley's quotation marks are a truly objectionable license. The world *did* cave in. The quotes undo the main premise and the effect of the story. However, this unjustifiable intervention has the virtue of showing, despite itself, precisely where the force of Borges's story resides.

emphasis) ["Manuales, antologías, resúmenes, versiones literales, reimpresiones autorizadas y reimpresiones piráticas de la Obra Mayor de los hombres abarrotaron y siguen abarrotando la tierra. *Casi inmediatamente, la realidad cedió en más de un punto*" (OC 442)]. Reality yields under the weight of Tlönian bibliography and ends up conforming and adapting to it. Later, the narrator says: "contact with Tlön, the habit of Tlön, has disintegrated this world" (CF 81) ["El contacto y el hábito de Tlön han desintegrado este mundo" (OC 443)]. The framed (fictional) reality finally overtakes the framing (real) one. It is the *idea* of Tlön that brings Tlön about: Tlön *is* because the perception of it (through magazines, encyclopedias, textbooks, etc.) has become widespread.

The narrator states: "The nations of that planet [Tlön] are, congenitally, idealistic. Their language and those things derived from their language—religion, literature, metaphysics—presuppose idealism" (CF 72) ["Las naciones de ese planeta [Tlön] son— congénitamente—idealistas. Su lenguaje y las derivaciones de su lenguaje—la religión, las letras, la metafísica—presuponen el idealismo" (OC 435)]. This should not be surprising, given that Berkeley was one of the founding members of the Uqbar society (CF 78; OC 440). And "Tlön, Uqbar, Orbis Tertius" is, in more than one way, a philosophical joke based on a double misreading of Berkeley's dogmatic idealism. The first misreading is the result of excess, while the second derives from lack. On the one hand, his doctrine is taken to fanatical extremes. If Berkeley shows it "to be impossible that any . . . sensible quality whatsoever should exist in an unthinking subject without the mind, or in truth, that there should be any such thing as an outward object" (Berkeley 30), Tlönians take this in a radical sense and turn the mind into the material, formal, and efficient *cause* of objects—the hrönir:

> Century upon century of idealism could hardly have failed to influence reality. In the most ancient regions of Tlön one may, not infrequently, observe the duplication of lost objects: Two persons are looking for a pencil; the first finds it, but says nothing; the second finds a second pencil, no less real, but more in keeping with his expectations. These secondary objects are called *hrönir*, and they are, though awkwardly so, slightly longer. (CF 77)

> [Siglos y siglos de idealismo no han dejado de influir en la realidad. No es infrecuente, en las regiones más antiguas de

Tlön, la duplicación de objetos perdidos. Dos personas buscan un lápiz; la primera lo encuentra y no dice nada; la segunda encuentra un segundo lápiz, no menos real, pero más ajustado a su expectativa. Esos objetos secundarios se llaman *hrönir* y son, aunque de forma desairada, un poco más largos. (OC 439)]

In Tlön, something perceived in the mind, immediately *is* in the world, even though Berkeley clearly states "it is impossible for an idea to do anything, or, strictly speaking, to be the cause of anything" (34). This is, then, the excessive interpretation of Berkeley. The lack, on the other hand, the gaping hole in this misreading is, absurdly enough, god, without whom Berkeley's entire argument simply collapses. One of the objections (the fourth) he presents himself in *A Treatise Concerning the Principles of Human Knowledge* reads: "It will be objected that from the foregoing principles it follows, things are every moment annihilated and created anew. The objects of sense exist only when they are perceived. . . . Upon shutting my eyes all the furniture in the room is reduced to nothing, and barely upon opening them it is again created" (Berkeley 42). Berkeley's response to this objection is that "wherever bodies are said to have no existence without the mind, I would not be understood to mean this or that particular mind, but all minds whatsoever" (44), which ultimately leads to god: "all objects are eternally known by God or, which is the same thing, have an eternal existence in his mind," says Philonous in the third *Dialogue* (196). Without god, there is no ontological stability: thinking of an object would be enough to conjure it up materially and ceasing to perceive it would cause its obliteration.

Things duplicate themselves on Tlön; they also tend to fade away and to lose detail when people forget them. The classic example is the threshold that persisted so long as a certain beggar frequented it, but which was lost to sight when he died. Sometimes a few birds, a horse, have saved the ruins of an amphitheater. (CF 78; edited)

[Las cosas se duplican en Tlön; propenden asimismo a borrarse y a perder los detalles cuando los olvida la gente. Es clásico el ejemplo de un umbral que perduró mientras lo visitaba un mendigo y que se perdió de vista a su muerte. A veces unos pájaros, un caballo, han salvado las ruinas de un anfiteatro. (OC 440)]

As Borges writes in "Berkeley at the Crossroads" ["La encrucijada de Berkeley"], his first (untranslated) essay on the Bishop, published in 1923, "God is not the maker of all things, but rather the one who meditates about life, or an immortal and ubiquitous spectator of life. *His eternal vigilance prevents the universe from being annihilated or reconstituted capriciously according to the attention of individuals*, and it also provides the entire system with firmness and grave prestige" ["Dios no es hacedor de las cosas; es más bien un meditador de la vida o un inmortal y ubicuo espectador del vivir. *Su eterna vigilancia impide que el universo se aniquile y resurja a capricho de atenciones individuales*, y además presta firmeza y grave prestigio a todo el sistema" (I 122; my emphasis)]. The hrönir, those objects produced by merely conjuring up the idea of them, and the complementary disappearance of forgotten things and places are testimony to Tlön's godlessness.

"Hume declared for all time that while Berkeley's arguments admit not the slightest refutation, they inspire not the slightest conviction" ["Hume notó para siempre que los argumentos de Berkeley no admiten la menor réplica y no causan la menor convicción"], the narrator says in "Tlön, Uqbar, Orbis Tertius" (CF 72; OC 435).[56] Without god, however, very little of Berkeley's arguments remains standing. Why, then, do away with the theological foundation of his philosophical edifice? The answer can be found where theology and politics converge. The American capitalist funding the Tlön society has a clear political agenda: create a religion-free world. Ezra Buckley fosters the development of Tlön with the main purpose of elevating man to the stature of demiurge in order to deny god. "Buckley did not believe in God, yet he wanted to prove to the nonexistent God that mortals could conceive and shape a world" (CF 79) ["Buckley descree de Dios, pero quiere demostrar al Dios no existente que los hombres mortales son capaces de concebir un mundo" (OC 441)]. He is also the one who turns the endeavor into a conspiracy—"to that giant of an idea he added another, the brainchild of his nihilism: The enormous enterprise must be kept secret" (CF 79) ["a esa gigantesca idea añade otra, hija de su nihilismo: la de guardar en el silencio la empresa enorme" (OC 441)]. The secret society and its invention follow, after all, a clear ideological program—and the

---

[56] Borges self-plagiarizes this quote from "The Postulation of Reality" ["La postulación de la realidad"], in his 1932 *Discusión* (OC 217; SNF 59).

way to carry it out is precisely by knitting a fiction large enough to completely enshroud reality.

As we have seen, in many of Borges's stories, power consists in the imposition of a reality, which, taken to its ultimate consequences, can have divine qualities—the creation of a new order that others accept as an unquestionable reality is, in the end, godlike. Therefore, politics eventually becomes a theological issue. As the Tlön society, the Congress, the Sect of the Phoenix, the Babylonian lottery company, the circular dreamers, or the chess players superimpose an order onto the world that coincides inch by inch with it (again, like that perfect map stretching over the entire empire). These are all subsets that overtake the superset. In this sense, "totalitarianism" can be understood quite literally as that instance when one particular order or configuration (which is necessarily partial and therefore *contained* within reality) expands and elevates itself to the entirety of reality. The political dimension of framing does not escape Borges. As said, after the flood of Tlönian bibliography,

> almost immediately, reality caved in more than one point. The truth is it wanted to cave in. Ten years ago [1937] any symmetry with an appearance of order—dialectical materialism, anti-Semitism, Nazism—was enough to spellbind mankind. How could the world not fall under the sway of Tlön, how could it not yield to the vast and minutely detailed evidence of an ordered planet? It would be futile to reply that reality is also orderly. Perhaps it is, but orderly in accordance with divine laws (I translate: inhuman laws) that we never quite manage to perceive. Tlön may be a labyrinth, but it is a labyrinth forged by men, a labyrinth destined to be deciphered by men. (CF 81)
>
> [casi inmediatamente, la realidad cedió en más de un punto. Lo cierto es que anhelaba ceder. Hace diez años [1937] bastaba cualquier simetría con apariencia de orden—el materialismo dialéctico, el antisemitismo, el nazismo—para embelesar a los hombres. ¿Cómo no someterse a Tlön, a la minuciosa y vasta evidencia de un planeta ordenado? Inútil responder que la realidad también está ordenada. Quizá lo esté, pero de acuerdo a leyes divinas—traduzco: a leyes inhumanas—que no acabamos nunca de percibir. Tlön será un laberinto, pero es un laberinto urdido por los hombres, un laberinto destinado a que lo descifren los hombres. (OC 442)]

There is a direct line from totalitarian regimes (National Socialism, Communism) that impose a "simetría con apariencia de orden" to the fiction of Tlön. Any order that pretends to be absolute is both tyrannical and absurd. What is remarkable is how eagerly everyone adopts the new reality of Tlön, despite being clearly a fiction. And it is precisely this noncoercive acceptance of the representation that turns it into a reality.

Ezra Buckley's deicide has been a full success: a human (subordinated, partial) order has displaced the divine, all-embracing one. Again, Borges resorts to chess: "Spellbound by Tlön's rigor, humanity has forgotten, and continues to forget, that it is the rigor of chess masters, not of angels" (CF 81) ["Encantada por su rigor [el de Tlön], la humanidad olvida y torna a olvidar que es un rigor de ajedrecistas, no de ángeles" (OC 443)]. The sonnets on chess offer the best exegesis of this passage.

But why even bother to mention Berkeley, if Buckley will ultimately do away with god? Precisely because his dogmatic idealism provides the philosophical support for the key element in the story: the fact that something *is* by virtue of being perceived ("Buckley," by the way, sounds like a slightly disfigured version—very much like a hrön—of "Berkeley"[57]). This explains the hrönir, of course, and also the story as a whole. After all, Tlön is, in its entirety, a

---

[57] Aside from the Buckley/Berkeley connection, there is another strong hrön-like correlation—that between Ezra Buckley and Silas Buckley. The latter is the alias with which Lazarus Morell (from "The Cruel Redeemer Lazarus Morell," in *Universal History of Infamy*) checks into hospital shortly before dying. Both Silas Buckley and Ezra Buckley are Southerners, and both are strong supporters of slavery: "[Ezra] Buckley was a freethinker, a fatalist, and a defender of slavery," Borges writes in "Tlön, Uqbar, Orbis Tertius" (CF 79 fn) ["Buckley era librepensador, fatalista y defensor de la esclavitud" (OC 441 fn)]. Silas Buckley, a.k.a. Lazarus Morell, instigated slaves to flee from their masters only to resell them, over and again (cf. the section called "The Method" in "The Cruel Redeemer Lazarus Morell" CF 9–10; OC 297–98). Thus, "Buckley" is a Russian doll: Ezra Buckley contains Silas Buckley, who contains Lazarus Morell, who contains John Murrell, the historical figure that Mark Twain describes in Chapter XXIX of *Life on the Mississippi* (404–13).

Furthermore, the name "Silas" also appears in "Tlön, Uqbar, Orbis Tertius" Silas Haslam (Borges borrowed the last name from his paternal grandmother) is the author of a *History of the Land Called Uqbar* (CF 70; OC 432). In other words, Silas Buckley, the protagonist of the opening story of Borges's first book of fiction, appears dismembered in "Tlön, Uqbar, Orbis Tertius" split into *Silas* Haslam and Ezra *Buckley*. And both names merit footnotes in the story as if stressing that they both point to something beyond the text.

hrön—an world that, just by virtue of being perceived intellectually, ends up becoming a real presence.

According to Borges's beloved Schopenhauer, "Berkeley . . . arrived at *idealism* proper; in other words, at the knowledge that what is extended in space, and hence the objective, material world in general, exists as such simply and solely in our *representation*, and it is false and indeed absurd to attribute to it, *as such*, an existence outside all representation and independent of the knowing subject, and so to assume a matter positively and absolutely existing in itself. But this very correct and deep insight really constitutes the whole of Berkeley's philosophy, and in it he had exhausted himself" (Schopenhauer 4). Once again it becomes fundamental to underscore the notion of *representation* without which the entire tradition of idealism, from Plato to Berkeley, is unthinkable. As was suggested earlier on, it is precisely this notion (often exaggerated and parodied, as is the case in "Tlön, Uqbar, Orbis Tertius") that constitutes the cornerstone of Borges's conception of politics. Toward the end of "Avatars of the Tortoise," Borges writes: "Let us admit what all idealists admit: the hallucinatory nature of the world. Let us do what no idealist has done: seek unrealities which confirm that nature. We shall find them, I believe, in the antinomies of Kant and in the dialectic of Zeno" (L 208) ["Admitamos lo que todos los idealistas admiten: el carácter alucinatorio del mundo. Hagamos lo que ningún idealista ha hecho: busquemos irrealidades que confirmen ese carácter. Las hallaremos, creo, en las antinomias de Kant y en la dialéctica de Zenón" (OC 258)]. This is a marvelous paradox: if the ultimate truth of idealism resides in the unreal quality of the world, the only way to confirm "reality" is by producing unrealities. This is exactly what Tlön and all the other "superimposed" (or unreal) realities in Borges are. The political dimension of this aporia emerges in the following (and final) paragraph of Borges's essay:

"*The greatest magician* (Novalis has memorably written) *would be the one who would cast over himself a spell so complete that he would take his own phantasmagorias as autonomous appearances. Would this not be our case?*" I conjecture that this is so. We (the undivided divinity operating within us) have dreamt the world. We have dreamt it as firm, mysterious, visible, ubiquitous in space and durable in time; but in its architecture we have allowed tenuous and eternal crevices of unreason which tell us it is false. (L 208)

["*El mayor hechicero* (escribe memorablemente Novalis) *sería el que se hechizara hasta el punto de tomar sus propias fantasmagorías por apariciones autónomas. ¿No sería ése nuestro caso?*" Yo conjeturo que es así. Nosotros (la indivisa divinidad que opera en nosotros) hemos soñado el mundo. Lo hemos soñado resistente, misterioso, visible, ubicuo en el espacio y firme en el tiempo; pero hemos consentido en su arquitectura tenues y eternos intersticios de sinrazón para saber que es falso. (OC 258)]

Once again, as was the case with the "Ode Written in 1966," the world is conceived as a dream, a dream that ultimately refers to god in some shape or form ("the undivided divinity operating within us"). And we have come to believe that our spectral projections are indeed the truth—very much like the conjurer in "The Circular Ruins" or the overly eager citizens of the 1940s, desperate to adopt the fiction of Tlön. Following Novalis's quote, reality is merely an effective self-deception. This is then the political aspect of Borges's take on idealism: the shared conviction that a hallucination, an imposed representation, is real. The disturbing detail in "Tlön, Uqbar, Orbis Tertius" is that everyone *knows* that this framed order is fake, and yet this is no impediment for embracing it as the truth.[58]

The last quote has a second political resonance. What we consider the world to *be* depends to an enormous extent on the imposition of a philosophical paradigm. Once again, "Tlön, Uqbar, Orbis Tertius" serves as an eloquent example: dogmatic idealism ends up shaping

---

[58] As Borges notes in his article on dubbed films, included in *Discussion*: "worse than dubbing, worse than the substitution that dubbing implies, is the general conscience of a substitution, of a deceit" ["peor que el doblaje, peor que la sustitución que importa el doblaje, es la conciencia general de una sustitución, de un engaño" (OC 284)]. Dubbing is in, a way, a perfect parallel of the situation in "Tlön, Uqbar, Orbis Tertius." In a footnote in the same essay, Borges ridicules dubbing with an absurd fractal model: "Since the voices have already been usurped, why not also usurp the figures? When will the system become perfect? When will we just see Juana González playing Greta Garbo playing Kristina, Queen of Sweden?" ["Ya que hay usurpación de voces, ¿por qué no también de figuras? ¿Cuándo será perfecto el sistema? ¿Cuándo veremos directamente a Juana González en el papel de Greta Garbo, en el papel de la Reina Cristina de Suecia?" (OC 284 fn)].

reality—and not in a merely metaphorical sense. The establishment, dissemination, and enforcement of a philosophical paradigm are always intertwined with a political struggle—both as its cause and effect.

In the first centuries of our era, the Gnostics disputed with the Christians. They were annihilated, but we can imagine their possible victory. Had Alexandria triumphed and not Rome, the bizarre and confused stories that I have summarized would be coherent, majestic, and ordinary. Lines such as Novalis's "Life is a sickness of the spirit," or Rimbaud's despairing 'True life is absent; we are not in the world,' would fulminate in the canonical books. (SNF 68)

[Durante los primeros siglos de nuestra era, los gnósticos disputaron con los cristianos. Fueron aniquilados, pero nos podemos representar su victoria posible. De haber triunfado Alejandría y no Roma, las estrambóticas y turbias historias que he resumido aquí serían coherentes, majestuosas y cotidianas. Sentencias como la de Novalis: *La vida es una enfermedad del espíritu*, o la desesperada de Rimbaud: *La verdadera vida está ausente; no estamos en el mundo*, fulminarían en los libros canónicos. (OC 216)] .

What would our reality be like had other philosophical paradigms prevailed? What would the world look like if idealism or Christianity had been just marginal trends or sects? These are the questions "Tlön, Uqbar, Orbis Tertius" renders visible through its parodic amplification. A political order may further the imposition of a philosophical paradigm, but it is also true that there is always a philosophical paradigm supporting and driving every political order. Our very conception of the world—the framed fiction we adopt as our reality—is determined at the intersection of politics and metaphysics.

PART TWO

The United States of America

Introduction

Just like Poe's purloined letter, the importance of North American literature in Borges's writing seems to have "escape[d] observation by dint of being excessively obvious" (Poe, *Poetry and Tales* 694). Borges read North American literature voraciously and wrote profusely about it throughout his entire career, from his first book of essays to the last. Furthermore, he has several North American short stories and poems, either set in the States or overtly inspired by North American writers. It could even be said that North American literature plays a more decisive role than the English canon (in a wide sense, including Scottish, Irish, and even Anglo-Saxon literature), although the latter includes most of Borges's dearest writers. Shakespeare, Berkeley, De Quincey, Conrad, Stevenson, and Chesterton are no doubt central figures for Borges, but his writing would not have taken its shape without two North American authors—Edgar Allan Poe and Walt Whitman.

Borges often joked that the year of his birth, 1899, made him a nineteenth-century writer. This was more than a quip: even the avant-garde experiments of his youth show a nineteenth-century sensibility, and many of the writers and philosophers from that era who influenced him were American. From Emerson he learned, among other things, to be an "intellectual poet" (SP 51; OC 79). Hawthorne taught him the wonders and dangers of allegory.[59] From his father,

---

[59] Borges's lengthy essay "Nataniel Hawthorne" (originally a lecture delivered in 1949, later published in *Otras Inquisiciones* [1952]) is an important text for two interrelated reasons. First, because of the extreme novelty of a Latin American writer discussing Hawthorne in such depth (over almost a century, numerous Latin American authors had written plenty of essays on Poe, Whitman, and Emerson, but Hawthorne was largely ignored in the southern hemisphere). But it is also an interesting essay in the context of Borges's own work: "Nathaniel Hawthorne" is the testing ground for one of Borges's most important contributions to the study of literary history—the fact that each writer creates her own precursors. This thesis, which he will publish two years later in the newspaper *La Nación*, under the title of "Kafka and His Precursors," appeared beforehand in this lecture. By linking Hawthorne to Kafka, Borges intervenes in the North American canon and reassesses the meaning of one of its central authors. The relevant paragraph reads: "Here, without any discredit

he inherited a passion for William James. He thought one of the few truly American (in a continental sense) writers was Mark Twain, who also was one of his earliest influences: "The first novel I ever read through," Borges wrote in his autobiographical essay for the *New Yorker*, "was *Huckleberry Finn*. Next came *Roughing It* . . ." (42). However, Borges also dealt with American twentieth-century literature: although averse to novels, he translated Faulkner's *The Wild Palms*,[60] and reviewed (and admired) his work.[61] Except

---

to Hawthorne, I should like to insert an observation. The circumstance, the strange circumstance, of perceiving in a story written by Hawthorne at the beginning of the nineteenth century the very flavor of Kafka's stories, written at the beginning of the twentieth, must not cause us to forget that the Kafkaesque flavor [in Hawthorne] has been created, and determined by Kafka. 'Wakefield' prefigures Franz Kafka, but Kafka modifies and sharpens the reading of 'Wakefield.' The debt is mutual; a great writer creates his precursors. He creates and somehow justifies them" (OI 56–57; very heavily edited) ["Aquí, sin desmedro alguno de Hawthorne, yo desearía intercalar una observación. La circunstancia, la extraña circunstancia, de percibir en un cuento de Hawthorne, redactado a principios del siglo XIX, el sabor mismo de los cuentos de Kafka que trabajó a principios del siglo XX, no debe hacernos olvidar que el sabor de Kafka ha sido creado, ha sido determinado por Kafka. *Wakefield* prefigura a Franz Kafka, pero éste modifica, y afina, la lectura de *Wakefield*. La deuda es mutua; un gran escritor crea a sus precursores. Los crea y de algún modo los justifica" (OC 678)].

[60] The translation (1950) does not rank among Borges's finest work. In addition to its patchiness, it is unforgivably prudish. Borges actually *alters* Faulkner's text in order to get rid of "dirty" words or scenes. In a novel like *If I Forget Thee, Jerusalem*, which revolves to such an enormous extent around sex, this self-imposed modesty is, to say the least, absurd. Examples abound. For instance, "males and females but without the pricks or cunts" (Faulkner, *Novels* 509) becomes "machos y hembras pero sin sexo" (*Las palmeras salvajes* 54). And the very last line of the novel is completely deprived of its force: "'Women, shit,' the tall convict said" (Faulkner 726) is rendered as "'¡Mujeres! . . .' dijo el penado alto" (*Las palmeras salvajes* 321). Perhaps the explanation may be that it was Borges's mother, Leonor Acevedo, who was taking dictation from her son, or, even, as Borges suggests, actually translating the text. In his "Autobiographical Notes," he wrote that his mother "translated some of Hawthorne's stories and one of Herbert Read's books on art, and she also produced some of the translations of Melville, Virginia Woolf, and Faulkner that are considered mine" (41). I will discuss Borges's prudishness and his view on censorship later on, when analyzing his take on Whitman. The explanatory notes in the Faulkner translation are also curious (and unmistakably penned by Borges) and reflect his obsession with outlaws from both hemispheres. When Faulkner mentions Diamond Dick and Jesse James, Borges believes it pertinent to footnote: "Léase los *Juan Moreira*, los *Hormiga Negra*, etc." (*Las palmeras salvajes* 27). This contextual translation (Jesse James for Hormiga Negra) will be discussed more carefully when considering *Universal History of Infamy*.

for his reverence for Faulkner, Borges's taste when it came to his contemporaries was quite eccentric—he preferred peripheral figures to the central, more canonical ones, such as Bret Harte and H. P. Lovecraft. Part of what makes the map of American literature that Borges draws interesting, then, are his omissions and his dislikes. Whether one agrees with them or not, Borges's dismissal of e.e. cummings and Ezra Pound, for instance, show him at his cantankerous best.

Even North American pop culture plays a crucial role in Borges's work. He loved Hollywood films, dime novels, gangsters, and cowboys. He reviewed numerous films and was acquainted with several pop icons (Krazy Kat, Mickey Mouse, or King Kong, for example, are mentioned here and there throughout his work). More importantly, Borges started his fiction career rewriting stories about the New York hoodlum Monk Eastman and, among other infamous characters, Billy the Kid. At the same time, the relevance of detective fiction in his career (as a writer, as a critic, and even as an editor) cannot be underestimated, and he was instrumental in making the genre accessible for Spanish-speaking readers.[62] In addition to showing that he was very much a man of his time, the evident relish with which Borges approached these (supposedly) lowbrow objects debunks his image as a rarified elitist.[63]

---

[61] See, for instance, his reviews on ¡Absalom, Absalom!, The Unvanquished, and The Wild Palms (TC 76; 245, 319). In the first review he writes: "¡Absalom, Absalom! is comparable to The Sound and the Fury. I know of no better compliment" ["¡Absalom, Absalom! es equiparable a El Sonido y la Furia. No sé de un elogio mayor" (77)]. In the last, he declares that "William Faulkner may be the first novelist of our time" ("Es verosímil la afirmación de que William Faulkner es el primer novelista de nuestro tiempo" [320]).

[62] Together with Adolfo Bioy Casares, Borges started a collection called El séptimo círculo, named after the Seventh Circle in Dante's Hell, which houses the violent. From 1945 to 1956 Borges and Bioy selected 139 titles and wrote the back covers for all of them. The collection focused more on classic, procedural detective fiction, as opposed to the hardboiled take on the genre (James Cain, with three titles in the collection, may be the sole exception during Bioy and Borges's tenure). Juan Rodolfo Wilcock and Rodolfo Walsh were among the translators. The collection, published by Emecé was a wild success (some titles were even adapted for television [cf. Bioy 719]) and helped make detective fiction visible and even respectable throughout the Spanish-speaking world.

[63] Or expands it. Here is just an example of how Borges enjoyed mixing high and low: "'Good,' for the Hollywood thinkers, means a steady relationship with decent and wealthy Lana Turner; 'Evil' (which so deeply concerned David Hume and the

Borges also wrote several pieces on all of these writers. In 1967, he even published a brief *Introduction to North American Literature*, a somewhat uneven book whose value resides in showing his idiosyncratic reconfiguration of the American canon. However, more important than the numerous references to North American authors is the fact that these influences are mostly ingrained *in* his texts and the fact that they became aesthetic materials.

Borges's investment in North America extends to his creative work, which includes numerous poems (about 20 of them) dedicated to American landscapes, cities, and, of course, writers. If formally, the influence of Whitman (and, to some extent, Emerson) was decisive, content-wise, the history, the cities, the heroes, and even the native animals of the United States provided Borges with valuable poetic material. Many of these poems were written from afar, inspired by books; others were motivated by Borges's trips to New England, New York, the South, and the Midwest.[64] Additionally, the place of the United States in his short stories is far from marginal. To a certain extent, Borges's fiction writing is bookended by American literature. As noted in the previous section, some of his first attempts, in *Historia universal de la infamia*, were rewritings of some American texts (including Twain's *Life on the Mississippi*). Forty years later, in his last proper collection of short stories, North America once more played a prominent role. Here, the United States is not a mere setting, interchangeable with some other location—stories like "The Bribe" ["El soborno"] or "The Ethnographer" ["El etnógrafo"] would be unimaginable outside American academia; these stories work *because* they take place in

---

heresiarchs from Alexandria), the illegal cohabitation with Fröken Ingrid Bergman or Miriam Hopkins" ["El Bien, para los pensadores de Hollywood, es el noviazgo con la pudorosa y pudiente Lana Turner; el Mal (que de tal modo preocupó a David Hume y a los heresiarcas de Alejandría), la cohabitación ilegal con Fröken Ingrid Bergman o Miriam Hopkins" (OC 285)].

[64] "Texas," "Emerson," "Edgar Allan Poe," "Camden, 1892," "The stranger" ["El Forastero"] "Otro poema de los dones," and "Un soldado de Lee (1862)" (in *The Other, the Same* [*El otro, el mismo*]); "New England, 1967" and "Acevedo" (in *In Praise of Darkness* [*Elogio de la sombra*]); "El pasado," "On His Blindness," "1971," "East Lansing," and "Al coyote" (in *The Gold of the Tigers* [*El oro de los tigres*]); "El bisonte" and "E.A.P." (in *The Deep Rose* [*La rosa profunda*]); "Herman Melville" (in *The Iron Coin* [*La moneda de hierro*]); "The Cloisters" (in *The Cipher* [*La cifra*, 1981]).

the States. Borges also wrote stories in the style of Henry James[65] (a recurrent presence in Borges's work), Hemingway (whom he actually disdained),[66] and H. P. Lovecraft, of whom he didn't think much, but whom, inexplicably, he mentioned quite often.[67]

In short, there is a vast Borgesian corpus dealing with the American tradition from Lincoln to JFK, from Ellery Queen to Langston Hughes, from Pound to Sandburg, from O. Henry to Steinbeck, from T. S. Eliot to Eugene O'Neill, from King Vidor to Orson Welles, from Billy the Kid to Charles Chaplin. That these texts were written over such a long period of time (from the early thirties to the mid-eighties), and spanning so many genres (from newspaper columns to sonnets), proves that, far from fleeting, Borges's interest in the United States was lifelong and deeply felt.

With the exception of a handful of Argentine authors who obsessed him (such as Macedonio Fernández and Leopoldo Lugones), it is hard to think of two writers who shaped Borges's literature in a more definite way than Poe and Whitman. Borges not only wrote detective stories that helped redefine the genre but also theorized extensively on the *policial* (as detective fiction is known in Argentina) and even transgressed its boundaries. As will be shown in the following section, detective fiction provided Borges with a new lens through which he reread the history of literature and philosophy. Regarding Whitman, there simply is no other author who explicitly influenced Borges from his first book (1923) to his last (1985) in such visible, decisive ways. In all the books of poetry he wrote during those 62 years, Whitman is constantly there, mentioned explicitly in prologues and afterwords, his name dropped in verses here and there, and (above all), his style and form impregnating numerous of Borges's poems.

"Contemporary literature is inconceivable without Whitman and Poe" ["La literatura actual es inconcebible sin Whitman y

---

[65] "The Duel" ["El duelo"] in *Brodie's Report*.

[66] "The Wait" ["La espera"] in *The Aleph*.

[67] The story is "There are More Things" (the original title is in English), in *The Book of Sand* (1975). And of Lovecraft, Borges wrote: "Fate . . . would not leave me in peace until I had perpetrated a posthumous story by Lovecraft, a writer I have always considered an unwitting parodist of Poe" (CF 484–85) "El destino . . . no me dejó en paz hasta que perpetré un cuento póstumo de Lovecraft, escritor que siempre he juzgado un parodista involuntario de Poe" (OC III: 72)].

sin Poe" (OC IV: 646), Borges wrote toward the end of his life. Similar statements can be found, as we will see, throughout Borges's work. It is the purpose of these pages to follow the presence of these two North American writers in Borges's texts and to show to what extent they informed his literature. In the process, it will also become clear that these North American authors helped Borges shape his particular articulation of the historical and the universal.

Finally, there is an important corollary: both Borges's particular take on North American literature and the way in which he was appropriated later by US writers make Borges a very special case. Not only was he influenced by North American literature but he also reverted the North-South current: toward the end of his life (and to the present), it was *he* who became a critical figure in North American literature, influencing directly such writers as Thomas Pynchon, John Barth, William Gass, William Gibson, and David Foster Wallace. In other words, North American writers got their own canon back, filtered through and transformed by Borges.

1

Edgar Allan Poe (on murder considered as metaphysics)

In "The Other Whitman" ["El otro Whitman"], Borges writes: "The men of the diverse Americas remain so disconnected that we barely know each other second hand, narrated by Europe. In such cases, Europe is often a synecdoche for Paris" ["Los hombres de las diversas Américas permanecemos tan incomunicados que apenas nos conocemos por referencia, contados por Europa. En tales casos, Europa suele ser sinécdoque de París" (OC 206)]. The essay was first published in 1929, when the hemispheric disconnection that Borges describes was, at least within the realm of literature, most certainly a fact. South and North America were each focused on defining their status in relation to Europe, either by seeking the Old Continent's approval or by emphasizing their originality and lack of ties with it, but there was little literary commerce between the hemispheres. If the very notion of an American (in the continental sense of the word) literature is still problematic, a century ago, it was completely unthinkable. Borges's dictum, then, seems to apply only to the literature of a particular period. More specifically, the triangulation that Borges draws (North America-Paris-South America) seems to be an allusion to *modernismo*, the literary movement lead by Rubén Darío that completely reshaped Latin American letters in the late nineteenth century—a movement Borges helped demolish in the

1920s.[68] Even more specifically, the vertices of this triangle can be specified even further: Edgar Allan Poe, Charles Baudelaire, and Rubén Darío. In a 1980 conversation with Willis Barnstone at the New York PEN Club, Borges declared:

> You can't think of *modernismo* without Hugo, Verlaine, and not least Edgar Allan Poe. And Edgar Allan Poe came to us through France, although we are fellow Americans. You may like or dislike what he wrote, but his influence cannot be denied. He begat Baudelaire, who begat Mallarmé, and so on. (*Borges at Eighty*, 120)[69]

Here, Borges is smuggling in a quotation from his own short story "Pierre Menard, author of the *Quixote*" (1939). Menard is "a *symboliste* from Nîmes, a devotee essentially of Poe—who begat Baudelaire, who begat Mallarmé, who begat Valéry, who begat M. Edmond Teste" (CF 92) ["un simbolista de Nîmes, devoto esencialmente de Poe, que engendró a Baudelaire, que engendró a Mallarmé, que engendró a Valéry, que engendró a Edmond Teste" (OC 447)]. Adequately enough, this biblical lineage in "Pierre Menard, author of the *Quixote*" ends with a shift toward a fictional character, M. Teste.[70] Poe and Whitman (via Paris) are, according to Borges the foundation of *modernismo*:

> Two North American poets, Edgar Allan Poe and Walt Whitman, had an essential influence on French literature, both because of

---

[68] Martí and Lugones, two key figures in the *modernista* movement wrote quite extensively about the United States. During and immediately after World War I, Leopoldo Lugones proved to be ardently pro-American (and a fervent supporter of President Wilson), as can be seen in such books as *Mi beligerancia* (1917) and, more significantly, *La torre de Casandra* (1919). However, nothing of this enthusiasm survived by the time Borges wrote his essay on Whitman—by then, Lugones had become an ultranationalist and severed any possible tie to the nation he had once extolled for its republican and democratic values. Martí's relationship with the United States is a complex matter that unfortunately cannot be explored here. His active denunciation of US expansionism did not prevent him from living in the United States, and even appreciating the positive sides of North American history, as can be seen in his "Cartas de Nueva York" and many of his "Crónicas."

[69] Borges made a very similar statement in his 1971 talk at NYU (C 132).

[70] A third occurrence of this lineage can be found in "Edgar Allan Poe," a 1949 article published in the newspaper *La Nación*: "Mirror of the arduous schools that practice a lonely form of art and do not aspire to become the voice of many, father

their theory and their work. Rubén Darío, a man from Hispanic America, picks up this influence through the symbolist school and takes it to Spain.

[Dos poetas norteamericanos, Edgar Allan Poe y Walt Whitman, habían influido esencialmente, por su teoría y por su obra, en la literatura francesa; Rubén Darío, hombre de Hispanoamérica, recoge este influjo a través de la escuela simbolista y lo lleva a España. (LL 22–23)]

Poe, then, comes to Darío through Baudelaire and the symbolists. In fact, Poe is the only North American mentioned in *Los raros* (sometimes translated as *The Eccentrics*, although *The Weirdoes* would do the original title more justice), Darío's personal canon of strange or "degenerate" writers, as Max Nordau (also included in Darío's book) would have it. First published in 1896, *Los raros* already confirms Borges's triangulation quite explicitly: "Every day," Darío writes, "Edgar Poe's unshadowed glory affirms itself ever so brightly, since his prestigious introduction by Baudelaire, later crowned by the transcendentally comprehensive and seductive spirit of Stephane Mallarmé" ["Cada día se afirma con mayor brillo, la gloria ya sin sombras de Edgar Poe, desde su prestigiosa introducción por Baudelaire, coronada luego por el espíritu trascendentalmente comprensivo y seductor de Stephane Mallarmé" (*Los raros* 9)]. Borges's radical rereading of Poe serves two simultaneous purposes. While reclaiming Poe from Darío and his followers, Borges lays the foundation of his Pan-American view of literature, and at the same time takes distance from *modernistas*.

For the most part the *modernistas*' relationship with the North was fraught with anxiety: the United States constituted not only an imperial threat but also tended to be perceived as a metaphysical menace. Politically, North America was, as Darío put it in one of his poems ("A Roosevelt") "the future invader/of the naive America . . . /that still speaks Spanish." ["El futuro invasor/de la América ingenua . . . /que aún habla español" (*Poesías* 640)].

---

of Baudelaire, who begat Mallarmé, who begat Valéry, Poe belongs indissolubly to the history of Western literature, which cannot be understood without him" ["Espejo de las arduas escuelas que ejercen el arte solitario y no quieren ser voz de los muchos, padre de Baudelaire, que engendró a Mallarmé, que engendró a Valéry, Poe indisolublemente pertenece a la historia de las letras occidentales, que no se comprende sin él" (TR II: 264)].

Culturally, the United States was simply the land of crass materialism, a nation of philistines driven by soulless commercial interests. "And though you [the United States] have it all, you lack one thing: God!" concludes the poem ["Y, pues contáis con todo, falta una cosa: ¡Dios!" (641)]. The *modernistas* saw in the United States a combination of instrumental reason, vulgarity, and territorial and financial greed, a nation ready to stomp on the noble and subtle ideals of the Latin (i.e. *classical*) traditions of South America. Rubén Darío inaugurated the long habit of associating the United States with Caliban, the monster shackled by Prospero in Shakespeare's *The Tempest*. The first mention occurs in *Los raros*, but two years later, in 1898, Darío published an article titled "Caliban's Triumph" ["El triunfo de Calibán"], a vehement attack on the Monroe Doctrine, and a rant against American coarseness and gigantism— "we are in the country of Brobdingnag" ["estamos allí en el país de Brobdingnag" (*Textos* 25)]. From the very first sentence, Darío pitches South against North in a stark antagonism,[71] which quickly escalates in its viciousness, before finally comparing the Americans to Prospero's slave. According to Darío, Americans are

> cyclops eating raw meat, bestial blacksmiths, dwellers of mastodontic houses. Red-faced, heavy, crass they go through their streets pushing and rubbing against each other like animals, hunting for dollars. The ideal of those Calibans is restricted to the stock market and the factory. They eat, they eat, they make calculations, they drink whisky, and they make millions.

> [cíclopes, comedores de carne cruda, herreros bestiales, habitadores de casas de mastodontes. Colorados, pesados, groseros, van por sus calles empujándose y rozándose animalmente, a la caza del *dollar*. El ideal de esos calibanes está circunscrito a la bolsa y a la fábrica. Comen, comen, calculan, beben whisky y hacen millones. (*Textos* 29)]

---

[71] The text opens thus: "No, I cannot, I do not want to be on the side of those buffalos with silver teeth. They are my enemies, they are the haters of the Latin blood, they are the Barbarians. Thus trembles every noble heart, thus protests every man with dignity in whom something of the she-wolf's milk remains" ["No, no puedo, no quiero estar de parte de esos búfalos de dientes de plata. Son enemigos míos, son los aborrecedores de la sangre latina, son los Bárbaros. Así se estremece hoy todo noble corazón, así protesta todo digno hombre que algo conserve de la leche de la Loba" (*Textos* 25)]. Note the opposition between the "Barbarians" and the *Latin* American children of Rome—those in whom "something of the she-wolf's milk remains."

The article concludes by completing the Shakespearian parallel and equating Latin America with Ariel:[72]

Miranda will always prefer Ariel! Miranda is the spirit's grace, and all the mountains of stone, iron, gold and bacon will never be enough to prostitute my Latin soul for Caliban!

[¡Miranda preferirá siempre a Ariel; Miranda es la gracia del espíritu; y todas las montañas de piedras, de hierros, de oros y de tocinos, no bastarán para que mi alma latina se prostituya a Calibán! (33)]

The Uruguayan essayist José Enrique Rodó picked up this allegory and expanded it in *Ariel*, a sort of lyrical essay published in 1900. Rodó, one of the main ideologues of *modernismo*, provided turn-of-the-century Latin America with the arguments and the rhetoric with which to oppose the United States: "If one could say of utilitarianism that it is the word of the English spirit, the United states may be considered the incarnation of that word" (Rodó 1922, 89) ["Si ha podido decirse del utilitarismo que es el verbo del espíritu inglés, los Estados Unidos pueden ser considerados la encarnación del verbo utilitario" (1985, 33)]. Opposed to Caliban's utilitarian, positivistic, materialistic, mercantile spirit, is, of course, the ethereal Ariel: "Ariel triumphant signifies ideality and order in life, noble inspiration in thought, unselfishness in conduct, high taste in art, heroism in action, delicacy and refinement in manners and usages" (1922, 144) ["Ariel triunfante, significa idealidad y orden en la vida, noble inspiración en el pensamiento, desinterés en moral, buen gusto en arte, heroísmo en la acción, delicadeza en las costumbres" (1985, 53)]. *Latin* America, partly because of its classical heritage, is closer to Ariel's interior freedom, elevated feelings, and noble intentions, while the United States is shackled, like Caliban, by crass material ambitions, its spirit "mutilated by the tyranny of a single and self-interested object" (1922, 33) ["mutilación [del espíritu] por la tiranía de un objetivo único e interesado" (1985, 13)].

Given this opposition (Caliban vs. Ariel; North vs. South; Anglo vs. Latin), Poe appears as an odd bird. It goes without saying that in the Calibanistic United States, ruled solely by instrumental reason, there cannot be pure, disinterested art: "In such a surrounding,"

---

[72] For lack of space, I cannot consider here the texts Darío wrote extolling the United States, such as "Salutación al águila."

Rodó writes, "true art can only exist as the rebellion of an individual. Emerson, Poe, are as estrays of a fauna expelled from their true habitat by some geological catastrophe" (Rodó 1922, 110) ["El arte verdadero sólo ha podido existir, en tal ambiente, a título de rebelión individual. Emerson, Poe, son allí como los ejemplares de una fauna expulsada de su verdadero medio por el rigor de una catástrofe geológica" (Rodó 1985, 41)]. For Rodó, Poe irrupts as an exception, a phenomenon his own context cannot account for. This is also the case for Rubén Darío, who first introduces the Caliban analogy in *Los raros*, but it is highly significant that he does so in his chapter on Poe—the only North American writer in the book. "Caliban rules the island of Manhattan, San Francisco, Boston, Washington, the entire country. He has managed to establish the rule of materialism . . . " ["Calibán reina en la isla de Manhattan, en San Francisco, en Boston, en Washington, en todo el país. Ha conseguido establecer el imperio de la materia . . . " (*Los raros* 16)]. Remarkably enough, a few pages later, Darío moves on to compare Poe to Ariel and, like Rodó, sees him as a paradox in the North American utilitarian context:

> One could say that Poe, Ariel as a man, spent his life under the floating influence of a strange mystery. Born in a country with a practical and material way of life, his environment influenced him in the opposite way. From a land of calculation springs a stupendous imagination.
>
> [Poe, como un Ariel hecho hombre, diríase que ha pasado su vida bajo el flotante influjo de un extraño misterio. Nacido en un país de vida práctica y material, la influencia del medio obra en él al contrario. De un país de cálculo brota imaginación tan estupenda. (*Raros* 19)]

And two years later, in "El triunfo de Calibán" (1898), Darío insists on the same idea: "and their Poe, their great Poe," he writes, "that poor swan inebriated with grief and alcohol, was the martyr of his own dream in a country where he will never be understood" ["y su Poe, su gran Poe, pobre cisne borracho de pena y de alcohol, fue el mártir de su sueño en un país en donde jamás será comprendido" (*Textos* 29)]. In fact, this paragraph was lifted almost verbatim from Baudelaire's "Poe, His Life and Works." "Americans are practical people," Baudelaire writes. "They do not have time to feel sorry for a poet who could be driven insane by grief and loneliness" (Baudelaire 40).

It is clear that, influenced by Baudelaire, both Darío and Rodó chose a particular, extremely partial side of Poe's work (and of his mythology). Theirs is the Romantic, melancholy, heroic, delirious, illuminated Poe; the poet, the mystic, the writer of grotesques and arabesques. Unsurprisingly, the other Poe, the one of the tales of ratiocination, the critic, the author of "The Philosophy of Composition" goes unmentioned. There is in Poe a clear struggle between a Classical and a Romantic spirit, and the *modernistas* only chose to see the latter. In other words, the "rational" side of Poe's work is ignored, for the simple motive that it could more easily be identified with the "utilitarian spirit" the *modernistas* attached to North American culture. The author of "The Rationale of Verse," the man who penned a treatise on secret writing, or, in brief, the creator of detective fiction (at whose core is, obviously, a particular take on reason and the scientific method) is thoroughly left out of Darío's and Rodó's appreciation. In short, the *modernistas* were able to see a precursor in Poe only by turning him into the most un-American of American writers.[73]

This version of Poe is, once again, attributable to Baudelaire. It is, in fact, Baudelaire who establishes the myth of a Romantic and anti-American Poe in "Poe, His Life and Works." Baudelaire's entire essay illustrates this point, which makes it hard to single out one particular passage. One example out of many: "The life of Edgar Poe was a painful tragedy with an ending whose horror was increased by trivial circumstances. . . . For Poe the United States was a vast cage, a great counting-house, and . . . throughout his life he made grim efforts to escape the influence of that antipathetic atmosphere" (Baudelaire 39). Borges overtly addressed this mystification:

Baudelaire started (and Shaw extended) the perfidious tradition of admiring Poe against the United States, of considering the poet

---

[73] This is also the case with Emerson and Whitman. It is a rather remarkable how, in his essays and chronicles, Martí "de-Americanizes" both these authors (and a similar operation can be seen in Darío). Emerson and Whitman are great writers because they are "universal" and even are represented as forces of nature. In short, it is as if they had to lose their North American specificity (and become timeless, cosmic entities) in order to be appreciated. Martí's 1882 article on Emerson (4–14) and his 1887 chronicle on Whitman (86–96) abound in examples.

an angel lost, to his doom, in that cold and avid hell. The truth is
that Poe would have suffered in any country. On the other hand,
no one admires Baudelaire against France, or Coleridge against
England.

[*Inaugurada por Baudelaire, y no desdeñada por Shaw, hay la
costumbre pérfida de admirar a Poe contra los Estados Unidos,
de juzgar al poeta como un ángel extraviado, para su mal, en
ese frío y ávido infierno. La verdad es que Poe hubiera padecido
en cualquier país. Nadie, por lo demás, admira a Baudelaire
contra Francia o a Coleridge contra Inglaterra.* (TR II: 265; my
emphasis)]

Borges may have been the first Latin American to read Poe as a
North American author (rather than a French or context-deprived
one). He expands on this in "Vindicación de Mark Twain," his very
first piece for the journal *Sur*, published in 1935:

Since Charles Pierre Baudelaire's amazement over the fact that
Edgar Allan Poe had been born in the state of Massachusetts, no
one can ignore that *if an American happens to be a novelist or a
musician, he is one despite all of America, and even against all of
America. . . . It has been said infinite times that that inventor* [Poe]
*is accidental in America. . . . I cannot agree. Not only American,
but also a Yankee is terrible and humoristic Poe.* This can be seen
both in in the ceaseless precision and practicality of his diverse
games with darkness, with secret writings and with poetry, and
in his bursts of enormous charlatanry, reminiscent of Barnum.

[Desde que Charles Pierre Baudelaire se maravilló de que Edgar
Allan Poe hubiera nacido en el estado de Massachusetts, nadie
puede ignorar que *el americano, si novelista o músico o pintor, lo
es a pesar de toda América, y aun en contra. . . . Infinitamente se ha
declarado que ese inventor* [Poe] *es accidental en América. . . . Yo
no puedo asentir. No sólo americano sino yankee, es el terrible y
humorístico Poe*: ya en la continua precisión y practicidad de sus
variados juegos con la tiniebla, con las escrituras secretas y con
el verso, ya en las ráfagas de enorme charlatanería que recuerdan
a Barnum. (PJLB 121–22; my emphasis)]

Was Poe, then, an "inebriated swan" (as Darío, via Baudelaire,
perceived Poe) or a technocrat (which the author of "The Philosophy

of Composition" could certainly be considered to be)? Borges, who was well aware of the internal tension found in Poe's work between Romantic and Classical tendencies, claimed he was both. "Poe was an extraordinary romantic poet" (cf. SNF 493) ["Poe fue un extraordinario poeta romántico" (BO 67)], writes Borges, while also arguing that Poe "saw himself as an intellectual," and that from him "derives the idea of literature as an intellectual practice" ["se veía a sí mismo intelectual [y de él] deriva la idea de la literatura como un hecho intelectual" (69; 68)]. Borges, then, reaches beyond the commonplace of Romanticism as a hypersensual, decadent and almost opiate aesthetic program that is opposed to rigorous critical thought. While doing so, he also draws a clear line between the tales of ratiocination, and Poe's more contrived ideas of order, chiefly his constrained "Philosophy of Composition," where "Poe *argued* [razonó] . . . *or pretended to argue* that the writing of a poem is an operation of the intelligence" (CF 346; my emphasis) ["Poe . . . *razonó o fingió razonar* que la escritura de un poema es la operación de la inteligencia" (OC 1021). A similar statement appears in his *Introduction to North American Literature*: "In 'The Philosophy of Composition' [Poe] explains how he wrote is famous poem 'The Raven,' and he *analyzes, or pretends to analyze*, the different stages of his work" ["En un trabajo titulado 'The Philosophy of Composition' explica de qué modo escribió su famoso poema 'El cuervo' y *analiza, o finge analizar*, las diversas etapas de su labor" (30; my emphasis)].[74] In brief, Borges sees Poe as a Romantic, without associating the term with capricious formlessness. Borges locates this contradiction within Poe's own writing. In his "Philosophy of Composition," Poe denounces the fact that "most writers . . . prefer having it understood that they compose by a species of fine frenzy—an ecstatic intuition" (14). It is in such passages that Borges sees the contradiction between Poe's romantic drive and his classical dogma: "In 'The Philosophy of Composition' the great Romantic declares that the execution of a poem is an intellectual operation, not a gift from the muses"

---

[74] In both these passages, Borges suggests that Poe "pretends" to reason or analyze the process of poetical composition. This opens the possibility of considering Poe's essay a hoax or, perhaps better, a game. Games, however, are not opposed to reason, but rather their product—as Poe himself showed in his analysis of the nature of games in "Murders in the Rue Morgue."

["En 'The Philosophy of Composition' el gran romántico declara que la ejecución de un poema es una operación intelectual, no un don de la musa" (OC IV: 647)]. Perhaps the most elegant and succinct enunciation of this problem is to be found in "Flaubert y su destino ejemplar" (in *Discusión*) where, in a footnote, Borges refers to the "'classical' doctrine of the Romantic Poe" ["la doctrina 'clásica' del romántico Poe" (OC 263)]. In a 1935 text published in the newspaper *La Prensa* ("La genesis de'El cuervo' de Poe"), Borges elaborates on this claim. He begins by stressing the "scandalous" nature of Poe's essay. Poe, he writes, had the nerve to go against the Romantic conception of artistic creation (an entranced, raptured genius taking dictation from the muses) in favor of a demystified view of the aesthetic production in which reason played a prominent (yet not exclusive) role:

> From the interlocutor of the muses, from a dark god's amanuensis, the poet is demoted to a mere winder of reasons! Lucidity instead of inspiration, comprehensible intelligence and not genius—what a blow for the contemporaries of Hugo, and even of Breton and Dalí! . . . I—naively, perhaps—believe in Poe's explanations.

> [¡Del interlocutor de las musas, del poeta amanuense de un dios oscuro, pasar al mero devanador de razones! La lucidez en lugar de la inspiración, la inteligencia comprensible y no el genio, ¡qué desencanto para los contemporáneos de Hugo y aun para los de Bretón y Dalí! . . . Yo—ingenuamente acaso—creo en las explicaciones de Poe. (TR II: 121)]

Borges subscribes to Poe's poetic program, but with one important caveat:

> Each link [in Poe's theory] is valid, but between each link remains a particle of darkness or of incoercible inspiration. In other words, Poe states the diverse moments of the poetic process, but between each one and the subsequent remains—infinitesimal— the moment of invention. And still another arcane matter remains: the one of personal preferences [i.e. why the poet makes certain choices over others that are relatively equivalent].

> [Cada eslabón [de la teoría de Poe] es válido, pero entre eslabón y eslabón queda su partícula de tiniebla o de inspiración incoercible.

Lo diré de otro modo: Poe declara los diversos momentos del proceso poético, pero entre cada uno y el subsiguiente queda— infinitesimal—el de la invención. Queda otro arcano general: el de las preferencias. (TR II: 122)]

The preceding quotation may be a long gloss of Borges's notion of the "'classical' doctrine of the Romantic Poe"—the "links" are forged in a classical mold, but their ties are somewhat more elusive, and are thus related to Romantic darkness ("tiniebla"). But despite these mysteries ("arcano"), Borges leaves no room for doubt: he declares "the validity of the analytical method carried out by Poe" ["la validez del método analítico ejercido por Poe" (TR II: 123)].[75]

If the "Romantic" Poe is the author of the grotesque and arabesque tales, then the "Classical" Poe is doubtlessly the one behind his tales of ratiocination. In an essay on Chesterton, Borges claims that Poe never combined these two sides in his fiction (the gothic and the enlightened, the grotesque and the rational, the Romantic and the Classical).

Edgar Allan Poe wrote stories of pure fantastic horror or of pure *bizarrerie*; Edgar Allan Poe was the inventor of detective fiction. These facts are as certain as the one that he never combined both genres. He did not charge Dupin with the mission of solving the ancient crime of the Man of the Crowd or of explaining the simulacrum that struck down, in the black and scarlet chamber, masked prince Prospero.

[Edgar Allan Poe escribió cuentos de puro horror fantástico o de pura *bizarrerie*; Edgar Allan Poe fue inventor del cuento policial. Ello no es menos indudable que el hecho de que no combinó los dos géneros. No impuso al caballero Auguste Dupin la tarea de fijar el antiguo crimen del Hombre de las Multitudes o de explicar el simulacro que fulminó, en la cámara negra y escarlata, al enmascarado príncipe Próspero. (OC 694)]

---

[75] Nevertheless, he insists on the "impossibility of reducing the creative act to a purely logical scheme, since the preferences of each writer are irreducible" ["imposibilidad de reducir el acto de creación a un puro esquema lógico, ya que las preferencias del escritor son irreducibles" (TR II: 123)].

The distinction between these two kinds of stories is, of course, part of a taxonomy proposed by Poe himself. But I would claim that the boundaries between these categories are not as stark as Borges suggests. In fact, the very first detective story ever written, "The Murders in the Rue Morgue," is *precisely*, the confluence of ratiocination and *bizarrerie*. Yes, Dupin, Poe's detective, is a prodigy of analytical thought. But the murderer he finally tracks down with his unusual talents is . . . an orangutan. The most analytical of genres is thus inaugurated by a *bizarrerie*. It is precisely the tension between these two sides of Poe—the "rational" Poe neglected by the *modernistas* and, on the other hand, his excessive, grotesque violence—that Borges will focus on to ultimately propose a new relationship between the Americas.

As we have seen, for the most part, in Latin America, the United States was perceived as the realm of mercantile, instrumental reason. At the core of this discussion was a particular take on modernization. A few Latin American thinkers, beginning with Sarmiento, thought North America was a model to look up to, but most believed, as the *modernistas* did, that it was a threat to be avoided at all cost; for some, the United States represented the virtues of modernization (industrialization, education, wealth); for most it represented its horrors (alienation, utilitarianism, greed). Borges, however, completely disarticulates this opposition, for he links North and South America not through a take (affirmative or negative) on modernization. Quite the contrary: what North and South have in common are their residues of barbarism. Both hemispheres are linked by violence, brought together by the common denominator of brutality. Initially, then, Borges is *not* interested in the enlightened side of the States—although later, of course, he will write profusely on the North American canon. In this first approach, he completely leaves aside North America's political, economic, and even literary "achievements," to focus on the bestial, dark side of the United States, a side the entire continent seems to share. This becomes particularly clear in Borges's very first book of fiction, *Universal History of Infamy* (1935).

In the foreword to the 1954 edition, Borges described the book as "the irresponsible game of a shy sort of man who could not bring himself to write short stories, and so amused himself by changing and distorting . . . the stories of other men" (CF 4) ["el irresponsable juego de un tímido que no se animó a escribir cuentos y que se distrajo en falsear y tergiversar . . . ajenas historias" (OC 291)].[76] Three out of seven of such rewritten stories are set in the United States.[77] The one that opens the book, "The Cruel Redeemer Lazarus Morell" ["El atroz redentor Lazarus Morell"][78] draws from Mark Twain's *Life on the Mississippi* (and also on Bernard Devoto's classic book on Twain).[79] Morell, a ruthless criminal, helps slaves to escape only to resell them over and over again in different states and ultimately kills them and sinks their disemboweled bodies in the Mississippi.[80] The second short story with an American setting is "Monk Eastman, Purveyor of Iniquities" ["El proveedor de iniquidades Monk Eastman"], based on Herbert Asbury's *Gangs of New York*. Here, Borges overtly compares New York criminals to the ones of Buenos Aires to show that both hemispheres are united by crime and violence—the titles of the first two sections of the story are eloquent: "This America" (meaning South America) and "The Other." What is striking is that Argentine gangsters (or *compadritos*) are quite tame and docile when compared to their New York counterparts: "The story of the thugs and ruffians of New york is more vertiginous and less graceful [than ours]" (CF 25) ["La historia . . . de los hombres de pelea de Nueva York es más vertiginosa y más torpe [que la de nuestro malevaje]" (HUI 51–52)]. This, it should be noted, destabilizes the idea (fostered mainly by Sarmiento) of a barbaric South and a civilized North. Borges claims that not

---

[76] In his "Autobiographical Notes," Borges writes: "I . . . read up on the lives of known persons and then deliberately varied and distorted them according to my own whims. For example, after reading Herbert Asbury's *The Gangs of New York*, I set down my free version of Monk Eastman, the Jewish gunman, in flagrant contradiction of my chosen authority. I did the same for Billy the Kid, for John Murrel (whom I rechristened Lazarus Morell) . . ." (78).

[77] Furthermore, the book is inscribed *in English* (HUI 7).

[78] The story was originally titled "El espantoso redentor Lazarus Morell" in the 1935 edition. "Espantoso" was changed to "atroz" in all subsequent ones.

[79] Before Twain, in 1857, Melville mentions "Murrel, the pirate of the Mississippi" in the opening chapter of *The Confidence Man* (841).

[80] See footnote 57 in "When Fiction Lives in Fiction" for connections between "The Cruel Redeemer Lazarus Morell" and "Tlön, Uqbar, Orbis Tertius."

only can barbarism be found in the United States[81] but also that
it is even more brutal than in Latin America. The third and final
North American Story, "The Disinterested Killer Bill Harrigan,"
is an appropriation of *A Century of Gunmen* (Watson) and *The
Saga of Billy the Kid* (Noble Burns). In another attempt at finding
common denominators between North and South, Billy the Kid
is described as a "chúcaro" and a "compadrito," two profoundly
Argentinean words (used for rural and urban ruffians, respectively)
applied now to a North American context. What is remarkable,
then, is that Borges, so well acquainted with the North American
canon (especially the nineteenth century, on which he wrote
extensively) chooses to draw a link between "This America" and
"The Other," not by comparing New England Brahmins to the
"salones literarios" of Buenos Aires but by following a vein of
barbarism running through both hemispheres.

The first story in the collection, "The Cruel Redeemer Lazarus
Morell," begins with a historical account of the barbarous thread that
brings North and South together into one single America. "In 1517,"
Borges writes, "Fray Bartolomé de las Casas, feeling great pity for
the Indians who grew worn and lean in the drudging infernos of the
Antillean gold mines, proposed to Emperor Charles V that Negroes
be brought to the islands of the Caribbean, so that they might
grow worn and lean in the drudging infernos of the Antillean gold
mines" (CF 6) ["En 1517 el P. Bartolomé de las Casas tuvo mucha
lástima de los indios que se extenuaban en los laboriosos infiernos
de las minas de oro antillanas, y propuso al emperador Carlos V la
importación de negros, que se extenuaran en los laboriosos infiernos
de las minas de oro antillanas" (HUI 11)]. Father Bartolomé de
las Casas's, *Short Account of the Destruction of the Indies*, first
published in 1552, denounced the systematic enslavement, torture,
and annihilation of indigenous Americans by the Spanish in the
New World. The myth that followed the book was that Las Casas
had suggested importing slaves from Africa to relieve the "indios"
from their forced labor. Even if this is nowhere to be found in the

---

[81] North American barbarism is, curiously enough, something Sarmiento chooses
either to ignore or to romanticize and aestheticize in his letters and journal entries
written while touring North America. Wild, untamed characters and landscapes that
he found censurable in the South somehow become alluring in the North.

Short Account,[82] Borges (who never was a stickler for truthfulness when it came to bibliographical references anyway) latches on to this notion, according to which Las Casas is responsible for the presence of Africans in the American continent. And according to Borges, this act of original violence inaugurates a new form of American unity. "To that strange variation of a philanthropist we owe an infinitude of things" ["A esa curiosa variación de un filántropo debemos infinitos hechos"], Borges writes, and then proceeds to list (in a long, typically Borgesian enumeration[83]) the many consequences of Las Casas's proposal: the blues; the work of Uruguayan painter Pedro Fígari, which often features scenes from "candombes"; the American Civil War; Vicente Rossi, author of *Cosa de negros* (1926); the mythical stature of Abraham Lincoln; Falucho, a Black hero of the South American Independence War; the Haitian revolutionary and dictator Toussaint Louverture; the Black man Martín Fierro kills in José Hernández's poem; tango. This abbreviation of Borges's extensive enumeration is enough to reveal its main intention: despite its diversity, the American continent (from the United States to Argentina through the Caribbean) is united by one foundational barbaric event—slavery. Here, Borges seems to claim, is the violent point of departure of any "Pan-American" perception of the continent. Slavery, this "remote cause" ["causa remota"], as he titles the first section of the first story of the book, is the murderous link that unites north and south. This, according to Borges, is the first form of continental union: north and south are brought together by crime and brutality. Paradoxically, as Borges's enumeration shows, this original crime ends up producing unique and untranslatable (i.e. *American*) art forms—paradoxically, but not surprisingly, as for Borges there tends to be an intimate relationship between criminal violence and art.

---

[82] Furthermore, since the early sixteenth century (before Las Casas had any presence in court), King Ferdinand had started the importation of African slaves to the New World. For more details that debunk the myth about Las Casas as an advocate of the importation of African slave labor into the Americas, see Parish (10, 49), who painstakingly rectifies an "old slander" (6) and even includes a little-known text where the Spanish friar denounces the use of African slaves (201–08).

[83] The importance of enumerations in Borges's work is discussed in the following section, on Whitman.

If "The Cruel Redeemer Lazarus Morell" flags crime as the *beginning* of a shared continental history, it also hints at the possibility that the *final* Pan-American unity will be criminal as well. Betrayed by his accomplices and cornered by the law, Morell comes up with a last resort plan: "Morell, crushed and almost undone by treachery, contemplated *a continental response*—a response in which criminality was exalted to the point of redemption and history" (my translation; also in CF 11) ["Morell, despeñado y casi deshecho por la traición, meditaba *una respuesta continental*: una respuesta donde lo criminal se exaltaba hasta la redención y la historia" (HUI 24; my emphasis)].[84] The coalition of the American continent would thus begin and end with crime—from Las Casas to Morell's Pan-American union.

Borges's two other North American Stories in *Universal History of Infamy* insist on this same point: violence translates easily from one hemisphere to the other, and all the local manifestations of brutal thuggishness are nothing but the particular embodiments of archetypal or *universal* savagery. There is a fluent, seamless transition from one context to the other, which does not seem to require explanations or comments of any kind. For instance, Borges insists in calling Eastman, a New York gangster, a "malevo," a decidedly Argentinean term for "thug," as in "odd—this tempestuous *malevo* was Jewish" (CF 26) ["cosa extraña, ese malevo tormentoso era hebreo" (HUI 55)]. By using this unmistakably Argentinean word (and a local oral intonation—"cosa extraña"), Borges is "translating" Eastman into an Argentine context (and vice versa), a procedure quite frequent in his literature. But among its many contextual translations, "Monk Eastman, Purveyor of Iniquities" offers an ambitious transhistorical and transcontinental amalgamation. Borges describes the Battle of Rivington, a street fight between two rival gangs: "A hundred heroes as insignificant or splendid as those of Troy or Junín fought that black deed of arms in the shadow of the elevated train" (CF 28) ["unos cien héroes tan insignificantes o espléndidos como los de Troya o Junín, libraron ese renegrido hecho de armas, en la sombra de los arcos del *Elevated*" (HUI 59)]. At the heart of this passage is a typically Borgesian questioning of boundaries and hierarchies, and it unfolds in two movements. First

---

[84] This quote is followed by an entire paragraph translated, word for word, from Twain's *Life in the Mississippi* (407–08).

Borges questions the very relevance of the battle: all heroes may be futile or glorious ("heroes as insignificant or splendid"), depending on the perspective—universal or historical. The truly interesting operation, however, is the second one, where he equates a dirty street fight with the most epic of all wars (Troy) and with one of the battles in the war of Argentinean independence (where one of his ancestors fought). By triangulating different traditions and events that obviously operate in different historical registers (the Trojan siege, the Argentine war of independence, the clash of two street gangs), Borges completely dilutes all sense of hierarchy. In the midst of a battle, a valorous action is the same, whether the fight is over a street corner or an empire. Achilles, hoodlum Paul Kelly, and Colonel Manuel Isidoro Suárez (Borges's great grandfather) all coexist on the same level. This elimination of historical and geographical distance and this complete homogenization of historical values, of symbolic relevance, of prestige, of contextual determinations are achieved, once again, through violence.

These three stories show, then, that Borges's first approach to the United States (and his first attempts at fiction writing) did *not* revolve around the process of modernization. Quite the opposite. All these brutal figures (the *gaucho*, the cowboy, the *malevo*, the hoodlum, the *compadrito*, etc.) have certain primitiveness in common: each in his own way questions the very existence of State and law. They are all in a constant war of all against all, close to a state of nature where, as Hobbes would have it, life is "solitary, poor, nasty, brutish, and short." Far from being the mercantile technocrats depicted by the *modernistas*, these figures are regressive forces in societies striving to become, in one way or another, "modern." Borges's is the "barbaric United States" ("los bárbaros Estados Unidos" [PJLB 167]). The novelty of Borges's approach resides in refusing to array South and North on a teleological timeline that goes from a primitive to a modern state, and insisting, rather, that both hemispheres are equally brutal at heart.

The cipher

Around this time (the second half of the nineteenth century), appears a figure that articulates violence, State, and law in a completely new way—the detective. The detective civilizes crime. Violence no longer is a brute force of nature that can only be addressed through more violence (like, for instance, the bludgeon-wielding thugs bashing each other's skulls in "Monk Eastman, Purveyor of Iniquities") but an act to be subjected to and understood through reason. Violence of any kind can be confronted in a clinical, rational way. This brings us back to Edgar Allan Poe. In this context, it is not irrelevant or whimsical that the murderer in the first detective story ever written actually *is* a brute force of nature—an orangutan. This raises important questions about the relationship between criminality and humanity[85] and also makes another crucial point: even the most senseless and, literally, *bestial* crime can be subordinated to reason.

For the *modernistas*, Poe was in between two worlds—Ariel in the land of Caliban. In his own way, Borges also sees Poe suspended between two realms, which are crucial for the Argentine writer. Dupin allows Borges to articulate the lettered, bookish world and the barbaric, bloody one. The coexistence of these two orders defines a great number of Borges's fictions. It should also be noted that Dupin also upsets every *modernista* opposition by conjugating the poet with the mathematician;[86] the coldness of analytical

---

[85] The criminal has often been seen as inhuman—as if transgressing the juridical law implied a simultaneous infringement of biological laws. In addition to literalizing this metaphor, Poe's story raises further issues—is it possible to speak of a "crime" when the agent (for lack of a better word, since "criminal" will not do) is in fact a being that is *not* subjected to the law? In a way, crime fiction is inaugurated by a story without either a criminal or a crime. Given the legal system in place, there is no murderer in "The Murders in the Rue Morgue." Proof of this is the fact that, even if the agent (the orangutan) is caught, a conviction is not possible.

[86] Dupin (and his alter ego and nemesis, Minister D—in "The Purloined Letter") fashions himself *both* "as a poet *and* a mathematician"—and this is why he "reasons well." If the Minister were a "mere mathematician, he could not have reasoned at all, and thus would have been at the mercy of the Prefect," a well-learned mathematician who feels "all fools are poets," embodies this kind of pure instrumental reason (the one Darío and Rodó objected to), completely deprived of poetic inspiration (Poe, *Poetry and Tales* 691).

thought with the rush of aesthetic pleasure;[87] the disinterested aesthete with the profit-seeking mercenary.[88] "Observing him," the narrator of "The Murders in the Rue Morgue" says referring to the detective, "I often dwelt meditatively upon the old philosophy of the Bi-Part Soul, and amused myself with the fancy of a double Dupin—the creative and the resolvent" (Poe, *Poetry and Tales* 402). But once again: if Poe is a decisive influence for Borges, it is because he conjugates the world of the intellect with the world of physical violence. And he does so by showing how barbarism can become a problem of ratiocination.

Detective fiction was one of Borges's constant concerns and a lens through which he read other genres and traditions. A good example is what may well be his very first mention of the detective genre, which can be found in his third collection of essays, *El idioma de los argentinos* (1928). In "La fruición literaria," Borges refers to "los novelones policiales de Eduardo Gutiérrez" (IA 91). Thus, in one of his typical displacements and contextual translations, Borges looks at the *gauchesca* tradition through the prism of detective fiction. The fact that Gutiérrez actually has very little to do with detective literature[89] is precisely why this first mention of the genre by Borges is so relevant—because Borges uses genres not so much

---

[87] "The mental features discoursed of as the analytical . . . are always to their possessor, when inordinately possessed, a source of the liveliest *enjoyment*. . . . He derives *pleasure* from even the most trivial occupations bringing his talent into play" (Poe 397; my emphasis).

[88] Even if Dupin leads the life of a Parisian bohemian, and seems only interested in the intangible rewards of intellectual life, in "The Purloined Letter" it becomes clear that (personal vendettas aside) he is working for money. Dupin actually refuses to hand over the retrieved letter before the Prefect signs him a check for 50,000 francs.

[89] As often occurs in *Universal History of Infamy* (where gangsters are called "compadritos" and cowboys, "chúcaros"), this is a drastic form of translation or, rather, relocation. Eduardo Gutiérrez (1851–1889) was a prominent writer of novels by installments. His "folletines" usually glorified gaucho outlaws, and (in opposition to most gaucho literature which was highly stylized) they are characterized by an "uncivil style" ["incivilidad del estilo"], which has the "satisfactory, the never used, the almost scandalous flavor of reality" ["el satisfactorio, el no usado, el casi escandaloso sabor de la veracidad"], as Borges puts it in "Eduardo Gutiérrez, escritor realista," a brief essay written in 1937 (TC 118). Qualifying, for instance, *Hormiga negra* (Borges's favorite of Guitérrez's texts) as detective fiction would require a long justification. Even though there are many arguments to be made in favor of Borges's "translation" (Gutiérrez and Poe were, each in his own way, pop writers; their stories

as a template for writing but rather as a model for reading. Borges explains in one of his 1979 lectures at the University of Belgrano:

> *Literary genres may depend less on the texts than on the way texts are read....* There exists a certain species of contemporary reader: the reader of detective fiction. This reader ... was invented by Edgar Allan Poe. Let us imagine that this reader ... is someone far removed from us. He may be a Persian, a Malaysian, a peasant, a child. In any case, this reader is told that *Don Quixote* is a detective novel; we will suppose that this hypothetical figure is familiar with detective novels, and that he begins to read: "In a place of La Mancha whose name I do not wish to recall, there lived, not long ago, a gentleman ... " Already this reader is full of suspicion, for the reader of detective novels reads with incredulity, with suspiciousness, with a special kind of suspiciousness. For example, if he reads: "In a place of La Mancha ... " he naturally assumes that none of it really happened in La Mancha. Then: " ... whose name I do not wish to recall ... "—and why didn't Cervantes want to remember? Undoubtedly, because Cervantes was the murderer, the guilty party. . . . *Detective fiction has created a special type of reader.* This tends to be forgotten when Poe's work is evaluated, for *if Poe created the detective story, he subsequently created the reader of detective fiction.* (SNF 491–92; my emphasis)

> [*Los géneros literarios dependen, quizás, menos de los textos que del modo en que éstos son leídos....* Hay un tipo de lector actual, el lector de ficciones policiales. Ese lector ha sido ... engendrado por Edgar Allan Poe. Vamos a suponer que [ese lector es] una persona muy lejana de nosotros. Puede ser un persa, un malayo, un rústico, un niño, una persona a quien le dicen que el *Quijote* es una novela policial; vamos a suponer que ese hipotético personaje haya leído novelas policiales y empiece a leer el *Quijote*. Entonces, ¿qué lee? "En un lugar de la Mancha de cuyo

---

are obviously concerned with crime and the law; their writings were shaped by the media in which they were published; they would often draw from real chronicles; etc.), there is one fundamental difference: the defining element of detective fiction, ratiocination, is absent from Gutiérrez. The procedural element is simply not there. Furthermore, Gutiérrez's heroes are usually criminals or social outcasts rather than truth-seeking gentlemen. If anything, Gutiérrez's antiheroes (despite being fully rural) are closer to Sam Spade than they are to Auguste Dupin.

nombre no quiero acordarme, no hace mucho tiempo vivía un hidalgo . . ." y ya ese lector está lleno de sospechas, porque el lector de novelas policiales es un lector que lee con incredulidad, con suspicacias, una suspicacia especial. Por ejemplo, si lee: "En un lugar de la Mancha . . . ," desde luego supone que aquello no sucedió en la Mancha. Luego: ". . . de cuyo nombre no quiero acordarme . . ." ¿Por qué no quiso acordarse Cervantes? Porque sin duda Cervantes era el asesino, el culpable. . . . *La novela policial ha creado un tipo especial de lector.* Eso suele olvidarse cuando se juzga la obra de Poe; porque *si Poe creó el relato policial, creó después el tipo de lector de ficciones policiales.* (BO 66–67)]

As we shall see, this is exactly how Borges reads a number of genres originally unrelated to detective fiction, from *gauchesca* literature to theology and metaphysics and turns them into detective stories by virtue of this "deflected reading," to use an expression he employs in "Kafka and His Precursors."[90]

"The End" ["El fin"] (in *Ficciones*) and "Biography of Tadeo Isidoro Cruz" ["Biografía de Tadeo Isidoro Cruz"] (in *El Aleph* [1949]) retell and expand two crucial scenes of *Martín Fierro*, Argentina's national poem and, in many ways, the pinnacle of the *gauchesca* genre. But in each case, the narrative is structured as a detective fiction—organized around an enigma (which in these stories is of a literary nature). At first, these appear to be simply two of Borges's typical texts set in the Argentine plains in the nineteenth century, but toward the end (and in a flash) it becomes clear that they are new takes on *Martín Fierro* and that the protagonist is the eponymous hero of Hernández's book. The main point in these two texts, why they *work*, is that the readers do not know that the stories

---

[90] The deflected reading of Guitérrez is closely linked to the argument Borges puts forward in his famous essay on Kafka and his precursors, the main argument of which I outlined when discussing his essay on Hawthorne. To sum up briefly, Borges perceives that there is something in Browning's "Fears and Scruples" (among other texts written before Kafka's birth) that anticipates Kafka—something proleptically Kafkaesque. But it is our having read Kafka that makes this affinity perceptible in the first place: "The poem . . . prophesies the work of Kafka, but our reading of Kafka noticeably refines and *deflects* our reading of the poem" (SNF 365; edited. My emphasis) ["El poema . . . profetiza la obra de Kafka, pero nuestra lectura de Kafka afina y *desvía* sensiblemente nuestra lectura del poema" (OC 711)]. It is by virtue of this deflection ("desvío") that Gutiérrez can be perceived as the writer of "novelones policiales."

are new takes on *Martín Fierro* until reaching the final lines where the identities of the characters are revealed. If these two stories are such effective revisions of the *gauchesca*, it is because they recast this genre in a different one—they turn these *gauchesca* scenes into detective-like enigmas (furthermore, in "El fin," the solution of the enigma of Martín Fierro's identity coincides with his death[91]). Both stories are structured as detective narratives, with hints that point to the solution to a riddle. But what makes them unique is that the readers are not even aware that there *is* an enigma until they reach the end of the story. Only then do they realize that the whole narrative had been, in fact, ciphered, and that seemingly irrelevant details were clues that a good reader (acting here as a detective) could have deciphered before the conclusion. The story reveals to be a riddle at the very moment it presents the solution to the riddle. Put differently, only at the end do the readers become aware of the fact that they *should have been* looking for something—and this reminds us of what Borges deems to be the crucial contribution of detective fiction to literature: *detective fiction has created a special kind of reader*. The revelation of the fact that "El fin" and "Biografía de Tadeo Isidoro Cruz" refer to *Martín Fierro* coincides with the revelation of the fact that they are detective stories. These two revelations are one and the same. At the end of these stories, and with one single stroke, Borges intervenes in both genres.

Borges thus brings together two traditions that, at first sight, have very little in common. However, Borges shows that these two genres share at least two traits. First, they are both inherently American (in a continental sense). Second, they both (albeit in very different ways) deal with the problem of the law—its constitution, its infringement, and (sometimes) its reinstatement. In this sense, the *gauchesca* has a very important common denominator with detective fiction: it also is a hinge between lettered culture and physical violence. The analytical element of classic detective fiction is of course absent from the *gauchesca*, whose sole concern typically is the biography of the hero (how the gaucho came to be an outcast, what he learned in the process, and what his final fate is). Despite this and other differences (from their setting to their form—most *gauchesca* literature feigns to be oral, and is rhymed), both genres see the literary virtues of violence. In this regard, according to

---

[91] For the implications of Borges's narration of Martín Fierro's death in the context of Argentine literary tradition, see Sarlo 85–93.

Borges, Edgar Allan Poe seems to be, yet again, an exception in the North American nineteenth century. In a review of Steinbeck's *Of Mice and Men*, Borges writes:

Brutality can also be a literary virtue. We know well that nineteenth-century North Americans were incapable of that virtue. Happily or unhappily incapable. (Not so with us: we could already show *La refalosa* by Colonel Ascasubi,[92] and "The Slaughterhouse" by Esteban Echeverría,[93] and the scene of the murder of the Negro in *Martín Fierro*, and the monotonous scenes of atrocities profusely dispatched by Eduardo Gutiérrez ...).[94]

[También la brutalidad puede ser una virtud literaria. Nos consta que en el siglo XIX los americanos del Norte eran incapaces

[92] Ascasubi (1807–1875) wrote "La refalosa" ("The Slippery One") in 1843, an extremely gory poem in octosyllables describing how the *federales* (supporters of Rosa's dictatorship, in whom Borges saw a direct antecedent of Perón) would slit their opponents throats.

[93] Echeverría (1805–1851) wrote "The Slaughterhouse" in 1837, but it was only published in 1871. "El matadero," Argentina's first short story, is remarkable (leaving its undeniable literary merits aside) for its explicit, incredibly gruesome violence. As Ascasubi's poem, it also denounces the terror regime of the *federales*.

[94] This passage appears, almost verbatim, in a 1941 review for *Sur* of Bret Harte's *Stories of the Old West* (BS 240). In both cases it should be noted that Borges surreptitiously introduces brutality as a literary value—a notion that would have required some kind of explanation instead of being presented as a *petitio principii*. He also discusses the presence of violence in North and South American literature in his "Nathaniel Hawthorne," where, once again, brutality seems to be the common trait that makes the comparison between both hemispheres possible: "In comparison with the literature of the United States, which has produced several men of genius and has had its influence felt in England and France, our Argentine literature may possibly seem somewhat provincial. Nevertheless, in the nineteenth century it produced some admirable works of realism—some admirable cruelties by Echeverría, Ascasubi, Hernández, and the forgotten Eduardo Gutiérrez—the North Americans have not surpassed (perhaps not equaled) to this day" (OI 64) ["Comparada con la de Estados Unidos, que ha dado varios hombres de genio, que ha influido en Inglaterra y en Francia, nuestra literatura argentina corre el albur de parecer un tanto provincial; sin embargo, en el siglo XIX, produjo algunas páginas de realismo—algunas admirables crueldades de Echeverría, de Ascasubi, de Hernández, del ignorado Gutiérrez—que los norteamericanos no han superado (tal vez no han igualado) hasta ahora" (OC 684)]. In other words, if Argentina can, here and there, outshine the United States, it is because its literature is unrivaled in its brutality. Once again, why this is a desirable trait (when Borges, for instance, detested hardboiled detective novels *precisely* because of their brutality) remains a mystery. At all events, this seems to be the way Borges finds to overcome the anxiety of belonging in a "provincial" literature.

de esa virtud. Feliz o infelizmente incapaces. (Nosotros, no: nosotros ya podíamos exhibir *La refalosa* del coronel Ascasubi y *El matadero* de Esteban Echeverría, y la escena del asesinato del negro en el *Martín Fierro* y las monótonas escenas atroces que despachaba con profusión Eduardo Gutiérrez . . .). (TC 250)]

This North American "incapability" for literary violence (in the nineteenth century) probably explains why Borges's sources for his chronicles of North American brutality are *not* literary—with the exception of Twain, the authors cited are, in a loose sense, historians. But Poe was clearly no stranger to brutality (examples abound, but it may be sufficient to recall the gruesome descriptions in his two first detective stories). In this, he represents a clear exception in the context outlined in the previous quotation. It seems, however, that, compared to the extensive tradition of violent literature in Argentina, Poe was not violent *enough*. Furthermore, Poe was insufficiently brutal compared to his own context:

No one ignores that detective fiction was invented about one hundred years ago by that ingenious North American inventor called Edgar Allan Poe. This genre (perhaps the most artificial of all literary genres) could not compete with the thundering reality of Monk Eastman and Al Capone, and thus migrated to the British Isles, where crime shows more modesty.

[Nadie ignora que el género policial fue inventado hará unos cien años por el ingenioso inventor norteamericano Edgar Allan Poe. Ese género (acaso el más artificial de cuantos la literatura comprende) no logró competir con la atronadora realidad de Monk Eastman y de Al Capone y emigró a las Islas Británicas, donde es pudoroso el delito. (TC 323)]

Once again, Borges sets out to debunk the image of the United States that both its most fervent proselytizers and its most virulent attackers promoted. Borges claims that the United States is *not* the center of rationality that Sarmiento idolized and the *modernistas* reviled. On the contrary, North America's brutality makes Latin America's *barbarie* pale in comparison. Furthermore, detective fiction was unable to prosper in this context, Borges hyperbolically claims (ignoring, as he always did, the hardboiled exponents of the genre[95]), because its moderate violence was unable to match the atrocious reality of North American life. Detective fiction is not, it seems, the proper genre to do the violence pervading the United States justice. Instead, that genre is the *gauchesca*.

If Borges rewrites the *gauchesca* in a detective-like key, he performs the opposite operation in his three North American stories in *Universal History of Infamy*, giving the United States the "brutal" and literary depiction of lowlifes it never, according to him, had (once again, it should be remembered that almost none of Borges's references in *Universal History of Infamy* are literary).

---

[95] Borges always lamented the turn detective fiction took in the United States in the late 1920s, and even believed that the hardboiled take on the genre was not detective fiction at all. "Currently, the detective genre has greatly declined in the United States, where it has become realistic and about violence—sexual violence, as well. In any event, *it has disappeared. The intellectual origins of the detective story have been forgotten*" (SNF 499; my emphasis) ["Actualmente el género policial ha decaído mucho en Estados Unidos. El género policial es realista, de violencia, un género de violencias sexuales también. En todo caso, *ha desaparecido. Se ha olvidado el origen intelectual del relato policial*" (BO 79)]. In a 1970 interview published by *Atlántida*, Borges declares: "What is called detective fiction in the United States nowadays is a sadistic or gory take on adventure novels. In Dashiell Hammett's novels, for instance, detectives use and abuse physical force. They are not intellectuals; they are criminals who happen to side with the law" ["Lo que se llama novela policial en Estados Unidos, ahora, es una forma sadista o sanguinaria de la novela de aventuras. En las novelas de Dashiell Hammett, por ejemplo, los detectives hacen uso y abuso de la fuerza física, no son intelectuales, son criminales que están de parte de la ley" (in Lafforgue and Rivera 126)]. Bioy Casares transcribes a conversation with Borges: "He [Borges] talks about American realism, hardboiled fiction (exemplified by [James] Cain's *The Postman Always Rings Twice*). Borges: 'It shows violent, vulgar people. It shows them without a hint of irony. One suspects the author is one of them'" ["Habla del realismo americano, *hard-boiled* (ejemplificado en *El cartero llama dos veces* de Cain), Borges: 'Muestra gente violenta, vulgar. La muestra sin ironía. Uno sospecha que el autor es uno de ellos'" (620)]. Borges even thought that the tough, gritty qualities of hardboiled detective fiction had affected North American literature as a whole: "the naïve fear of not being hardboiled enough is one of the most obvious (and less agreeable) traits of North American letters today" ["el temor candoroso de no ser lo bastante *hardboiled*, que es uno de los signos más evidentes (y menos agradables) de las letras norteamericanas de hoy" (BS 240)]. Oddly enough, in Latin America, "[b]rutality can also be a literary virtue," as Borges claimed reviewing Steinbeck (TC 250), but in the North this same brutality is perceived as crass and vulgar. A further paradox is that, for Borges, violence seems to demand a great degree of delicacy and finesse: it requires a very delicate fine-tuning, a subtle balance that North American literature seems unable to achieve: it is either not brutal enough (Poe) or much too brutal (Hammett, Cain, etc.).

And to do so he resorts not to detective fiction (which, as said, is not sufficiently brutal) but to the template of the *gauchesca*. It is hard to think of a material better suited for the detective form than the crooks, murders, and impostors in these stories (Who is Monk Eastman? What is his real identity? Will the police anticipate his next move? Will they get him?). Yet, these texts are not structured along the main lines of the detective genre. Every vestige of enigma is completely gone, and there are neither clues to read nor questions to be answered. Rather, they are presented in the straightforward biographical way that defines *gauchesca* narratives (from their rhymed origins to Gutiérrrez's novels).[96] The life story, the central aspect of *gauchesca* literature, has completely displaced and done away with every procedural vestige. Lazarus Morell, Monk Eastman, and Bill Harrigan are biographical subjects. We see them evolve from the cradle into a criminal adulthood, where they live

---

[96] "The biographical story . . . narrates the series of actions whereby a gaucho is accused of a crime or confronted by the representatives of the law. . . . The oral autobiography is a juridical narration, entirely constituted by the interplay between different codes of law; its subject is guilty before a modern, written, hegemonic legal code, but innocent before another one, his own. . . . The biographical function [i.e., a narrative in third person] served to attack the subject and proffer him as an example of criminal barbarism[,] while the autobiographical function was used to defend the writing subject and attack his political enemies" (Ludmer 627). Here, in a nutshell, are the main traits of the *gauchesca*, beginning with the biographical element (and the issue of the oral register vs. the written code, the tension with the law, the dissonance with modernization, and the friction between civilization and barbarism). Ludmer's last distinction between autobiographies and biographies in the third person is also relevant in this context. All of Borges's infamous North Americans in *Universal History of Infamy* are subjected to what Ludmer calls "the biographical function." This renders them "examples of criminal barbarism," which is in accord with Borges's book, whose aim, as its title eloquently states, is "universalization." Borges, it should be added, wrote numerous essays on the *gauchesca* and often thought of this genre through the prism of North American literature. A clear example is "La poesía gauchesca," included in *Discusión*. This essay on the most Argentine of genres is bookended by the North American tradition: it begins with a quote by Whistler (and then, briefly, considers the western as a genre) and ends with a reflection on *Huckleberry Finn*. Regarding the supposed similarities between gauchos and cowboys, Borges is quick to dismiss this facile parallel: "pastoral life is typical of many American regions, from Montana and Oregon to Chile. But hitherto, those territories have vigorously abstained from composing *The Gaucho Martín Fierro*. Rough herdsmen and the desert, then, are not enough. Cowboys, despite Will James's documentary books and despite the insistence of motion pictures, are less important in the United States than the farmers from Midwest or the Black men from the South" ["la vida pastoril ha sido típica de muchas regiones de América, desde Montana y Oregón hasta Chile, pero esos territorios, hasta ahora, se han

according to a moral code of their own (opposed to the written law) and then meet their more or less pathetic end. There is no room in these narratives for enigmas or riddles of any kind. The biographical drive consumes these stories. If Borges, as we saw, "detectivizes" the *gauchesca* (by turning the identity of the characters and the texts they refer to into an enigma), here he recasts detective fiction in the mold of the *gauchesca* (by reversing the former process and neutralizing the enigma in these criminal narratives in favor of the biographical component).

This, as has been shown, emerges from Borges's claim that genres are primarily habits of reading—Poe invented not the detective story but the detective *reader*: "When we read a detective novel, we are an invention of Edgar Allan Poe" (my translation. Also in SNF 497) ["Nosotros, al leer una novela policial, somos una invención de Edgar Allan Poe" (BO 75)]. The remarkable turn in this quote is

---

abstenido enérgicamente de redactar *El gaucho Martín Fierro*. No bastan, pues, el duro pastor y el desierto. El *cowboy*, a pesar de los libros documentales de Will James y del instistente cinematógrafo, pesa menos en la literatura de su país que los chacareros del Middle West o que los hombres negros del Sur" (OC 179—and there is an almost verbatim version of this passage in his micro-biography of Will James (TC 195)]. However, Borges finds a common denominator between both genres: both the western and the *gauchesca* are lettered, urban, inventions of rough, rural myths. Neither of them is truly popular literature (a notion Borges would find hard to grasp anyway). Rather, Borges views both as complex constructs, fictional worlds that are supposed to be realities with their own weight—almost like Tlön. "I should say that the West was invented by New Englanders, no?" (C 80). The source for this parallel between the *gauchesca* and the western can be tracked back to Borges's reading of Van Wyck Brooks: "*The Flowering of New England* is an excellent book. Just like there would not have been *gauchesca* literature without Buenos Aires (the gauchos would never have written it; it was written by gentlemen), the legend of the West would never have existed without New England. It was the people from New England who felt there was something poetic in the conquest of the West, and in the Californian gold rush" ["*The Flowering of New England* de Van Wyck Brooks es un excelente libro. Así como no habría literatura gauchesca si no hubiera habido Buenos Aires—los gauchos no la hubieran escrito, son los señores quienes la escribieron—sin New England no existiría la leyenda del Oeste. Es la gente de New England la que sintió como poética la conquista del Oeste, la busca de oro en California" (Bioy 994)]. Borges believed the very notion that this literature had been written by "primitive people, gauchos, etc."—rather than by men of letters—was a populist approach, an "*ur-Peronist* idea" ["una idea *ur-peronista*" (Bioy 1062)] that relied on a fetishized idea of *Volk*. Regarding Twain, there are numerous instances (OC 197, 271, 733, 736, 761; ILN 52; TR I: 100; TC 103) where Borges links him to the *gauchesca* genre—particularly to Hernández and Güiraldes. *Don Segundo Sombra* (by Güiraldes) and the *Adventures of Huckleberry Finn* were, for Borges, the two inherently American bildungsromans.

that Borges does not claim that Poe invented detective fiction (that would be a mere commonplace) but a particular kind of reader, a particular kind of disposition—*we*, the readers, are Poe's creations each time we approach a text with the suspicion and paranoia he inculcated in us. More than a few formal devices and stereotypes, this attitude in the reader is Poe's main creation. The corollary to this is that any text can become a detective fiction. The only condition is that the readers (of any text) become detectives themselves, that "reading" and "detection" are taken as strict synonyms. In "A Survey of the Works of Herbert Quain" ("Examen de la obra de Herbert Quain"), Borges stresses this affinity between detective and reader and even places the latter above the former. Quain (an apocryphal writer) started out his career with a detective novel, *The God of the Labyrinth*:

> There is an undecipherable murder in the early pages of the book, a slow discussion in the middle, and a solution of the crime toward the end. Once the mystery has been cleared up, there is a long retrospective paragraph that contains the following sentence: *Everyone believed that the chessplayers had met accidentally.* That phrase allows one to infer that the solution is in fact an error, and so, uneasy, the reader looks back over the pertinent chapters and discovers *another* solution, which is the correct one. The reader of this remarkable book, then, is more perspicacious than the detective. (CF 108)

> [Hay un indescifrable asesinato en las páginas iniciales, una lenta discusión en las intermedias, una solución en las últimas. Ya aclarado el enigma, hay un párrafo largo y retrospectivo que contiene esta frase: *Todos creyeron que el encuentro de los dos jugadores de ajedrez había sido casual.* Esa frase deja entender que la solución es errónea. El lector, inquieto, revisa los capítulos pertinentes y descubre *otra* solución, que es la verdadera. El lector de ese libro singular es más perspicaz que el *detective.* (OC 462)]

Borges turns his maxim about detective fiction ("Detective fiction has created a special kind of reader") not just into the literal premise that drives Quain's novel but also into the *material* condition thanks to which the text works—"detection," here, is the reader's task more than the hero's, and it is in the actual process of reading itself that the story finds its resolution. By showing the affinities between reader and detective, the very notion of "reading" acquires a completely new dimension. Both for the detective and for the detective fiction reader, there is a saturation of meaning; nothing merely *is*, but everything signals to something else. Literality, in this over-interpreted world, is simply unthinkable. Nothing can ever be what it seems, because everything, in brief, is a *clue*. To return to Borges's own example: "if [the reader of detective fiction] reads 'In a place of la Mancha . . . ' he will of course guess that events did not take place in la Mancha." A lipstick-stained cigarette is not just that but "stands for" the woman who smoked it. Clues, furthermore, mark the convergence of different temporalities—the trace of *rouge* takes the detective back to the scene where woman smoked it (or brings the past scene into the present). For this reason, clues distort the opposition between presence and absence—the woman is gone, but the cigarette she held and smoked conjures up her presence *in absentia*. Finally, even though clues are, in their own way, signs, they complicate the relationship between language (in a wide sense) and the world (its referent). Even if they stand for something else, they also *are* what they represent—they are, at least partly their referent (the lady *is* on the cigarette filter, her material, concrete traces—the lipstick, the concave mark left by her fingers—remain there).[97]

This is how Erik Lönnrot, the detective in "Death and the Compass," reads the world. "Lönnrot," writes Borges, "thought of himself as a pure reasoner, an Auguste Dupin, but there was something of the adventurer in him, even something of the gambler"

---

[97] There are clear affinities between the notion of clue and C. S. Peirce's concept of index. A thorough consideration of Peirce's theory of signs exceeds the purpose of these pages, but a brief account is in order. "Indices are signs which stand for their object *in consequence of a real relationship to them*. An index is a sign which stands for its object *in consequence of having a real connection with it*. . . . The index asserts nothing; it only says 'There!'" (V: 379; my emphasis). Some of Peirce's frequent examples are a pointing finger and demonstrative and relative pronouns. "An index *represents its object by a real correspondence with it*—as a tally does quarts of milk, and a vane the wind" (I: 475; my emphasis). In "An Elementary Account of the Logic of Relatives," however, Peirce provides an example that is illuminating in the context of detective fiction: "For example, I wanted one day to know whether it was raining. I looked out of the window, and could not be sure that I saw any rain. However, I noticed a number of people with their umbrellas up, and concluded it was raining" (V: 379). For a full definition of "index," see Peirce I: 476; II: 56; V: 163. Borges, oddly enough, never wrote about Peirce, even though the intellectual affinities between both are apparent and even if Borges was deeply interested in pragmatism (and William James in particular).

(CF 147) ["Lönnrot se creía un puro razonador, un Auguste Dupin, pero algo de aventurero había en él y hasta de tahúr" (OC 499)]. A Hebraist has been murdered in his hotel room (across the hall from the suite Tetrach of Galilee's suite). The scholar was sitting at his typewriter and slain midsentence (he had typed "The first letter of the Name has been articulated" (CF 149) ["La primera letra del Nombre ha sido articulada" (OC 500)]. The police commissioner immediately presents his reconstruction of the facts:

"No need to go off on wild-goose chases here[98]. . . . We all know that that the Tetrarch of Galilee owns the finest sapphires in the world. Somebody intending to steal the sapphires broke in here by mistake. Yarmolinsky woke up, the burglar had to kill him. What do you think?"

"Possible, but uninteresting," Lönnrot replied. "You will answer that reality has not the slightest obligation to be interesting. I will answer in turn that reality may get along without that obligation, but hypotheses may not." (CF 148)

[—No hay que buscarle tres pies al gato. . . . Todos sabemos que el Tetrarca de Galilea posee los mejores zafiros del mundo. Alguien, para robarlos, habrá penetrado aquí por error. Yarmolinsky se ha levantado; el ladrón ha tenido que matarlo. ¿Qué le parece?

—Posible, pero no interesante—respondió Lönnrot—. Usted replicará que la realidad no tiene la menor obligación de ser interesante. Yo le replicaré que la realidad puede prescindir de esa obligación, pero no las hipótesis. (OC 500)]

Lönnrot's response is a distilled, concentrated manifesto of the detective-fiction reader (who, in this, mimics the detective himself). Facts may be trivial, but the explanation *behind* them (the preposition is crucial—there is always an unseen motive lurking in the dark side of every object and action) can never be. This is the

---

[98] The original reads "No hay que buscarle tres pies al gato," which resists a literal translation (Borges reflects on this adage in Bioy 1114). However, Treviranus's use of the adage is relevant, given that the whole story hinges on the numbers 3 and 4 (among other references, "Treviranus," the "Tetrarch," the Third Talmudic Conference, the crimes committed on the third day of the month (which is, in fact, the fourth), and, of course, the "Tetragrammataton," which inspires Lönnrot to expand the triangle of murders into a rhombus.

drive that sustains the genre: everything is bursting with meaning, every single triviality demands to be deciphered, as if Occam's razor (the principle according to which the simplest explanation is most likely the correct one) had been inverted and was now being held by its blade. Typically, Borges presents this basic law of the genre only to subvert it. Since its inception with Poe, a basic rule of detective fiction is that the institutional solution, the one offered by the police (as opposed to the detective), is always erroneous and *trivial*. In "Death and the Compass," however, the opposite is true. Trivial Treviranus,[99] the police commissioner, is correct, and the would-be Dupin is duped.

What Borges ultimately took from detective fiction is precisely this state of constant hermeneutical alert. Detective stories showed him that even the most minute, insignificant traces could be read and interpreted as clues; that even though life may seem random and chaotic, there is (if one cares to come up with it) a hidden unifying thread. The paradoxical conclusion, then, is that these stories that deal with violence, crime, and the infringement of the law are governed by a stern idea of order—no matter how anarchic, dirty, and confusing things may seem, in the end *it all makes sense*. As Borges puts it in his lecture on detective fiction, this genre can be credited with having "safeguarded order in an era of disorder" (SNF 499) ["salvado el orden en una época de desorden" (BO 80)].[100]

From Poe, then, Borges learned that suspicion is a powerful literary engine. There is always an explanation; there is always a (rational) cause. This means, of course, that there is no room for chance or randomness. In this pan-determined view of the universe, there is always an intentional source. And the consequences of this premise pervade Borges's entire poetics.

---

[99] It should be noted that "trivial" derives from "trivium" (the lower division of the seven liberal arts, which included grammar, rhetoric, and logic). In the story, the number four (the four-lettered name of god, the four cardinal points) is the central element of the trap that Scharlach, the criminal, sets Lönnrot. By complicating the simple solution offered by Treviranus, and going beyond the trivial (in its double sense of "simple" and "triple"), Lönnrot meets his end.

[100] "As opposed to chaotic literary forms, I was attracted to detective fiction because it was a way in which order could be defended, a way to look for classical forms, to appreciate form" ["Frente a una literatura caótica, la novela policial me atraía porque era un modo de defender el orden, de buscar formas clásicas, de valorizar la forma" (in Lafforgue and Rivera 47)].

If there is an order, if the world can be read (and this is precisely what detectives do—they turn their surroundings into a legible surface), there is, in the end, no difference between literature and life. This constant semiotic alarm informs many of Borges's more "metaphysical" texts, stories that, at a first glance, have nothing to do with detective fiction, such as "The Writing of the God," "Tlön, Uqbar, Orbis Tertius," or "The Library of Babel." In these texts, the relationship between words and things is in crisis precisely because *everything* is a clue: there is a saturation of meaning that paradoxically tends to make the act of reading meaningless. These are, in their own way, detective fictions.

"The Writing of the God" ["La escritura del dios"] can help illustrate this point. Tzinacán, a Mayan priest has been thrown into a cell by a Spanish conquistador. In his confinement, Tzinacán sets to reconstruct a magical sentence god wrote (in an encrypted language) when he created the universe, in order to prevent—when the day came—the ruin of his people and the end of the world.

He wrote it in such a way that it would pass down to the farthest generations, and remain untouched by chance. *No one knows where he wrote it, or with what letters*, but we do know that it endures, a *secret text*, and that a chosen one will read it. . . . *I might have seen Qaholom's inscription thousands of times, and need only to understand it*. . . . A mountain might be the word of the god, or a river or the empire or the arrangement of the stars. . . . I thought of the generations of grains, of grasses, of birds, of men. Perhaps the spell was written on my very face. . . . (CF 251; my emphasis)

[La escribió de manera que llegara a las más apartadas generaciones y que no la tocara el azar. *Nadie sabe en qué punto la escribió ni con qué caracteres*, pero nos consta que perdura, *secreta*, y que la leerá un elegido. . . . *Acaso yo había visto mil veces la inscripción de Qaholom y sólo me faltaba entenderla*. . . . Una montaña podía ser la palabra del dios, o un río o el imperio o la configuración de los astros. . . . Pensé en las generaciones de los cereales, de los pastos, de los pájaros, de los hombres. Quizá en mi cara estuviera escrita la magia. . . . (596–97)]

Tzinacán, the sorcerer, is the absolute and ultimate detective: for him the entire creation is a ciphered message. And as the highlighted passages suggest, the entire issue resides in the ability to *recognize* writing where others just see "things"—a river, crops, a face. This, more than actually deciphering the writing, is the crucial matter. "To detect" is to see the potential for meaning where, at first glance, there is none.

The narrator of "The Library of Babel" faces a similar challenge. Just like "The Writing of the God," this story could not seem farther removed from the detective genre—it is, in fact, one of Borges's best-known "metaphysical" and even "mystical" stories. However (and though it is set in a timeless, floating, almost incorporeal world), it follows the basic premises of detective fiction. In fact, one could even say that the text consists in taking the metaphorical principle of the genre literally. "The universe is readable," is the detective's first and guiding metaphor. This becomes literal in the opening line of "The Library of Babel": "The universe (which others call the Library) . . ." (CF 112) ["El universo (que otros llaman la Biblioteca) . . ." (OC 465)]. "Universe" and "library" are here strict synonyms.

The story is an "epistle" (CF 118; OC 470) describing the library where the narrator and his fellow librarians live in. It is an infinite space that contains all the possible combinations of 25 orthographic symbols in 410 page-long books. It is suspected that once this vast combination is exhausted, the library recommences, cyclically, endlessly. Needless to say, there is no "outside" of the library. Here, order is one of the random results of chaos: by sheer combinatorial effect, the answer to "the fundamental mysteries of humanity—the origin of the Library and the origin of time" (CF 115) ["la aclaración de los misterios básicos de la humanidad: el origen de la Biblioteca y del tiempo" (OC 468)] is there, buried among the gibberish.[101] The problem is, of course, that by virtue of that same combinatorial excess,[102] there is no way to crack the

---

[101] The narrator believes in "the formless and chaotic nature of virtually all books" (CF 113) ["la naturaleza informe y caótica de casi todos los libros" (OC 466)]. Even so, amidst the chaos there has to be an order, a "catalog of catalogs" (CF 112) ["catálogo de catálogos" (465)].

[102] It is worth making a marginal (and rather quirky) remark regarding the combinatorial ripples in "The Library of Babel." The text, which so obviously is concerned with the effect of statistical excess, plays with different combinations that echo or foretell previous or later texts by Borges. A few examples: (1) "*The*

code. The library contains "the faithful catalogue of the Library, thousands and thousands of false catalogs, the proofs of the falsity of those catalogs, a proof of the falsity of the true catalog" (CF 115) ["el catálogo fiel de la Biblioteca, miles y miles de catálogos falsos, la demostración de la falacia de esos catálogos, la demostración de la falacia del catálogo verdadero" (OC 467–68)]. Where different possible senses ceaselessly collide against one another, nothing, in the end, makes sense—and the narrator, in a chilling address to the reader, turns this radical uncertainty to the very text he is writing: "You, who read me—are you certain you understand my language" (CF 118) ["Tú, que me lees, ¿estás seguro de entender mi lenguaje?" (OC 470)]. In this, the library resembles the world as perceived by a detective (and also by Tzinacán), for whom everything *may* mean something. Even more than the actual meaning itself, the problem here is *how* and *to what* meaning is assigned. The issue is not really *what* is signified (the semantic content) but being able to tell a signifier from a mere object; being able to discern what is language and what is merely a thing or a random trace—drawing the line between sense and nonsense (or even those things or actions where sense is not even at stake), between scrambled letters and a sentence, between a cloud and a divine inscription, between a dead rabbi and a Hasidic conspiracy.

The nameless narrator of "The Library of Babel," Tzinacán, and the detective all *know* that the universe is legible, but they

---

Library is a sphere whose exact center is any hexagon and whose circumference is unattainable" (CF 113) ["La Biblioteca es una esfera cuyo centro cabal es cualquier hexágono, cuya circunferencia es inaccessible" (OC 466)] is quite obviously a reference to Pascal's sphere: "A frightful sphere, the center of which is everywhere, and the circumference nowhere" (SNF 353) ["Una esfera espantosa cuyo centro estás en todas partes y la circunferencia en ninguna" (OC 638)]. (2) "axaxaxas mlö" is a quote out of one of the Library of Babel's books (CF 117; OC 470), but it is also one of the examples of the language of Tlön (CF 73; OC 435). (3) The Babylonian librarian writes: "Let heaven exist, though my own place be in hell" (CF 117) ["Que el cielo exista, aunque mi lugar sea el infierno" (OC 470)]. This is exactly what Otto zur Linde writes (in the first person plural) toward the end of "*Deutsches Requiem*" (CF 234; OC 581). (4) One of the most widely studied passages in the Library of Babel reads ("*O time your pyramids*" (CF 114) ["*Oh tiempo tus pirámides*" (OC 466)], which becomes "O time, your ephemeral pyramids" (SP 155; 157) ["¡Oh Tiempo! tus efímeras pirámides" (OC 866)] in "Del cielo y del infierno," a poem in *El otro, el mismo.*

cannot make it out. They are enlightened enough to be aware of the presence of meaning, but also limited enough not to be able to bring it forth. This is the tragic condition of the detective—knowing there is something *beyond* appearances but not being quite able to reach it (a cigarette butt is not merely that, just like *dhcmrlchtdj* are not merely a few letters haphazardly thrown together in a volume in the Library of Babel—they both *have to mean* something). To be a detective or a Babylonian librarian means knowing that although the world seems completely random there is an order, even if it is beyond our grasp: "Man, the imperfect librarian, may be the work of chance or of malevolent demiurges; the universe, with its elegant appointments—its bookshelves, its enigmatic books . . . —can only be the handiwork of a god" (CF 113) ["El hombre, el imperfecto bibliotecario, puede ser obra del azar o de los demiurgos malévolos; el universo, con su elegante dotación de anaqueles, de tomos enigmáticos . . . sólo puede ser obra de un dios" (OC 466)]. Chaos is only a more complex order—that I cannot understand. And there is an extreme, unwavering optimism in this idea of order: even though I am lost and, quite literally, *clueless*, there is a direction, a purpose, and a system. As the Babylonian librarian says, "let heaven exist, though my own place be in hell" (CF 117) ["que el cielo exista, aunque mi lugar sea el infierno" (OC 470)].

The concern with order and how it may relate to the chaos and haphazardness of life is at the center of "The Lottery of Babylon." There is an attempt at canceling chance by its amplification. In other words, if *everything* is the result of lottery draws (some believe that even the cry of a bird and the hues of dust and rust are determined by the lottery), chaos has effectively been managed—there is no spontaneous randomness but an administered disorder. "If the lottery is an intensification of chance, a periodic infusion of chaos into the cosmos, then would it not be appropriate that chance intervene in every aspect of the drawing, not just one? . . . In reality, *the number of drawings is infinite*. No decision is final; all branch into others" (CF 104–05; emphasis in original) ["Si la lotería es una intensificación del azar, una periódica infusión del caos en el cosmos, ¿no convendría que el azar interviniera en todas las etapas del sorteo y no en una sola? . . . En la realidad *el número de sorteos es infinito*. Ninguna decisión es final, todas se ramifican en otras" (OC 459)]. There is, then, the superimposition of a will (in this case, an institutional will) onto the entire surface of the world.[103] Put differently, nothing merely *is* (in a spontaneous way) but everything is the calculated and intentional result of a design. "Order" is, in this sense, a neutral word for "conspiracy"—and conspiracies tend to trigger infinite readings.

Borges's true contribution when it comes to detective fiction is to have taken these premises (which all stem, as we have seen, from a particular conception of reading) beyond a merely personal realm (the individual "case") and to have given them a *total* dimension.[104] It is not about an individual conflict (a stolen letter, a lady in a lake) but about the entire universe. Anything, if one reads hard enough into it, can be turned into a detective-like plot. This principle is Borges's blueprint for his "metaphysical" or "mystical" fiction. From detective fiction, Borges takes an attitude of universal suspicion and a tendency toward over interpretation and gives them a theological rank. Thus, Borges's famous maxim in "Tlön, Uqbar, Orbis Tertius," according to which "metaphysics is a branch of fantastic literature" (CF 74) ["la metafísica es una rama de la literatura fantástica" (OC 436)] could actually be reinterpreted as "metaphysics is a branch of detective fiction."

In the United States, Borges is best known for what I have called here (with a grandiloquent vagueness that I believe adequate) his "metaphysical" or "mystical" stories. Even those who have appropriated his literature in a productive, complex fashion, like John Barth, focus on these "philosophical" texts. It is remarkable that none of these writers and critics really consider Borges's ties to the United States. Furthermore, most of Borges's compilations (at least until his almost complete fiction was published by Penguin in 1990) featured mostly stories dealing either in philosophical paradoxes (like "The Aleph" or "The Circular Ruins") or, on the other hand, addressing classical, central problems of literary theory

---

[103] This, of course, related to the argument presented in "When Fiction Lives in Fiction," in the first half of this book.

[104] "The Zahir" is particularly interesting in this context. In this story, the notion of "clue" (an object saturated with meaning, glowing with semantic aura, but yet irreducible and untranslatable from its particular, individual material constitution) is taken to hyperbolic extremes—this object becomes *the* only meaning of life (and the meaning is, tautologically, the object itself).

(like in "Pierre Menard, Author of the Quixote"). But the Borges fascinated by gangsters and hoodlums is hardly read in the States. Beyond, perhaps, "Death and the Compass," Borges's obsession with outlaws (from Billy the Kid to New York hoodlums) tends to be overlooked. It is also vastly ignored that this is his first link to the United States—it is through crooks and murderers that he initially addresses the North American tradition. And it is thanks to these lowlifes that we get detectives, and it is thanks to them that we arrive at the art of suspicion that makes stories like "The Lottery in Babylon" possible. It is thanks to these criminals that Borges arrives at the semiotic anxiety that leads to the conception of the world as a text. These thugs and crooks are, then, in a way the humble source of some of the lofty metaphysical speculations that American readers seem to love most in Borges. Thus, through these philosophical considerations about language and the universe, North American literature, inadvertently, gets part of its own tradition back, while hemispheric stereotypes and hierarchies are questioned and subverted.

2

Walt Whitman, an American, a kosmos

According to Borges, all modern literature springs from two sources. One, as we have seen, is Poe. The other is Whitman:

> Undeniably, all that is specifically modern in contemporary poetry comes from two North Americans of genius: Edgar Allan Poe and Walt Whitman. From Edgar A. Poe derive Baudelaire, symbolism, Valéry, and, in a way, Joyce[105]—and one might add that Poe's theory is perhaps more important and more productive than its practice. From Whitman derives the civil poetry of humanity, often called engaged.[106]

---

[105] Later, in the same lecture, Borges draws a direct line from Whitman to Joyce's *Finnegans Wake*, although "the relative failure of this deliberately enigmatic work could be used as a yardstick to measure the almost miraculous victory achieved by Walt Whitman" ["el relativo fracaso de esta obra deliberadamente enigmática puede servirnos para medir la casi milagrosa victoria lograda por Walt Whitman" (TR III: 44)]. Borges first links Whitman and Joyce in his 1957 article "Montaigne, Walt Whitman": "In 1939, Joyce published *Finnegan's* [sic] *Wake*, whose protagonist . . . aspires to encompass all humanity, but the gods did not let him repeat Whitman's feat" ["En 1939, Joyce ha publicado *Finnegan's Wake*, cuyo protagonista . . . quiere abarcar la humanidad, pero los dioses no dejaron que repitiera la proeza de Whitman" (TR III: 39)]. In 1969, in the foreword to his abridged translation of *Leaves of Grass*, Borges insists on the comparison with the "inextricable and certainly unreadable *Finnegans Wake*" ["el inextricable y ciertamente ilegible *Finnegans Wake*" (P 173)].

[106] Borges repeats this judgment in his 1979 lectures at the University of Belgrano, almost in the same terms. The only interesting addition is the mention of Neruda

[Es innegable que todo lo específicamente moderno de la poesía de nuestro tiempo procede de dos hombres de genio norteamericano: Edgar Allan Poe y Walt Whitman. De Edgar A. Poe descienden Baudelaire, el simbolismo, Valéry y, de algún modo, Joyce, y cabría agregar que la teoría de Poe es quizá más importante y más generadora que su práctica. De Whitman desciende la poesía civil de la humanidad, la que ha dado en llamarse comprometida. (TR III: 42)]

According to Borges, then, from Poe stems the literature concerned with formal experimentation (it is worth pointing out Borges's emphasis on Poe's "theory," condensed in his "Philosophy of Composition," which is, after all, a list of procedures or techniques—almost a manual, in the most technical sense of the word), whereas from Whitman derives what would later be called *littérature engagée* and social literature in general. Together, these two streams cover both the political and aesthetic sides of vanguardism.[107] Proof of the fact that this division is, at best, questionable can be found in one of Borges's early texts, where the opposite statement is made: here, Whitman is the source of expressionism, understood as "art *underscored*," an aestheticist idea of literature that contradicts the social quality he later attached to

---

(not one of Borges's favorite poets) as one of Whitman's descendants: "It could be said that there are two men without whom contemporary literature would not be what it is, both of them Americans, and of the past century: Walt Whitman—from whom derives what we can call civic-minded poetry, from whom derives Neruda, along with so many things, good or bad—and Edgar Allan Poe, from whom derives the symbolism of Baudelaire" (SNF 492) ["Podría decirse que hay dos hombres sin los cuales la literatura actual no sería lo que es; esos dos hombres son americanos y del siglo pasado: Walt Whitman—de él deriva lo que denominamos poesía civil, deriva Neruda, derivan tantas cosas, buenas o malas—; y Edgar Allan Poe, de quien deriva el simbolismo de Baudelaire . . ." (BO 68)].

[107] This division first appears in "El otro Whitman," an essay in *Discusión*: "Those poor copies or memories [of Whitman] were Futurism and Unanimism; they were, and still are, the entirety of current French poetry, except the one deriving from Poe" ["esos remedos o recuerdos [de Whitman] fueron el futurismo y el unanimismo. Fueron y son toda la poesía francesa de nuestro tiempo, salvo la que deriva de Poe" (OC 206)]. This fragment shows that, for Borges, the "social" quality in the literature of Whitman's descendants is not a sign of political progressiveness—futurism, for instance, had a collective drive without being left-leaning.

Whitman's legacy.[108] But there is a more substantial argument against this schism between formal innovation and political commitment: as we shall see, Whitman's investment in that unprecedented event that was American democracy is the direct and inseparable cause of his radically new approach to poetry.

The course of North American literature bifurcates in Poe and Whitman for one further reason: they seem to have, Borges hesitantly claims, opposite views of their national tradition and of the legacy inherited from Europe. Paraphrasing John Brown, Borges writes that "Whitman and his followers represent the idea that America is a new event that poets ought to celebrate, while Edgar Allan Poe and his see it as a mere continuation of Europe. The history of American literature *could* be understood as the ceaseless conflict between these two conceptions" ["Whitman y sus continuadores representan la idea de que América es un nuevo acontecimiento que deben celebrar los poetas, en tanto que Edgar Allan Poe y los suyos la ven como una mera continuación de Europa. La historia de la literatura americana *sería* el incesante conflicto de esas dos concepciones" (ILN 46; my emphasis)]. Like the opposition between "decadent" and "social" literature, this is a rather questionable distinction. It is of course impossible to deny the place the United States (as a territory, as an institution, as an idea) has in *Leaves of Grass*, and that when compared to Whitman's epic and prophetic nationalism, Poe almost appears to be a mere epigone of the European tradition (beginning with the setting of many of his text to his compliance with inherited poetic forms). But what other writer can claim to have produced, singlehandedly, two specifically American genres—detective fiction and science fiction[109]—that later

---

[108] In "Lírica expresionista: síntesis," a text originally published in *Grecia* in 1920, Borges writes: "We could say that Expressionism . . . is, in the final analysis, nothing but art *underscored*. . . . Its source is the cyclopean and athletic vision of the pluriverse rhythmed by Whitman (who, in turn, departed from Fichte and Hegel)" ["Diríamos que el expresionismo . . . no es otra cosa en última exégesis que el arte *subrayado*. . . . Su fuente la constituye esa visión ciclópea y atlética del pluriverso que ritmara Walt Whitman (partiendo a su vez de Fichte y Hegel)" (TR I: 52)].

[109] While Poe is, with little or no dispute, the inventor of detective fiction, things are not that clear with science fiction. Thomas Disch, however, makes an excellent case for Poe as the creator of the latter genre (instead of, for instance, Mary Shelley) in *The Dreams Our Stuff Is Made Of* (32–52). Borges, it should be added, agrees with this assessment: as detective fiction "science fiction . . . also has Poe as one of its possible forefathers" (SNF 493) ["la ficción científica, que también tiene en Poe a uno de sus posibles padres" (BO 68)].

had such deep, widespread impact, and that define, even today, what we call "American literature"? Fortunately, Borges distances himself from Brown by using the conditional mood in his last sentence ("La historia de la literatura americana *sería* el incesante conflicto de esas dos concepciones"), thus tacitly conceding that the whole hypothesis is rather doubtful. With little rhetorical effort these oppositions (Poe is decadent and Europeanized; Whitman is social and local) could even be reverted: Poe could easily be considered the social-minded writer (his detective stories alone would be credit enough) and Whitman the self-indulgent hedonist (it doesn't take much to unearth this streak in his poetry). It even seems that by insisting on this rivalry, Borges is indulging in one of his favorite topics—dueling doubles, a passion inherited, no doubt, from Poe's stories (beginning with "William Wilson") and Whitman's own doubles in *Leaves of Grass* (discussed below). The potential interchangeability of the poles of this argument is reminiscent of the adversaries in "The Theologians," who sustain a lifelong rivalry only to discover, in the end, "that in the eyes of the unfathomable deity [they] were a single person" (CF 207) ["para la insondable divinidad . . . formaban una sola persona" (OC 556)]. The frailty of Borges's divisions reveal, in fact, that the relationship between Europe and America cannot be disentangled as easily (or as heroically, by one single author). The precariousness of the oppositions also shows that politics and aesthetics are not so easily extricated from one another either. Despite the dubious nature of these oppositions, it seems clear, however, that for Borges, Whitman had one main concern: American democracy. Ultimately, however, Borges's own appropriation of the American poet will completely undo this opposition between the *artiste* and the proselytizer.

The following pages aim to retrace and reconstruct the ways in which Borges read Whitman. Rather than establishing the accuracy of Borges's critical judgments, I am more concerned with the image he creates of *Leaves of Grass* (and its author) and what place and function this image has within his own work.

Borges's initial approach to Whitman might have been a tad overenthusiastic. When recounting his first encounter with Whitman, Borges even confesses to his near-plagiaristic appropriation:

It was . . . in Geneva that I first met Walt Whitman, through a German translation by Johannes Schlaf. . . . For a time I thought of Whitman not *only* as a great poet but as the *only* poet. In fact,

I thought all the poets the world over had been merely leading up to Whitman until 1855, and that *not to imitate him was a proof of ignorance.* (AN 51; the last emphasis is mine)[110]

The very first poem Borges ever published (never collected in any of the books he put out) already shows Whitman's overwhelming influence. "The winter of 1919–20 we spent in Seville, where I saw my first poem into print. It was called 'Hymn to the Sea' and appeared in the magazine *Grecia*[111]. . . . In that poem, I tried my hardest to be Walt Whitman" (AN 56). The first verse of the poem reads: "I have longed for a hymn to the Sea with rhythms as expansive as the screaming waves" ["Yo he ansiado un himno del Mar con ritmos amplios como las olas que gritan" (TR I: 24)]. The intonation is quite obviously Whitman's, as is its large-scale (almost planetary) ambition, as well as the emphasis on nature, and, lastly, the form—the long, free, blank verses, and, as the title and the first verse both declare, the conception of the poem as a hymn. Whitman's presence in the rest of this rather long poem (with its psalm-like cadence, with its invocations of brotherhood, with its repetitions, with its glorification of the body, etc.) is overwhelming—it almost feels like an overemphatic translation of some discarded poem that never made it into *Leaves of Grass*. Furthermore, it is doubly significant that the first verse has a programmatic quality to it, both in its overt enunciation of an intention ("Yo he ansiado") and in the declaration of formal principles ("ritmos amplios"—which, needless to say, define Whitman's poetry to an enormous extent). Examples in Whitman's work showing how close young Borges was to *Leaves of Grass* abound, and the blatant similarities (bordering plagiarism) render a close reading comparing both authors futile. For instance, Borges's first verse, "I have longed for a hymn to the Sea with rhythms as expansive as the screaming waves" clearly recalls

---

[110] Borges adds a few charming details in one of his Harvard lectures: "I was then [while in Geneva] a very unhappy young man. I suppose young men are fond of unhappiness; they do their best to be unhappy, and they generally achieve it. Then I discovered an author who doubtless was a very happy man. It must have been in 1916 that I came to Walt Whitman, and then I felt ashamed of my unhappiness. I felt ashamed, for I had tried to be still more unhappy by reading Dostoevsky" (CV 104).

[111] *Grecia* also printed the first Ultraist manifesto.

the end of Whitman' "Excelsior"—"And who has made hymns
fit for the earth? for I am mad with devouring ecstasy to make
joyous hymns for the whole earth" (Whitman 599). Furthermore,
in Borges, the unity between the poet and the sea, loudly echoes
section 22 of "Song of Myself" (208–09), but the similarities with
Whitman go well beyond a particular passage or a certain topic.
The repetitions, the claims for universal brotherhood, the young
poet fashioning himself as an old soul, the erotic yet innocent
representation of the body, the mythologies, the cosmogonies, the
rhapsodic tone in which one ecstatic illumination after the other
is conveyed—these Whitmanian commonplaces are all in Borges's
first poem. Borges translated a few of his own verses into English
for his "Autobiographical Notes":

> O sea! O myth! O sun! O wide resting place!
> I know why I love you. I know that we are both very old,
> that we have both known each other for centuries . . .
> O Protean, I have been born of you—
> both of us chained and wandering,
> both of us hungering for stars,
> both of us with hopes and disappointments . . . ! (AN 56)

Immediately after quoting himself, Borges comments: "Today, I
hardly think of the sea, or even of myself, as hungering for stars."[112]
Starting with this first poem, Whitman's trace is visible throughout
Borges's entire career. In 1969, Borges wrote a new foreword to his
first book, *Fervor de Buenos Aires* (and heavily edited its poems).
There he confesses that "the young man who wrote the book
in 1923 was already essentially . . . the mature author who either
resigns himself never to touch his earlier work or who endeavors to
rewrite it. We two are the same person; we . . . both are devoted to

---

[112] Almost 50 years later, Borges revisited this topic. From Bioy Casares's journal:
"The newspaper *La Nación* publishes a sonnet to the sea by Borges [29 January
1967]. About a month ago . . . he told me: 'Today I wrote, as an exercise, a poem
about the sea. I thought it would be amusing to compare it to another poem, also
about the sea, which was the first one I ever wrote'. . . . I asked him if still had that
first poem. He said he did not ["En *La Nación* aparece un soneto de Borges, al mar.
Hará cosa de un mes . . . me dijo: 'Hoy escribí, como ejercicio, un poema sobre el mar.
Me divertía compararlo con otro, también sobre el mar, que fue el primero que escribí
en mi vida'. . . . Le pregunté si tenía aquel primer poema. Dijo que no" (Bioy 1167)].

Schopenhauer, Stevenson and Whitman" (SP 3) ["aquel muchacho que en 1923 . . . escribió [este libro] ya era esencialmente . . . el señor que ahora se resigna o corrige. Somos el mismo . . . los dos somos devotos de Schopenhauer, de Stevenson y de Whitman" (OC 13)].[113] Whitman's formal influence, which never waned throughout the years, can still be seen in *Los conjurados*, Borges's last book of poetry.[114] In fact, it would be fair to claim that Whitman-like qualities (the cosmic yet intimate scope, the enumerations, the syntactical repetitions) become more prominent and more recurrent in Borges's later work—an adequate dividing point may be *Elogio de la sombra*, published in 1969, when Borges (as he declared in the foreword to this book reached "three score and ten (as Whitman said)" (SP 265) [("los setenta años de mi edad (la frase es de Walt Whitman)" [OC 975]).[115]

A crucial paradox should be pointed out at this juncture: as we have seen, Borges professed that literature was utterly divorced from politics, and yet, his lifelong influence is the father of "civil poetry," the poet who "intended to show an ideal democrat" ["Whitman se propuso exhibir un demócrata ideal" (OC 253)]. In a poem added to *Fervor de Buenos Aires* in the 1969 edition, Borges conjures up "Walt Whitman, whose name is the universe" (SP 31) ["Walt Whitman, cuyo nombre es el universo" (OC 51)]. And consistently with his whole career, in his last book of poetry (*Los conjurados*), he declares that "Walt Whitman . . . decided to be all men" ["Walt Whitman . . . decidió ser todos los hombres" (OC III: 471)].[116] These two statements bookending Borges's *oeuvre* (and there are many

---

[113] In a 1982 interview, he declared of his young self: the young poet who wrote *Fervor de Buenos Aires* "was trying to imitate Walt Whitman and failing, of course. He did his best to be Walt Whitman; he failed miserably" (C 204).

[114] "Christ on the Cross" ["Cristo en la cruz"], "*Doomsday*," and "Otro fragmento apócrifo" may be the clearest examples (only the first text is included in *Selected Poems*).

[115] Mysteriously enough, Alexander Coleman decided to exclude this parenthesis from his edition of *Selected Poems*.

[116] "Someone Dreams" ["Alguien sueña"], the prose poem where this quotation appears, revisits most of Borges's topics in a Whitman-like fashion—a long mantra (every sentence begins with "Ha soñado"), reviewing universal history, from the minute (plow, hammers, and tools) to the mythical (the history of the orb, from Thebes, through Greece, Rome, and the Crusades to the present), from the private (his grandmother) to the public (generations of kings), from small and seemingly meaningless nature (a cat) to the history of thought and literature (from Socrates, through Shakespeare, to Whitman).

similar ones between them) should not be taken in a metaphysical sense. Contradictory as it may seem, Whitman's "universality" is anchored in specific historic contingencies. Put differently, "universality" is here a different word for "democracy":

> In the nineteenth century, democracy was an utopia the young American states were realizing on Earth. Whitman wanted that new order to be projected in his book, just as the Medieval order had been projected in Dante's book. To the democrat, any given individual can never be less valuable than another; those reading the poem cannot be less valuable than the one writing it. The book [Leaves of Grass] is in the first person, but sometimes the author speaks, and others the reader: "Oh take my hand, Walt Whitman!" or "What do you hear, Walt Whitman?"[117] In reality, author and reader are both part of Whitman, who, as the famous giant in the frontispiece of Leviathan, is a plural figure, made up by a multitude of beings.[118]

> [En el siglo XIX, la democracia era una utopía que los jóvenes estados americanos estaban realizando en la tierra; Whitman quería que ese nuevo orden se proyectara en su libro, como el orden medieval se había proyectado en el libro de Dante. Para el demócrata, un individuo no vale menos que otro; quienes leen el poema no pueden valer menos que quien lo escribe. La obra [Leaves of Grass] está en primera persona, pero a veces habla el autor y a veces el lector: "Oh take my hand, Walt Whitman!" o "What do you hear, Walt Whitman?" En realidad, autor y lector son partes de Whitman, que, como el famoso gigante del frontispicio de Leviathan, es una figura plural, integrada por una muchedumbre de seres. (TR III: 38; my emphasis)]

However, Borges was not precisely a fiery democrat himself. He famously declared that he "had doubts about democracy, that

---

[117] Whitman 287; 288.

[118] It is no coincidence that this quote ends with the father of contractualism. In fact, the dictum on the seal of the United States, "E pluribus unum," is almost the verbal translation of what the picture in Leviathan's frontispiece conveys graphically. "E pluribus unum" is also a very tight synopsis of the myth of the Simurg that Borges quoted over and again through his life—those birds looking for their monarch, the Simurg, that finally realize that all of them (and each one of them) is the Simurg. This, as we have seen in "Political Theology" is, to a large extent, the foundation of Borges's political philosophy.

curious abuse of statistics" (SP 371) ["descreo de la democracia, ese curioso abuso de la estadística" (OC III: 122)] and believed it was an outdated concept, related, precisely, to an antiquated reading of authors such as Whitman:

> I would say that politicians are the last plagiarizers, the last disciples of writers. But they are usually a century behind, or perhaps a little more, yes. Because what is now called "current" is really . . . well, it is a museum, usually an archaic one. Now we are all spellbound by democracy. Well, all of that takes us back to Paine, to Jefferson, to all that which could have stirred up passion back when Walt Whitman wrote his *Leaves of Grass*. Year of 1855. All this is what we now call "current." So politicians would be backward readers, right? Antiquated readers, readers of old libraries. . . .

> [yo diría que los políticos vendrían a ser los últimos plagiarios, los últimos discípulos de los escritores. Pero, generalmente con un siglo de atraso, o un poco más también, sí. Porque todo lo que se llama actualidad es realmente . . . y, es un museo, usualmente arcaico. Ahora estamos todos embelesados con la democracia; bueno, todo eso nos lleva a Paine, a Jefferson, a aquello que pudo ser una pasión cuando Walt Whitman escribió sus *Hojas de Hierba*. Año de 1855. Todo eso es la actualidad; de modo que los políticos serían lectores atrasados, ¿no?, lectores anticuados, lectores de viejas bibliotecas. . . . (D: II 129)]

Despite his skepticism when it came to democracy,[119] Borges did acknowledge the radical novelty and the importance of the American Revolution.[120] The political order resulting from it was at the very

---

[119] In the foreword to his translation of *Leaves of Grass*, Borges insists on his idea that democracy is an exhausted, outdated model: "America was then the symbol of a famous ideal, which is now somewhat worn by the abuse of ballot boxes, and by the eloquent excesses of rhetoric, despite the fact that millions of men have given it—and still give it—their blood" ["América era entonces el símbolo de un famoso ideal, ahora un tanto gastado por el abuso de las urnas electorales y por los elocuentes excesos de la retórica, aunque millones de hombres le hayan dado, y sigan dándole, su sangre" (p 170–71)].

[120] "Let us not forget that the first revolution of our time, the one that inspired the French Revolution and our revolutions [in South America] was the American Revolution, and that democracy was its doctrine" ["No olvidemos que la primera de las revoluciones de nuestro tiempo, la que inspiró la revolución francesa y las nuestras, fue la de América y que la democracia fue su doctrina" (P 171)].

core of Whitman's poetry, which aspired "to define America, her athletic Democracy" (Whitman 167). Addressing such an original and unique event required, Borges claimed, an equally original and unique literary form. Whitman "thought democracy was a new phenomenon, and that extolling it would require an equally new procedure" ["pensó que la democracia era un hecho nuevo y que su exaltación requería un procedimiento no menos nuevo" (P 171)]. The form Whitman found could be called a "centerless epopee." The scope of his enterprise was epic: to represent the entire American experience—and even its planetary resonance. As Borges put it, "Whitman set himself the task of composing a messianic work, the epopee of American democracy" ["Whitman se propuso una obra mesiánica, la epopeya de la democracia de América" (ILN 44)]. However, the epic form is, by definition, the celebration of mainly *one* heroic character—who, additionally, in all the classic examples, from Homer to Ariosto, is a nobleman, and never a man of the people. This emphasis on individuality (and the aristocratic attributes attached to it) obviously did not fit into the representation of the nascent American democracy:

In each of the illustrious models young Whitman knew and called "feudal," there is a central character—Achilles, Ulysses, Aeneas, Roland, Cid, Siegfried, Christ—whose stature is superior to all the surrounding ones, who are always subordinated to him. This primacy, Whitman told himself, belongs in a world that has been abolished or that we aspire to abolish—the world of aristocracy. My epic cannot be like that. It has to be plural; it has to declare or presuppose the incomparable and absolute equality of all men.[121]

[En cada uno de los modelos ilustres que el joven Whitman conocía y que llamó feudales, hay un personaje central—Aquiles, Ulises, Eneas, Rolando, El Cid, Sigfrido, Cristo—cuya estatura resulta superior a la de los otros, que están supeditados a él. Esta primacía, se dijo Whitman, corresponde a un mundo abolido o que aspiramos a abolir, el de la aristocracia. Mi epopeya no puede ser así; tiene que ser plural, tiene que declarar o presuponer la incomparable y absoluta igualdad de todos los hombres. (P 171)]

---

[121] A similar argument can be found in ILN 44.

Whitman overcame this obstacle by giving his "epopeya americana" (P 170) a collective hero:

> He needed . . . a hero, but his hero, a symbol of the multiple nature of democracy, had to be, necessarily, innumerable and ubiquitous, like Spinoza's dispersed God. He created a strange creature that we still do not fully understand, and gave it the name of Walt Whitman.
>
> [Necesitaba . . . un héroe, pero el suyo, símbolo de la múltiple democracia, tenía forzosamente que ser incontable y ubicuo, como el disperso Dios de Spinoza. Elaboró una extraña criatura que no hemos acabado de entender y le dio el nombre de Walt Whitman. (P 172)]

This is the genesis of (and the justification for) a discrepancy that always obsessed Borges—the distinction between Whitman the man and Whitman the character. In "Notas sobre Walt Whitman," for instance, Borges insists on the difference between "Whitman, the man of letters, [and] Whitman, the semidivine hero of *Leaves of Grass*" ["Whitman hombre de letras [y] Whitman, héroe semidivino de *Leaves of Grass*" (OC 250)]. Virtually every essay or scattered remark about the North American author underscores this distinction: "there are two Whitmans: 'The friendly and flowing savage'[122] in *Leaves of Grass* and the poor man of letters who invented him" ["hay dos Whitman: el 'amistoso y elocuente salvaje' de *Leaves of Grass* y el pobre literato que lo inventó" (OC 250)].[123] Whitman, the character, is a polyphonic hero: "I am large, I contain multitudes," he famously declares toward the end of "Song of Myself" (Whitman 87). This is the choral character

---

[122] Whitman 231.

[123] Borges lists many discrepancies between Walter's biography and Walt's fictional itineraries in *Leaves of Grass* (and supports his thesis quoting a number of poems), and ends by writing: "The former was chaste, reserved and rather taciturn; the latter, effusive and orgiastic. It would be easy to multiply these discrepancies, but it is more important to understand that the simple, happy vagabond that the verses of *Leaves of Grass* put forth would have been incapable of writing them" ["Éste fue casto, reservado y más bien taciturno; aquél efusivo y orgiástico. Multiplicar esas discordias es fácil; más importante es comprender que el mero vagabundo feliz que proponen los versos de *Leaves of Grass* hubiera sido incapaz de escribirlos" (OC 250)]. This argument obsessed Borges, and can also be found in C 58; ILN 45; P 172; TR 45; OC 660.

Borges refers to: "Walt Whitman, an American, one of the roughs, a kosmos,/Disorderly fleshy and sensual . . . eating drinking and breeding. . . . I speak the password primeval. . . . I give the sign of democracy . . . " (Whitman 50).

As Borges puts it in his 1958 lecture on Whitman, "he believed in democracy, and this is why the hero of his book is not one man but, in a way, all men" ["Creía en la democracia, y por eso el héroe de su libro no es un hombre, sino, de algún modo, todos los hombres" (TR III: 46)]. But according to Borges (and this is crucial), Whitman takes this strategy one step further by blurring the line between author and reader: "Whitman wrote his rhapsodies based on an imaginary 'I,' which was constituted partially by himself, partially by each one of his readers" ["Whitman redactó sus rapsodias en función de un yo imaginario, formado parcialmente de él mismo, parcialmente de cada uno de sus lectores" (OC 686)].[124] And to muddle the line between "self" and "other" further, Whitman himself becomes a reader: "he confuses himself with [the reader] and converses with the other, with Whitman: 'What do you hear, Walt Whitman?'" ["se confunde con [el lector] y dialoga con el otro, con Whitman: '¿Qué oyes, Walt Whitman?'" (OC 253)]. These fluctuations between first and third person, this indetermination between individual and collective, and, more importantly, this problematic and sometimes impossible distinction between reader and writer—all conceived against the notion of a stable and bounded subject—will become decisive in the articulation of Borges's own poetics.

Borges's literature was consciously and even programmatically built on this dissolution of subjectivity he learned from Whitman. In fact, Borges's entire *oeuvre* opens with this Whitman-originated concern about the boundaries of subjectivity: the foreword to his first book (eliminated from subsequent editions) reads: "We are all one; barely different are our nothingnessess, and such is the influence of circumstances upon the soul that it is almost by chance that you happen to be the reader and I the writer . . . of my verses" ["Todos somos unos [sic]; poco difieren nuestras naderías, y tanto influyen en las almas las circunstancias, que es casi una casualidad esto de ser tú el leyente y yo el escribidor . . . de mis versos" (FBA 5)].

---

[124] Borges repeats this in his *Introduction to North American Literature*, where he writes that "Whitman," the character, is an embodiment of both "the author and, at the same time, each one of his readers" ["es el autor y es a la vez cada uno de sus lectores" (45)].

Again, the distinction between reader and writer is in crisis. Both instances seem to be almost indistinguishable and to depend on trivial contingencies (the untranslatable "naderías"). There is, however, a major difference with Whitman: young Borges stripped every political connotation away from this indetermination of subjectivity and turned it into an aesthetic principle. In "La nadería de la personalidad," a manifesto-like text included in *Inquisiciones*, his first book of essays published in 1925, he writes:

> *I want to tear down the exceptional preeminence now generally awarded to the self.* . . . I intend to prove that personality is a mirage maintained by conceit and habit, without metaphysical foundation or visceral reality. *I want to apply to literature the consequences that issue from these premises, and erect upon them an aesthetic* hostile to the psychologism inherited from the last century. . . . (SNF 3; my emphasis)

> [*Quiero abatir la excepcional preeminencia que hoy suele adjudicarse al yo.* . . . Pienso probar que la personalidad es una trasoñación, consentida por el engreimiento y el hábito, mas sin estribaderos metafísicos ni realidad entrañal. *Quiero aplicar, por ende a la literatura las consecuencias dimanantes de esas premisas, y levantar sobre ellas una estética,* hostil al psicologismo que nos dejó el siglo pasado. . . . (I 93)]

What is a political drive in Whitman (the need of a polymorphous, collective, nonindividual idea of subjectivity in order to forge his democratic hero) becomes a purely literary problem for Borges.[125]

---

[125] It is also a philosophical problem, of course. Borges traces the lack of distinction between one and many back to Socrates—if not to the pre-Socratics. In a footnote of "Avatars of the Tortoise," Borges writes: "In the *Parmenides*—whose Zenonian character is irrefutable—Plato . . . demonstrate[s] that the one is really many. If the one exists, it participates in being; therefore, there are two parts in it, which are being and the one, but each of these parts is one and exists, so that they enclose two more parts, which in turn enclose two more, infinitely" (L 204 fn.) ["En el *Parménides*—cuyo carácter zenoniano es irrecusable—Platón [demuestra] que el uno es realmente muchos. Si el uno existe, participa del ser; por consiguiente, hay dos partes en él, que son el ser y el uno, pero cada una de esas partes es una y es, de modo que encierra otras dos, que encierran también otras dos: infinitamente" (OC 255–56 fn.)]. The tension between one and many (the latter is here "being") could quite easily have a political reading—a reading that Borges does not engage in, but that Whitman certainly would have welcomed.

Whitman's distortion of the boundaries between the "real" author and his fictional image (either as a public figure or as a character in the texts) constitute some of Borges's life-long concerns. In fact, the fuzziness of this boundary also will prove extremely productive for his fiction. A case in point is his first book of fiction, *Universal History of Infamy*, made up entirely of rewritten texts. Here, the division between reader and writer is materially and effectively put into question—and with it, the very notion of authorship.[126] Who wrote "The Cruel Redeemer Lazarus Morell," Borges or Mark Twain? Are we reading a reading? Could we possibly be reading two authors at the same time? As a matter of fact, in many of Borges's stories this seems to be the case—the reader is reading a reading (or a rewriting, or a synopsis). This happens, for instance, in "Acercamiento a Almotásim," "Tlön, Uqbar, Orbis Tertius,"[127] and "Examen de la obra de Herbert Quain," among others.[128] In none of these texts are there only one writer and only one reader. Furthermore, the separation between these instances tends to become rather unclear. The culmination of this crisis of subjectivity as a literary problem is the 1939 story "Pierre Menard, Author of the *Quixote*."[129]

---

[126] For a detailed analysis of the distortion of the notion of authorship (and its often-tautological intersections with the figure of the reader), see Molloy 49–57, and what she calls (paraphrasing the title of one of Borges's early essays) "the nothingness of authority" ["la nadería de la autoridad" (56)].

[127] Furthermore, in "Tlön, Uqbar, Orbis Tertius" the link between this decentered or plural subjectivity and the issue of authorship is explicitly addressed. The narrator explains the "idealistic pantheism" (OC 438; CF 76) that lies behind the Tlönian notion of subjectivity (how all subjects are, in fact one), and then explores its consequences on literature: "Within the sphere of literature, too, the idea of the single subject is all-powerful. Books are rarely signed, nor does the concept of plagiarism exist. It has been decided that all books are the work of a single author who is timeless and anonymous" (CF 76–77) ["En los hábitos literarios también es todopoderosa la idea de un sujeto único. Es raro que los libros estén firmados. No existe el concepto de plagio: se ha establecido que todas las obras son obra de un solo autor, que es intemporal y es anónimo" (OC 439)].

[128] This clearly relates to Borges's frequent use of framed narratives, which I discussed in "When Fiction Lives in Fiction."

[129] Pierre Menard is a (fictional) French symbolist poet and essayist who, in 1918, embarked on an impossible task: he planned to write Cervantes's *Don Quijote*—not a sequel, not a copy, but, word for word, the same book, while retaining his own identity as Menard and refusing the shortcut of (somehow) become Cervantes.

If "Whitman, with impetuous humility, wants to resemble all men" ["Whitman, con impetuosa humildad, quiere parecerse a todos los hombres" (OC 250)], Borges will insist, throughout his entire work, on erasing the line between self and other. This can be found in his early books (beginning, as we have seen with the foreword to his very first volume of verse, and in several poems[130]) as well as in the late ones.[131] Furthermore, following Whitman, Borges lent his own name to some of his main characters (as in

---

"The undertaking was impossible from the outset, and of all the impossible ways of bringing it about, this [becoming Cervantes] was the least interesting. . . . Being, somehow, Cervantes, and arriving thereby at the Quixote—that looked to Menard less challenging (and therefore less interesting) than continuing to be Pierre Menard and coming to the Quixote through the experiences of Pierre Menard" (CF 91) ["la empresa era de antemano imposible y de todos los medios imposibles para llevarla a término, éste [transformarse en Cervantes] era el menos interesante. . . . Ser, de alguna manera, Cervantes y llegar al Quijote le pareció menos arduo—por consiguiente menos interesante—que seguir siendo Pierre Menard y llegar al Quijote, a través de las experiencias de Pierre Menard" (OC 447)]. Menard succeed in producing a few passages of the *Quijote*. Comparing Menard's work with Cervantes's original (both, of course, consist of *exactly* the same words), the narrator concludes that, mostly because of its new context, the Frenchman's version is "subtler" (SF 93; OC 448)—but Cervantes's style is better: he uses the Spanish of his time with great self-assurance, while Menard's prose feels like an archaic affectation Of course, Cervantes's novel itself is based on the questioning of authorship and originality and on the distortion of the boundaries separating reader and writer: let us remember that a nameless narrator finds some manuscripts in Arabic (by one Cide Hamete Benengeli), has them translated, and then sits down and reads the story of don Quijote. This reading is what we read. The "original" act of writing has been removed several steps. Menard adds one more coil to this fractal pattern. And toward the end of the story, the nameless narrator even suggests the need of a second Menard to get a full grasp of Menard's the palimpsest of drafts and versions that went into this new *Quijote*: "only a second Pierre Menard, reversing the labors of the first, would be able to revive those Troys . . ." (CF 95) ["sólo un segundo Pierre Menard, invirtiendo el trabajo del anterior, podría exhumar esas Troyas . . ." (OC 450)]. The final genealogy would then be: Benengeli: Translator: Nameless Reader/ Narrator: Menard[1]: Menard[2]. What does the distinction between reader and writer mean in this configuration?

[130] See, for instance, "Jactancia de Quietud," in *Luna de enfrente*: "My name is someone and anyone" (SP 43) ["Mi nombre es alguien y cualquiera" (LE 17)].

[131] Examples abound. For instance "Proteo" ("You, who are one and are many men" ["Tú, que eres uno y eres muchos hombres" (OC 1108)]), "Tú" (which begins: "One single man has ever been born, one single man has ever died on earth" ["Un solo hombre ha nacido, un solo hombre ha muerto en la tierra" (OC 1113)]), both in *El oro de los tigres*.

"Hombre de la esquina rosada" and "El Aleph"), and he and his ancestors appear in numerous poems.[132] Perhaps one of the most eloquent examples can be found in "Elegía," included in *The Other, the Same*, a title that quite obviously speaks to the instability of the terms considered here:

> Oh destiny of Borges,
> to have traversed the various seas of the world
> or the same solitary sea under various names,
> to have been part of Edinburgh, of Zurich, of the two
>   Córdobas,
> of Colombia, and of Texas,
> to have gone back across the generations,
> to the ancient lands of his forebears,
> . . .
> Oh destiny of Borges, perhaps no stranger than yours. (SP 231)

> [Oh destino el de Borges,
> haber navegado por los diversos mares del mundo
> o por el único y solitario mar de nombres diversos,
> haber sido una parte de Edimburgo, de Zürich, de las dos
>   Córdobas,
> de Colombia y de Texas,
> haber regresado, al cabo de cambiantes generaciones,
> a las antiguas tierras de su estirpe,
> . . .
> Oh destino de Borges, tal vez no más extraño que el tuyo. (933)]

"Borges's" itineraries may be backed by biographical facts (unlike "Whitman's"), but his metamorphosis into a third person projected onto the immensity of the world, traveling through space and time is unmistakably Whitmanesque—as are the poem's form (with its free unrhymed verses and its repetitions), and the invocation of the reader through the second person in the last verse, a reader with whom "Borges" ultimately merges by recognizing their fates are not,

---

[132] "Many poets (Virgil, Dante, Ronsard, Cervantes, Whitman, Browning, Lugones, the Persian poets) who have woven their names into their compositions" ["Muchos son los poetas (Virgilio, Dante, Ronsard, Cervantes, Whitman, Browning, Lugones, los persas) que han intercalado sus nombres en sus composiciones" (OCC 880)].

after all, that dissimilar. Borges even turns this idea to Whitman, and fuses with him in "Camden, 1892," a late poem (oddly enough, a sonnet) that is an homage to the North American poet: "I was once Walt Whitman" (SP 213) ["Yo fui Walt Whitman" (OC 913)].

This, then, is the first idea regarding subjectivity that Borges takes from Whitman, a notion resting on the fundamental correspondence or similarity between one and others: anyone is everyone.[133] This principle is based on a universal likeness, or, in political terms, on a radical form of egalitarianism. There is, however, a second articulation of Whitman's distortion of subjectivity, one expressed as absolute difference: "I am someone else" or, following Rimbaud's famous pronouncement in a letter to Paul Demeny, "Je est un autre." Put differently, through Whitman, Borges will say (and the paraphrase is mine): "I am like everyone else, but I am not myself;

---

[133] As we have seen, Borges found this idea of subjectivity extremely productive in shaping his own conception of literature, since it questions the very notion of authorship. Because Shakespeare functions in Borges as *The Author*, many references can be found where Whitman's impersonalized (or "pluripersonalized") subjectivity are turned to him. Shakespeare is everyone and no one. He is everything and nothing. "There was no one inside him," begins "*Everything and Nothing*" (CF 319) ["Nadie hubo en él" (OC 803)]. The text ends with Shakespeare in his deathbed saying, "*I, who have been so many men in vain, wish to be one, to be myself.* God's voice answered him out of a whirlwind: *I, too, am not; I dreamed the world as you, my Shakespeare, dreamed your own work, and among the forms of my dream are you, who like me are many, yet no one*" (CF 320) ["Yo, que tantos hombres he sido en vano, quiero ser uno y yo. La voz de Dios le contestó desde un torbellino *Yo tampoco soy; yo soñé el mundo como tú soñaste tu obra, mi Shakespeare, y entre las formas de mi sueño estás tú, que como yo eres muchos y nadie*" (OC 804)]. Many more examples can be found: "All men, in the vertiginous instant of coitus, are the same man. All men who speak a line of Shakespeare *are* William Shakespeare" (CF 76, fn.) ["Todos los hombres en el vertiginoso instante del coito, son el mismo hombre. Todos los hombres que repiten una línea de Shakespeare, *son* William Shakespeare" (OC 438, fn.)]; "Are the enthusiasts who devote themselves to a line of Shakespeare not literally Shakespeare?" (SNF 323) ["¿Los fervorosos que se entregan a una línea de Shakespeare no son, literalmente, Shakespeare?" (OC 763)]; "Schopenhauer may have been right—I am other men, any man is all men, Shakespeare is somehow the wretched John Vincent Moon" (CF 141) ["Acaso Schopenhauer tiene razón: yo soy los otros, cualquier hombre es todos los hombres, Shakespeare es de algún modo el miserable John Vincent Moon" (OC 494)]; "[Valéry is a symbol of] a man who transcends the differential traits of the self and of whom we can say, as William Hazlitt did of Shakespeare, 'he is nothing in himself'" (L 198) ["[Valéry es símbolo de] un hombre que trasciende los rasgos diferenciales del yo y de quien podemos decir, como William Hazlitt de Shakespeare: *He is nothing in himself*" (OC 687)].

the sameness that connects me to all the others cannot be found within myself." There is a constitutive difference *within* the subject, who is unable to reconcile himself with his own representations. A good example can be found in Whitman's "When I read the Book":

> When I read the book, the biography famous,
> And is this then (said I) what the author calls a man's life?
> And so will some one when I am dead and gone write my life?
> (As if any man really knew aught of my life,
> Why even I myself I often think know little or nothing of my
> real life,
> Only a few hints, a few diffused faint clews and indirections
> I seek for my own use to trace out here.) (Whitman 171)

This internal rift constitutes less an ontological problem than a reflection of the figure of the author as a social construct or, more plainly, as a celebrity. Borges knew Whitman's poem well and even translated it and included it in his essay "El otro Whitman" (OC 207).[134] And "When I Read the Book" is the clear, direct antecedent of "Borges y yo," one of Borges's most famous texts:

> It's the other one, Borges, that things happen to. I walk through Buenos Aires and I pause—mechanically now, perhaps—to gaze the arch of an entryway and its inner door; news of Borges reaches me by mail, and I see his name on a list of academics or in some biographical dictionary. . . . It would be an exaggeration to say that our relationship is hostile—I live, I let myself live, so that Borges can spin out his literature, and that literature is my justification. I willingly admit that he has written a number of sound pages, but those pages cannot save me, perhaps because what is good no longer belongs to any individual, not even to the other, but rather to language itself, or to tradition. Beyond that, I am doomed to disappear definitely, without a trace, and only instants of myself will survive in the other. Little by little, I turn everything over to him, though I know the perverse way he has of falsifying and magnifying everything. . . . I shall endure in

---

[134] And he also quoted it in the foreword he wrote to Ana María Barrenechea's *Borges, the Labyrinth Maker* (vii).

Borges, not in myself (if, indeed, I am anybody at all). . . . So my
life is an evasion, and I lose it all, and all belongs to oblivion, or
to the other.
    I don't know which one of us writes this page. (cf. CF 324)

[Al otro, a Borges, es a quien le ocurren las cosas. Yo camino por
Buenos Aires y me demoro, acaso ya mecánicamente, para mirar
el arco de un zaguán y la puerta cancel; de Borges tengo noticias
por el correo y veo su nombre en una terna de profesores o en un
diccionario biográfico. . . . Sería exagerado afirmar que nuestra
relación es hostil; yo vivo, yo me dejo vivir, para que Borges
pueda tramar su literatura y esa literatura me justifica. Nada me
cuesta confesar que ha logrado ciertas páginas válidas, pero esas
páginas no me pueden salvar, quizá porque lo bueno ya no es de
nadie, ni siquiera del otro, sino del lenguaje o la tradición. Por
lo demás, yo estoy destinado a perderme, definitivamente, y sólo
algún instante de mí podrá sobrevivir en el otro. Poco a poco voy
cediéndole todo, aunque me consta su perversa costumbre de
falsear y magnificar. . . . Yo he de quedar en Borges, no en mí (si
es que alguien soy). . . . Así mi vida es una fuga y todo lo pierdo
y todo es del olvido, o del otro.
    No sé cuál de los dos escribe esta página. (OC 808)]

Both texts present the same schism between the private and the
public subject; both show how the "inner self" (for lack of a better
expression) fades away and becomes inaccessible; and both end
with a self-referential moment—this ambiguity (and the attempt at
clarifying it) takes place in writing.
    This disjunction appears in other of Borges's texts, such as
"The Watcher" ["El centinela"]. Here "Borges" also is presented
as a highly fossilized collection of tics (his obsession with Anglo-
Saxon history, his fetishization of soldiers long dead, etc.) that has
"enslaved" Borges: "I revert to the servitude which has lasted more
than seven times ten years" (SP 325) ["vuelvo a la esclavitud que
ha durado más de siete veces diez años"] (OC 1115). Both these
incarnations—the first and the third person—coexist under one
single name ("his name which (it should now be clear) is mine"
["su nombre que es (ya se entiende) el mío"]). And they both come
together in literature, in the act of writing: "He dictates to me now
this poem, which I do not like" ["Me dicta ahora este poema que
no me gusta"]. However, a contradiction underlies these texts.

By insisting on the internal split of the subject, and, furthermore, by stressing the falseness of the public author, they are in fact emphasizing the coherence, unity, and ultimate authenticity of that secret, inaccessible self.

Whitman's faithfulness to the utopia of American democracy not only affected his conception of the subject (and some of its ancillary categories, such as the reader and the writer), but also led him to find a new voice and a new form. Borges, in turn, appropriated the innovations that resulted from Whitman's articulation of politics and literature in his own way. In his *Introduction to North American Literature*, Borges outlines what, for him, are Whitman's decisive formal traits:

> Whitman set himself a messianic task—the epopee of American democracy. His favorite poet was Tennyson, but his task demanded, he thought, a different language: the oral English of the American streets and the frontier. . . . Regarding form, he rejected regular, rhymed verses, and opted for long rhythmic stanzas inspired by the psalms in the Scriptures.

> [Whitman se propuso una obra mesiánica, la epopeya de la democracia de América. El poeta de su predilección era Tennyson, pero su obra exigía, le pareció, un lenguaje distinto: el inglés oral de las calles americanas y de las fronteras. . . . En cuanto a la forma, rechazó el verso regular y la rima y optó por largas estrofas rítmicas, inspiradas por los salmos de la Escritura. (ILN 44)]

This partial view of Whitman's work (with its highlights and omissions) already reveals much about Borges's own writing. Borges never had messianic ambitions or commanded an epic scope, but, as we shall see, he certainly appropriated all the other formal qualities he attaches to Whitman. The young Borges felt he needed "a different language" and also opted for transcribing, occasionally, the Spanish spoken on the streets and in the frontier—in Borges's case, the borderline between the city and the country, the *orillas*, which constituted his *locus amoenus*. Free, blank verse is predominant in his first three books of poems, and the second two of these teem with the rhythmic stanzas Borges attributes to Whitman—and in *Luna de Enfrente* (1925) and *Cuaderno San Martín* (1929) he embraces Whitman's longer verses and his "psalmodic" (to quote

Borges) repetitions. Examples abound. An almost random one from "Casi juicio final," in *Luna de enfrente*:

> In my secret heart I justify and praise myself:
> I have witnessed the world; I have confessed to the oddness of the world.
> I have sung the eternal: the clear returning moon, and the cheeks love hungers for.
> I have sanctified with verses the city that holds me: the infinitude of the suburbs, the vacant lots.
> Following the horizon down the streets, I have unleashed my psalms, and they bring back the taste of distance.
> I have spoken of the wonderment of living, where others only speak of habit.
> Opposing the song of the lukewarm, I lit my voice with sunsets, with all love and with fright of death.
> To the ancestors of my blood and to the ancestors of my spirit, I offered the sacrifice of my verses.
> I have been and I am.

> [En mi secreto corazón yo me justifico y ensalzo:
> He atestiguado el mundo; he confesado la rareza del mundo.
> He cantado lo eterno: la clara luna volvedora y las mejillas que apetece el querer.
> He santificado con versos las ciudad que me ciñe: la infinitud del arrabal, los solares.
> En pos del horizonte de las calles he soltado mis salmos y traen sabor de lejanía.
> He dicho asombro del vivir, donde otros dicen solamente costumbre.
> Frente a la canción de los tibios, encendí en ponientes mi voz, en todo amor y en el pavor de la muerte.
> A los antepasados de mi sangre y a los antepasados de mi espíritu, sacrifiqué con versos.
> He sido y soy. (LE 28)]

Not only the form but also the vocabulary clearly resembles Whitman's. Passages like "I justify and praise myself" or "I have sung the eternal" are Whitmanesque clichés—Borges even uses the word "psalm" (interestingly enough, deleted in subsequent editions), which is a term to which he often resorts in order to define Whitman's poetry. The general tone and pitch are also those of *Leaves of Grass*—the first person elevating himself to cosmic heights ("I have witnessed the world"), rediscovering and recording the marvel and the miracle of existence ("I have spoken of the wonderment of living, where others only speak of habit"), almost confrontationally self-reliant ("Opposing the song of the lukewarm, I lit my voice with sunsets"), and affirming his own presence with ontological emphasis ("I have been and I am"). History ("the ancestors of my blood") put in mythical perspective ("the forefathers of my spirit"—the 1969 edition reads "dreams") is also part of what Borges refers to as Whitman's "epic" quality. In fact, this sense of bewilderment ("rareza," "asombro") is, for Borges, a crucial feature of Whitman's poetry. In "El otro Whitman" he writes: "It is as if Whitman said: The world is unexpected and elusive, but its very contingency is a form of wealth, because we are unable even to determine how poor we are, because everything is a gift" ["Es como si dijera Whitman: Inesperado y elusivo es el mundo, pero su misma contingencia es una riqueza, ya que ni siquiera podemos determinar lo pobres que somos, ya que todo es regalo" (OC 208)]. The idea of the gift ("regalo") will be extremely productive for Borges—and a good example of this is, precisely, the Whitmanesque "Otro poema de los dones" (OC 936), a sequel to "Poema de los dones," one of his most famous poems.

In fact, the foreword to the first edition of *Luna de Enfrente* (which Borges eliminated from subsequent editions[135]) is quite revealing. It is a programmatic appropriation (almost a manifesto) of those traits that the older Borges found in Whitman and stated with professorial aplomb in the segment of *Introduction to North American Literature* quoted above. Part of the 1925 foreword reads:

A dialogue between death and life is our every day life, made up either by memories (forms of having been and being no

---

[135] In 1969, Borges wrote a new prologue to this book (the only of the two to be translated into English), gently mocking his young self for wanting to be modern (i.e. "contemporary") and Argentinean, which were, of course, inescapable contingencies. However, he finishes the prologue with a lie: "I have made few changes to this book" (SP 35) ["Poco he modificado este libro" (OC 55)]. The changes are countless and substantial. It is, in fact, a radically different book.

more) or plans—mere appetites of being. . . . May each rhymer praise those things that suit him best, for this, and nothing else, is poetry. I have celebrated those that suit me best, those that are intense within me—the light blue walls of the suburb, and the small little squares with their share of sky. . . . Today I do not wish to talk to you about technique. To be honest, I am not interested in the aural qualities of verse; I like strophic forms, as long as the rhymes are not too jarring. Many pieces in this book are in spoken *criollo*; not in gaucho parlance or in the slang of the slums, but in the heterogeneous vernacular language of the conversations of Buenos Aires. Others assume that timeless, eternal Spanish (which is neither from Castile nor the River Plate) registered in dictionaries.

[Diálogo de muerte y de vida es nuestro cotidiano vivir, tan hecho de recuerdos (formas del haber sido y no ser ya) o si no de proyectos: meras apetencias del ser. . . . Ensalce todo verseador los aspectos que se avengan bien con su yo, que no otra cosa es la poesía. Yo he celebrado los que conmigo se avienen, los que en mí son intensidá. Son las tapias celestes del suburbio y las plazitas [sic] con su fuentada de cielo. . . . Hoy no quisiera conversarte de técnica. La verdá es que no me interesa lo auditivo del verso y que me agradan todas las formas estróficas, siempre que no sean barulleras las rimas. Muchas composiciones de este libro hay habladas en criollo; no en gauchesco ni en arrabalero, sino en la heterogénea lengua vernácula de la charla porteña. Otras asumen ese intemporal, eterno español (ni de Castilla ni del Plata) que los diccionarios registran. (LE 6)]

The first striking aspect of this text is its orthography, which is a literal fulfillment of that need Borges saw in Whitman, the need for "a different language: the oral English of the American streets and the frontier." This is not such a decisive trait of Whitman's poetry, but it is vastly important for the young Borges. Most of the poems in *Luna de Enfrente* have some sort of transcription of "criollo" parlance. Consider, for instance, the title of the first poem in the book: "calle con almacén rosao" (instead of "rosado")—examples like this abound, mostly phonetic transcripts of oral language, certain morphological characteristics of the Spanish of Buenos Aires (different forms for second person singular pronouns and verbs), lexical peculiarities, and a particular approach to orthography (in fact, he signs the book as *Jorje* Luis Borges).[136] But in his foreword, Borges tries to make sure these experiments do not become a mere regionalist novelty by combining this idiosyncratic Spanish with a "timeless and eternal" approach to language. This tension between a particular and a universal language can also be seen in what Borges considers another of Whitman's fundamental qualities: the coexistence of local themes (in *Leaves of Grass*, as Borges points out, the concern with the idea of America; in *Luna de enfrente*, the outskirts of Buenos Aires) and universal concerns (there are plenty of examples of Whitman's "kosmic" reach; as far as *Luna de enfrente*, the first sentence of the quotation from the foreword reveals Borges's transcendental aspirations). Of course the celebratory spirit explicitly invoked in the foreword comes straight from Whitman—it can be found, quite famously, in the very first verse of *Leaves of Grass*.

Lastly, the prosodic qualities that Borges describes in his foreword are virtually the same he enumerates in his *Introduction to North American Literature*. These aspects deserve special consideration. Free verse is a decisive formal characteristic of a great part of Borges's poetry, but it is also the means through which he initially distinguished himself from the tradition preceding him. Young Borges's disdain for the aural qualities of verse ("no me interesa lo auditivo del verso") in favor of a strophic approach not only brings him closer to Whitman but also distances him from the *modernistas*, who had an eminently melopoetic—to borrow Pound's term—conception of poetry. Borges already had pitched his poetry against Darío and his followers in his first book (the original foreword to *Fervor de Buenos Aires*—which Borges also expurgated from later editions—explicitly goes up against the lyrical sumptuousness of the *modernistas*[137]), but there he also admits to

---

[136] Borges writes in his autobiography: "*Luna de enfrente* . . . was published in 1925 and is a kind of riot of sham local color. Among its tomfooleries were the spelling of my name in the nineteenth-century Chilean fashion as 'Jorje' (it was a halfhearted attempt at phonetic spelling); the spelling of the Spanish 'and' as 'i' instead of 'y' (our greatest writer, Sarmiento, had done the same, trying to be as un-Spanish as he could); and the omission of the final 'd' in words like 'autoridá' and 'ciudá.' In later editions, I dropped the worst poems, pruned the eccentricities, and, successively— through several reprints—revised and toned down the verses" (AN 74).

[137] In the foreword, Borges rants against the poet who is a "burnisher of feeblenessess [who] clutters his writing with gold and jewels" ["abrillantador de endebleces [que] abarrota su escritura de oro y de joyas"], and denounces the "shiny, decoratively

his strong tendency to hendecasyllables.[138] His second book, *Luna de enfrente*, is formally more innovative, beginning with the fact that it is almost entirely made up by free "strophic" verses.[139] The prominence *Leaves of Grass* gained in Borges's poetry in only two years is quite striking, and it is Whitman's overwhelming presence that makes *Luna de enfrente* such a radical book in the context of *modernismo*. Ten years later, even though the clash between the *modernistas* and the "new generation" had subdued, free verse (and Whitman's legitimizing role regarding it) was still, according to Borges, a matter for debate in Argentina: "Since [Sandburg's poetry] does not rhyme, those who oppose him decree it is not poetry; those in favor strike back quoting the exemplary names of Heinrich Heine, King David, and Walt Whitman. It is pointless to revisit this discussion, still ongoing in Buenos Aires, despite having become utterly obsolete in other countries . . ." ["Como [la poesía de Sandburg] no tiene rimas, los opositores resuelven que no es

---

visual lyric poetry bequeathed to us by don Luis de Góngora through his executor, Rubén [Darío]" ["lírica decorativamente visual y lustrosa que nos legó don Luis de Góngora por intermedio de su albacea Rubén [Darío]" (4)]. In addition to their euphonic ambition, the *modernistas* were defined by their fetishistic obsession with decadent atmospheres, exotic settings, and sumptuary trinkets—or, at least, this was what the young generation (Borges's) charged them with. Borges, in brief, feels a profound antipathy toward "this time, whose lyrical poetry is usually diluted in almost-musical rhythms or degrades itself to mere heaps of gaudy trinkets. There is no hatred in my statement, only justified rancor" ["esta época, cuya lírica suele desleírse en casi-músicas de ritmo o rebajarse a pila de baratijas vistosas. No hay odio en lo que asevero, sino rencor justificado"]. For a more detailed exposition of Borges's assessment of the *modernista* tradition, see his two first books of essays, particularly the devastating review of Lugones's *Romancero* in *El tamaño de mi esperanza* (95–97). Later on, however, Borges will constantly strive to undo his disdain for the *modernistas* and insist in numerous occasions on the importance of this poetic movement, not only for himself but also to the history of literature as a whole. The turning point may well be the long inscription to *El hacedor*, dedicated to Leopoldo Lugones. After this public (and posthumous) reconciliation, there are countless vindications of Darío, Lugones, and *modernismo* in general, which Borges (hyperbolically, no doubt) now considered to be his main influence.

[138] "Because hendecasyllables are a substantial part of our oral tradition, I wrote many verses in that meter" ["La tradición oral que además posee en nosotros el endecasílabo, me hizo abundar en versos de esa medida" (4)].

[139] There are a few exceptions, like "El general Quiroga va en coche al muere," "Tarde cualquiera," and "Versos del catorce," in alexandrines and "Soleares," in octosyllables.

poesía. Los partidarios contraatacan, invocando los nombres y los ejemplos de Enrique Heine, del rey David y de Walt Whitman. Inútil repetir la discusión, todavía corriente en Buenos Aires, aunque ya del todo arrumbada en otros países del mundo . . ." (TC 34)]. This last quotation shows the importance of the debate—it is not a mere formal preference that is in question, it is the very definition of poetry that is at stake (unmetered, blank verses do not seem to amount to poetry, according to the old guard).[140] Borges, however, featured poems in free verse in all of his books (except for *Para las seis cuerdas* [1965], entirely in octosyllables). Over 40 years after *Luna de enfrente*, in his foreword to *Obra Poética 1923–1967*, Borges reexamined his turn to free verse in a critical fashion: "As every young poet, I once believed free verse to be easier than regular meters. Now I know that it is in fact harder, and that writing free verse requires the intimate conviction of certain pages by Carl Sandburg or his father, Whitman" ["Como todo joven poeta, yo creí alguna vez que el verso libre es más fácil que el regular; ahora sé que es más arduo y que requiere la íntima convicción de ciertas páginas de Carl Sandburg o de su padre, Whitman" (OP 12)].[141] Given that, as we shall see, free verse (and other devices inherited from Whitman) plays an even more prominent role in late Borges, one cannot help but think that here he is saying (in a veiled way, through Whitman) that he has now mastered the form that he had somewhat recklessly handled in his youth.

A detailed analysis of Whitman's presence in Borges's late poetry and a comparative close reading of both authors would constitute

---

[140] For more on the problem of free verse and rhyme, see Borges's *Leopoldo Lugones*, particularly the chapter "Lugones, poeta" (OCC 470–84). Later, in that same book, Borges revisits this issue and cites "the Holy Scripture, Shakespeare, William Blake, Heine and Whitman" to demonstrate that "rhyme is less vital than Leopoldo Lugones believes" ["la rima es menos imprescindible de lo que cree Leopoldo Lugones" (OCC 498)]. *Borges on Writing* also has enlightening passages, where he addresses the main differences between working within inherited forms (like the sonnet) and writing free verse (70–71).

[141] In his 1967 lectures at Harvard, Borges insisted on the fact that "unless you take the precaution of being Walt Whitman or Carl Sandburg, then free verse is more difficult" (CV 110). In his seminar at Columbia University, he underscored the dangers of considering free verse an easier option. "I committed that mistake when I published my first volume, *Fervor de Buenos Aires*, way back in 1923. I wrote that book in free verse—I had read my Whitman, of course—because I thought it was easier. Now I know it is far more difficult" (BW 71).

a book-length project in itself—to begin with, there is a matter of sheer volume: the number of Borges's late poems where the trace of *Leaves of Grass* is unmistakable and simply impossible to ignore is overwhelming. However, certain decisive intersections ought to be noted and expanded on. In the prologue to *Elogio de la sombra*, Borges explicitly refers to the formal imprint Whitman left in his verses: "I once aspired to the vast breathing of the psalms[142] or of Walt Whitman. After many years I realize (not without a bit of sadness) that I just went from one classical meter to another—the alexandrine, the hendecasyllable, the heptasyllable" (SP 267) ["Yo anhelé alguna vez la vasta respiración de los psalmos o de Walt Whitman; al cabo de los años compruebo, no sin melancolía, que me he limitado a alternar algunos metros clásicos: el alejandrino, el endecasílabo, el heptasílabo" (OC 976)]. This "psalmodic breath" that Borges aspired to certainly makes itself felt through *Elogio de la sombra*. Furthermore, and in keeping with the religious tone, this book contains a poem called "Fragments from an Apocryphal Gospel" ["Fragmentos de un evangelio apócrifo"]. Here, Borges seems to have taken Whitman's project literally: "I will write the evangel-poem of comrades and of love," reads one of the last verses of section 6 of "Starting from Paumanok" (Whitman 179). The mystical fervor that Borges sometimes appropriates in subtle ways from Whitman appears here unbridled, and the joyous, self-reliant optimism that increases throughout the poem to conclude in an ecstatic tautology ("Happy are the happy" (SP 295) ["Felices los felices" (OC 1012)]) also harks back to *Leaves of Grass*. But "Buenos Aires" may be the most Whitmanesque poem in the collection, with its reverberations (24 of the 27 extremely long verses of the poem begin with "It is" ["Es"], reminiscent of certain passages of *Leaves of Grass*, such as sections 15, 31, and 33 of "Song of Myself"), its enumerations (which will be discussed momentarily), its invocation to the reader, and (as has been pointed out regarding other poems) the tension between the intimate and the transcendental, the anecdotal and the mystical. In fact, this poem contains a self-referential moment where this influence becomes explicit: the "I" of the poem mentions "Whitman, whose great echo hopefully will resound through this page" ["Whitman, cuyo gran eco ojalá resuene

---

[142] Borges links Whitman's enumerations to "los salmos de la Escritura" in his essay "El otro Whitman" (OC 206).

en esta página" (OC 1010)]. The foreword to *El otro, el mismo*, expresses the same hope: "the reader will note the influence . . . , I hope, of Walt Whitman" (SP 149) ["se advertirá la influencia . . . , así lo espero . . . , de Whitman" (OC 858)].[143] In fact, two of the poems that most clearly show Whitman's influence in this book are the "*Two English Poems*," written in 1934 (and omitted in Penguin's *Selected Poems*). Part of the second poem reads:

> . . . I offer you lean streets, desperate sunsets, the moon of the ragged suburbs . . .
> I offer you my ancestors, my dead men, the ghosts that living men have honoured in marble . . .
> I offer you whatever insight my books may hold, whatever manliness or humour my life.
> I offer you the loyalty of a man who has never been loyal.
> I offer you that kernel of myself that I have saved, somehow—the central heart that deals not in words, traffics not with dreams, and is untouched by time, by joy, by adversities.[144]
> I offer you the memory of a yellow rose seen at sunset, years before you were born.
> I offer you explanations of yourself, theories about yourself, authentic and surprising news of yourself.
> I can give you my loneliness, my darkness, the hunger of my heart; I am trying to bribe you with uncertainty, with danger, with defeat. (OC 861–62)

Parallels with Whitman of course abound. The litany-like, incantatory repetitions; the invocation of a second person; the long syntactic periods and the extended rhythmical patterns; the sense of an absolute present while conjuring up a legendary past; the absolute confidence of the first person shaped, somehow, as

---

[143] And indeed, Whitman *is* present in several poems of this 1964 book (see, for instance, "Insomnio," "To a Minor Poet of the Greek Anthology" ["A un poeta menor de la antología"], "A Page to Commemorate Colonel Suárez, Victor at Junín" ["Página para recordar al coronel Suárez, vencedor en Junín"], "Matthew XXV: 30" ["Mateo, XXV, 30"], "Fragmento," "España," "Elegy" ["Elegía"], "Otro poema de los dones," and "Ode Written in 1966" ["Oda escrita en 1966"].

[144] This verse appears in the inscription of *Historia Universal de la Infamia*, published a year after these verses were written: "I inscribe this book to S. D.: English, Innumerable and an Angel. Also: I offer her that kernel of myself that I have saved, somehow [etc.]" (OC 293).

self-effacing modesty. One of many examples is the final stanza of "Song of the Open Road":

> Camerado, I give you my hand!
> I give you my love more precious than money,
> I give you myself before preaching or law;
> Will you give me yourself? will you come travel with me?
> Shall we stick by each other as long as we live? (Whitman 307)

Structurally, the resemblances are obvious, but the poems are also quite similar in tone. In both, there is a dissonance between the humility implicit in every offering or gift and a certain arrogance of the giver (Borges: "I offer you explanations of yourself, theories about yourself, authentic and surprising news of yourself"; Whitman: "I give you my love more precious than money"). The gift does not seem to come from below (as if to ingratiate or appeal to the receiver) but handed down from above. Another similarity is the strong first person revealing itself (by offering itself up) in its utmost purity, in its absolute essence (Borges: "I offer you that kernel of myself that I have saved, somehow—the central heart that deals not in words, traffics not with dreams, and is untouched by time, by joy, by adversities"; Whitman: "I give you myself before preaching or law"). Here, as in many other poems, certain fundamental aspects of Whitman's poetry are combined with some of Borges's classical obsessions and themes, such as the suburbs and the margins; his genealogical fetishism; his self-deprecation; the fascination with treason and betrayal; the rose; the color yellow—the only one that could pierce through his blindness. However, the result is an oddly confessional poem. Whitman's devices were, for Borges, often reduced to mere gimmicks—an excuse for surprising and sometimes whimsical lists, a way of legitimizing his compulsion to repeat (particularly in his later poems), a means to escape the hendecasyllabic or alexandrine constraints to which he often confined himself. But in his "Two English Poems," Borges is more open (almost sensual) than in most of his poems, showing carnal desires and exposing his "hungry heart" (OC 861). "I am the poet of the body,/and I am the poet of the soul," wrote Whitman (46), who did not shy from "bathing [his] songs in Sex" (264). And this may be the greatest difference between these authors—in his writings Borges was quite prudish. It goes without saying that these two poems are, of course, quite bashful compared to Whitman's least explicit passages. Still, in relative terms, there is an urge in these poems hard to find elsewhere in Borges's poetry. Perhaps the English language offers here protection to that first person that preferred (in his poems in Spanish) to present himself as a chaste librarian wandering through dark bookshelves and labyrinths, musing on the kabbalah and dreaming of tigers, and seldom (if ever) talked about "the hunger of his heart."[145]

Whitman's impact is not restricted only to Borges's poetry. His prose also bears the imprint of *Leaves of Grass*. A minor but decisive trait of Borges's short stories and essays is the presence of enumerations. "Minor" because it is certainly not one of those crucial operations through which Borges helped reshape twentieth-century literature (like, for example, the distortion of the boundaries between discursive genres, the use of erudition as a narrative device,

---

[145] Borges was not quite turned on by Whitman's eroticism. He discussed the matter in several occasions. In fact, he always mistrusted Whitman's sensual side, arguing (in consonance with his theory of the two Whitmans) that it was an imposture, one of the attributes of the main character of *Leaves of Grass*. In "Nota sobre Walt Whitman," he points out that there was a great difference between Whitman, the man, and Whitman, the character in the poems. "The former was *chaste*, reserved and rather taciturn, while the latter was effusive and *orgiastic*" ["Éste fue *casto*, reservado y más bien taciturno; aquél efusivo y *orgiástico*" (OC 250; my emphasis)]. As we have seen, for Borges, Whitman was, first and foremost, what he called a "civic" poet— opposed to Poe and his decadent followers. "[Whitman] can be looked at in two ways: there is his civic side—the fact that one is aware of the crowds, great cities, and America—and there is also an intimate element, though we can't be sure whether it is genuine or not" (C 58). This suspiciously "intimate" side of Whitman always made Borges uncomfortable, as did anything related to physical drives. As Bioy Casares wrote in his journal, "Borges fosters a secret rancor against obscenity" ["en Borges gravita un secreto rencor contra la obscenidad" (Bioy 803)]. Furthermore, Bioy thought that Borges felt "a puritanical antipathy toward the subject of love" (1238). Borges even told his friend: "I am in favor of censorship. When there is censorship, literature becomes more virile, subtler, more composed" ["Yo soy partidario de la censura. Cuando hay censura, la literatura es más viril, más sutil, más decantada" (802)]. He also told Bioy "censorship stimulates writers. Without censorship we would not have Gibbon's or Voltaire's irony" ["la censura es un estímulo para los escritores. Sin censura no existiría la ironía de Gibbon ni la de Voltaire"]. Since Bioy's response was silence, Borges asked: "Do you think this idea is too perfidious?" ["¿Creés que es una idea demasiado pérfida?" (Bioy 1202)]. In 1960, the newspaper *La Razón* printed Borges's response to Judge Woolsey's ruling that removed the federal ban that had been placed on Joyce's *Ulysses* on grounds of its "obscenity." Strangely enough, Borges, who truly appreciated the book, made an absurd apology

or the destabilization of highly petrified notions through which we understand literature itself—such as "author" and "reader").

But some of these crucial operations (such as, for instance, the impression of overwhelming erudition[146]) are created precisely through enumerations—virtually any of his essays provides examples of how lists of names and texts contribute to create an immediate sense of superhuman learnedness. Furthermore, enumerations are one of Borges's most characteristic procedures, almost a trademark of his fiction and one of his obsessions as a critic.[147] Some essays contain the most beautiful and Lautréamont-like juxtapositions (the lovely and surprising lists in "El idioma analítico de John Wilkins"), others start out by enumerating texts and authors at breakneck speed as if to overwhelm the reader (an example completely at random—this, I insist is Borges's *modus operandi*—is the essay "La metáfora," whose first page mentions Snorri Sturluson, Bendetto Croce, Leopoldo Lugones, Charles Baudelaire, Middleton Murry, Lycophron, and the *I Ching* [OC 382]). Some stories are made

---

of censorship. Halfway through his response, Borges declares: "When it comes to eroticism, there is no poet, as far as I know, more explicit than Whitman. His best verses are not the rawest ones, but those in which he resorts to metaphor, following a millenary and instinctive poetic tradition" ["En materia erótica no hay, que yo sepa, poeta más explícito que Whitman: sus mejores versos no son los más crudos sino aquellos en que recurre a metáforas, según la milenaria e instintiva tradición poética" (TR III: 251–52)]. And in his *Introduction to North American Literature* he writes: "[*Leaves of Grass*] included poems whose erotic frankness (which may remain unmatched) scandalized many readers. During a long walk, Emerson tried to dissuade him. Years later, Whitman would admit the arguments of his friend were irrefutable, but was not swayed by them" ["[*Leaves of Grass*] incluyó composiciones cuya franqueza erótica, acaso jamás igualada, escandalizó a no pocos lectores. En una larga caminata, Emerson quiso disuadirlo; Whitman admitiría años después que las razones de su amigo eran irrefutables, pero no se dejó convencer" (43)]. Borges did see, however, that, for Whitman, "there is something sacred in physical love" ["en el amor físico hay algo sagrado" (OCC 852)].

[146] See Molloy (153–63) and Pauls (91; 96; 141–56).

[147] A good synopsis of Borges's own take on the matter can be found in "On Literary Description" ["Sobre la descripción literaria"], a 1942 article published in *Sur*. Here, enumerations are, for the most part, considered an objectionable procedure. There are, however, a few exceptions: the psalms, Blake, and, of course, Whitman (SNF 234; PJLB 171). Numerous critics have paid particular attention to the different implications of Borges's enumerations. See, for instance, Michel Foucault (xv–xviii), Alan Pauls (144–45), Sarlo (131–34), and, especially, Sylvia Molloy's brilliant analysis on Borges's "heterogeneous enumerations" (165–79).

up mostly by enumerations (about half of "Pierre Menard, autor del Quijote" is an apocryphal bibliography); others derive a great deal of their effect from partial lists that could go on and on into infinitude (the absolutely irrational numeric "method" in "Funes, el memorioso," where the decimal system is replaced by whimsical correspondences: 7,013 becomes "Máximo Pérez," 7,014 becomes "The Railway," and so on—the endless progression gives the reader a good sense of the accuracy of Funes's memory, which is precisely the story's point). There are, to be sure, more examples. However, I will to pause on just one of these many enumerations, the famous one in which "Borges," the narrator of "El Aleph" tries to describe what he sees when he looks into the Aleph, a circle no larger than a quarter that condenses the entire universe. The narrator is aware that he faces an impossible task:

> The central problem—*the enumeration, even partial enumeration, of infinity*—is irresolvable. In that unbounded moment, I saw millions of delightful and horrible acts; none amazed me so much as the fact that all occupied the same point, without superposition and without transparency. What my eyes saw was simultaneous; what I shall write is successive, because language is successive. Something of it, though, I will capture. (CF 282–83; my emphasis)

> [El problema central es irresoluble: *la enumeración, siquiera parcial, de un conjunto infinito.* En ese instante gigantesco, he visto millones de actos deleitables o atroces; ninguno me asombró como el hecho de que todos ocuparan el mismo punto, sin superposición y sin transparencia. Lo que vieron mis ojos fue simultáneo: lo que transcribiré sucesivo, porque el lenguaje lo es. Algo, sin embargo, recogeré. (OC 625)]

Then the narrator offers his necessarily partial account of what he saw:

> I saw the populous sea, I saw dawn and dusk, I saw the multitudes of the Americas, I saw a silvery spider web at the center of a black pyramid, I saw a broken labyrinth (it was London), I saw endless eyes, all very close, studying themselves in me as though in a mirror, I saw all the mirrors on the planet (and none of them reflecting me), I saw in a rear courtyard on Soler Street the same

tiles I'd seen twenty years before in the entryway of a house in
Fray Bentos, I saw clusters of grapes, snow, tobacco, veins of
metal, water vapor, I saw convex equatorial deserts and their
every grain of sand, I saw a woman in Inverness whom I shall
never forget, I saw her violent hair, her haughty body, I saw a
breast cancer, I saw a circle of dry soil within a sidewalk where
there had once been a tree, I saw a country house in Adrogué,
I saw a copy of the first English translation of Pliny (Philemon
Holland's), I saw every letter of every page at once (as a boy,
I would be astounded that the letters in a closed book didn't
get all scrambled up together overnight), I saw simultaneous
night and day, I saw a sunset in Queretaro that seemed to reflect
the color of a rose in Bengal, I saw my bedroom (with no one in
it), I saw in a study in Alkmaar a terrestrial globe placed between
two mirrors that multiplied it endlessly, I saw horses with wind-
whipped manes on a beach in the Caspian Sea at dawn, I saw the
delicate bones of a hand, I saw the survivors of a battle sending
postcards, I saw a Tarot card in a shop window in Mirzapur, I
saw the oblique shadows of ferns on the floor of a greenhouse,
I saw tigers, pistons, bisons, tides, and armies, I saw all the ants
on earth, I saw a Persian astrolabe, I saw in a desk drawer (and
the handwriting made me tremble) obscene, incredible, detailed
letters that Beatriz had sent Carlos Argentino, I saw a beloved
monument in Chacarita, I saw the horrendous remains of what
had once, deliciously, been Beatriz Viterbo, saw the circulation
of my dark blood, I saw the coils and springs of love and the
alterations of death, I saw the Aleph from everywhere at once,
I saw the earth in the Aleph, and the Aleph once more in the
earth and the earth in the Aleph, I saw my face and my viscera,
I saw your face, and I felt dizzy, and I wept, because my eyes
had seen that secret, hypothetical object whose name has been
usurped by men but which no man has ever truly looked upon:
the inconceivable universe. (CF 283–84)[148]

[Vi el populoso mar, vi el alba y la tarde, vi las muchedumbres
de América, vi una plateada telaraña en el centro de una negra

---

[148] I have introduced one main alteration in the translation: Hurley omits the subject
from each one of these repetitions (in other words, he writes "I saw" the first time,
and then merely "saw"). I have reintroduced the grammatical subject for reasons
that will become apparent.

pirámide, vi un laberinto roto (era Londres), vi interminables
ojos inmediatos escrutándose en mí como en un espejo, vi todos
los espejos del planeta y ninguno me reflejó, vi en un traspatio
de la calle Soler las mismas baldosas que hace treinta años vi
en el zaguán de una casa en Fray Bentos, vi racimos, nieve,
tabaco, vetas de metal, vapor de agua, vi convexos desiertos
ecuatoriales y cada uno de sus granos de arena, vi en Inverness
a una mujer que no olvidaré, vi la violenta cabellera, el altivo
cuerpo, vi un cáncer en el pecho, vi un círculo de tierra seca
en una vereda, donde antes hubo un árbol, vi una quinta de
Adrogué, un ejemplar de la primera versión inglesa de Plinio,
la de Philemon Holland, vi a un tiempo cada letra de cada
página (de chico yo solía maravillarme de que las letras de un
volumen cerrado no se mezclaran y perdieran en el decurso de
la noche), vi la noche y el día contemporáneo, vi un poniente en
Querétaro que parecía reflejar el color de una rosa en Bengala,
vi mi dormitorio sin nadie, vi en un gabinete de Alkmaar un
globo terráqueo entre dos espejos que lo multiplicaban sin fin, vi
caballos de crin arremolinada, en una playa del Mar Caspio en el
alba, vi la delicada osatura de una mano, vi a los sobrevivientes
de una batalla, enviando tarjetas postales, vi en un escaparate de
Mirzapur una baraja española, vi las sombras oblicuas de unos
helechos en el suelo de un invernáculo, vi tigres, émbolos, bisontes,
marejadas y ejércitos, vi todas las hormigas que hay en la tierra,
vi un astrolabio persa, vi en un cajón del escritorio (y la letra me
hizo temblar) cartas obscenas, increíbles, precisas, que Beatriz
había dirigido a Carlos Argentino, vi un adorado monumento en
la Chacarita, vi la reliquia atroz de lo que deliciosamente había
sido Beatriz Viterbo, vi la circulación de mi oscura sangre, vi el
engranaje del amor y la modificación de la muerte, vi el Aleph,
desde todos los puntos, vi en el Aleph la tierra, y en la tierra otra
vez el Aleph y en el Alpeh la tierra, vi mi cara y mis vísceras, vi
tu cara, y sentí vértigo y lloré, porque mis ojos habían visto ese
objeto secreto y conjetural, cuyo nombre usurpan los hombres,
pero que ningún hombre ha mirado: el inconcebible universo.
(OC 625–26)]

Despite being in prose, the passage, scanned by the repeated "I
saw," retains Whitman's cadence, his psalmodic repetitions, and
his universal yet intimate range. In fact, Whitman faced the same

difficulty the narrator of the Aleph had to deal with: "the central problem—*the enumeration, even partial enumeration, of infinity*—is irresolvable." From his very first collection of essays, Borges was obsessed with the titanic nature of Whitman's enterprise: to depict the world, the *entire* world. This immediately conjures up the problem of enumerations. Consider, for instance, the enumeration, beginning in section 4 of "Salut au Monde." Despite having been considerably abridged, this is a rather long quotation, but its length is relevant to the argument:

What do you see Walt Whitman?
. . .
I see a great round wonder rolling through space,
I see diminute farms, hamlets, ruins, graveyards, jails, factories, palaces, hovels, huts of barbarians, tents of nomads upon the surface,
I see the shaded part on one side where the sleepers are sleeping, and the sunlit part on the other side,
I see the curious rapid change of the light and shade,
I see distant lands, as real and near to the inhabitants of them as my land is to me.

I see plenteous waters,
I see mountain peaks, I see the sierras of Andes where they range,
I see plainly the Himalayas, Chian Shahs, Altays, Ghauts,
I see the giant pinnacles of Elbruz, Kazbek, Bazardjusi,
I see the Styrian Alps, and the Karnac Alps,
I see the Pyrenees, Balks, Carpathians, and to the north the Dofrafields, and off at sea mount Hecla,
I see Vesuvius and Etna, the mountains of the Moon, and the Red mountains of Madagascar,
I see the Lybian, Arabian, and Asiatic deserts,
I see huge dreadful Arctic and Antarctic icebergs,
I see the superior oceans and the inferior ones, the Atlantic and Pacific, the sea of Mexico, the Brazilian sea, and the sea of Peru,
The waters of Hindustan, the China sea, and the gulf of Guinea,
The Japan waters, the beautiful bay of Nagasaki land-lock'd in its mountains,

The spread of the Baltic, Caspian, Bothnia, the British shores,
  and the bay of Biscay,
The clear-sunn'd Mediterranean, and from one to another of its
  islands,
The White sea, and the sea around Greenland.

. . .

5

I see the tracks of the railroads of the earth,
I see them in Great Britain, I see them in Europe,
I see them in Asia and in Africa.

I see the electric telegraphs of the earth,
I see the filaments of the news of the wars, deaths, losses, gains,
  passions, of my race.

I see the long river-stripes of the earth,
I see the Amazon and the Paraguay,
I see the four great rivers of China, the Amour, the Yellow River,
  the Yiang-tse, and the Pearl,
I see where the Seine flows, and where the Danube, the Loire, the
  Rhone, and the Guadalquiver flow,
I see the windings of the Volga, the Dnieper, the Oder,
I see the Tuscan going down the Arno, and the Venetian along
  the Po,
I see the Greek seaman sailing out of Egina bay.

6

I see the site of the old empire of Assyria, and that of Persia, and
  that of India,
I see the falling of the Ganges over the high rim of Saukara.

I see the place of the idea of the Deity incarnated by avatars in
  human forms,
I see the spots of the successions of priests on the earth, oracles,
  sacrificers, brahmins, sabians, llamas, monks, muftis,
  exhorters,

I see where druids walk'd the groves of Mona, I see the mistletoe
  and vervain,
I see the temples of the deaths of the bodies of Gods, I see the
  old signifiers.

I see Christ eating the bread of his last supper in the midst of
  youths and old persons,
I see where the strong divine young man the Hercules toil'd
  faithfully and long and then died,
I see the place of the innocent rich life and hapless fate of the
  beautiful nocturnal son, the full-limb'd Bacchus,
I see Kneph, blooming, drest in blue, with the crown of feathers
  on his head

. . .

7

I see the battle-fields of the earth, grass grows upon them and
  blossoms and corn,
I see the tracks of ancient and modern expeditions.

I see the nameless masonries, venerable messages of the unknown
  events, heroes, records of the earth.

I see the places of the sagas,
I see pine-trees and fir-trees torn by northern blasts,
I see granite bowlders and cliffs, I see green meadows and lakes,
I see the burial-cairns of Scandinavian warriors,

. . .

I see the steppes of Asia,
I see the tumuli of Mongolia, I see the tents of Kalmucks and
  Baskirs,
I see the nomadic tribes with herds of oxen and cows,
I see the table-lands notch'd with ravines, I see the jungles and
  deserts,
I see the camel, the wild steed, the bustard, the fat-tail'd sheep,the
  antelope, and the burrowing wolf.

I see the highlands of Abyssinia,
I see flocks of goats feeding, and see the fig-tree, tamarind, date,
And see fields of teff-wheat and places of verdure and gold.

I see the Brazilian vaquero,
I see the Bolivian ascending mount Sorata,
I see the Wacho crossing the plains, I see the incomparable rider
    of horses with his lasso on his arm,
I see over the pampas the pursuit of wild cattle for their hides.

8

I see the regions of snow and ice,
I see the sharp-eyed Samoiede and the Finn,
I see the seal-seeker in his boat poising his lance,
I see the Siberian on his slight-built sledge drawn by dogs,
I see the porpoise-hunters, I see the whale-crews of the south
    Pacific and the north Atlantic,
I see the cliffs, glaciers, torrents, valleys, of Switzerland—I mark
    the long winters and the isolation.

I see the cities of the earth and make myself at random a part of
    them

. . .

10

I see all the menials of the earth, laboring,
I see all the prisoners in the prisons,
I see the defective human bodies of the earth,
The blind, the deaf and dumb, idiots, hunchbacks, lunatics,
The pirates, thieves, betrayers, murderers, slave-makers of the
    earth,
The helpless infants, and the helpless old men and women.

I see male and female everywhere,
I see the serene brotherhood of philosophs,
I see the constructiveness of my race,
I see the results of the perseverance and industry of my race,

I see ranks, colors, barbarisms, civilizations, I go among them, I
    mix indiscriminately,
And I salute all the inhabitants of the earth. (289–94)

It is hardly necessary to point out the resemblances between
Borges's and Whitman's fragments. Not only are both enumerations
structurally alike but they also leap between the small and the
monumental, between the loudness of the battlefront and the silence
of plants and minerals. They both jump between continents and
cultures, and they both surprise with moments of cold compassion
(Borges sees a breast tumor; Whitman sees the "defective human
bodies of the earth"). Although in prose, this passage may constitute
one of Borges's most profoundly Whitman-like moments. And it is
interesting to find (following the reverse affiliations that he proposes
in "Kafka and his Precursors") that, conversely, Whitman's poem
has a Borgesian premise. In "The Aleph," the narrator says: "What
my eyes saw was simultaneous; what I shall write is successive." And
in "Salut au Monde" there is a similar tension between simultaneity
and consecutiveness: "I see the shaded part on one side where the
sleepers are sleeping, and the sunlit part on the other side." Borges
even writes in "El Aleph": "I saw simultaneous night and day." This
speaks of a ubiquitous gaze that sees it all without superimpositions.
It would not be excessive to state that Whitman's verse (paraphrased
in Borges's story) is the kernel of "The Aleph."

Borges knew "Salut au Monde" well. Although he did not include
this poem in his 1969 abridged translation of *Leaves of Grass*,[149]
he quotes the first verse of section 3 ("What do you hear Walt
Whitman" [288]) in his "Nota sobre Walt Whitman" (OC 253). He
also makes a veiled allusion to the poem in his 1958 conference on
Whitman (TR III: 44), and in 1966, in a brief essay on the gaucho,
Borges even translates a few verses from section 7:

Veo al gaucho [Whitman writes "wacho"] atravesando los
    llanos,
Veo al incomparable jinete de caballos tirando el lazo,
Veo sobre las pampas la persecución de la hacienda brava.
    (TR III: 127)

---

[149] As Borges's mother interfered with or even took over his prose translations, it
seems Borges's first wife, Elsa Astete, may not have been the most reliable amanuensis
during the work on *Leaves of Grass* (see Bioy 1261).

Lastly, the poem resurfaces in his 1967 *Introduction to North American Literature*, where he focuses on the crucial passage describing the simultaneous (not overlapping) perception of the world: "'Salut au Monde' contains a total vision of the planet, with simultaneous day and night. Among the many things he sees, are our plains" ["'Salut au Monde' encierra una visión total del planeta, con el día y la noche simultáneos. Entre las muchas cosas que ve, está nuestra llanura" (ILN 45)].

However, not all enumerations in "The Aleph" or in *Leaves of Grass* are as successful. In fact, at the very core of Borges's story, there is a discussion about the pertinence and the effectiveness of enumerations. It should be remembered that, after all, "The Aleph" is a story about two rival poets, Carlos Argentino Daneri and the narrator, "Borges." Daneri is writing a bombastic poem that comprises the entire world, aided, precisely, by the Aleph he found, by sheer chance, in his basement: "[Daneri's] poem was entitled *The Earth*; it was a description of the planet" (CF 276) ["El poema [de Daneri] se titulaba *La Tierra*; tratábase de una descripción del planeta" (OC 619)]. To do so, Daneri writes a poem listing every single thing on the planet. Thus, Daneri's enterprise is not too different from the way in which Borges often characterizes Whitman's ambitious poem:

> Whitman was the first Atlas . . . to carry the world on his shoulders. He believed that it sufficed to *enumerate* things by their names to immediately convey how unique and surprising they are. This is why, in his poems, along with beautiful rhetoric, *there are garrulous strings of words—often traced from geography and history textbooks—ignited by erect exclamation marks, and merely resembling the highest enthusiasms.*

> [Whitman fue el primer Atlante que . . . se echó el mundo a cuestas. Creía que bastaba *enumerar* los nombres de las cosas, para que enseguida se tantease lo únicas y sorprendentes que son. Por eso, en sus poemas, junto a mucha bella retórica, *se enristran gárrulas series de palabras, a veces calcos de textos de Geografía o de Historia, que inflaman enhiestos signos de admiración, y remedan altísimos entusiasmos.* (I 100; my emphasis)]

The long quote from "Salut au Monde" justifies part of Borges's invective—Whitman's world seems, at times, to be a mere *coup d'encyclopedie.*[150] This is why the entire highlighted passage in Borges's last quote ("there are garrulous strings of words—often traced from geography and history textbooks . . . ") also could work as an accurate description of Daneri's poetry. Daneri "proposed to versify the entire planet" (CF 277) ["se proponía versificar toda la redondez del planeta" (620)]. The tone, the lexical choices, and the rhetoric that Borges attributes to Whitman could easily be applied to the samples of Daneri's work we find in "The Aleph." It should be added that Borges's harsh criticism is not merely a rash, youthful diatribe. Over 30 years later, he repeats the same judgment in very similar terms: "Whitman could have claimed that his subject was the universe. Some of his poems seem to have been inspired by maps, or by loose chapters from a geography textbook, but everything is brought to life by him" ["Whitman pudo haber dicho que su tema era el universo; hay poemas suyos que parecen inspirados por mapas, o por los capítulos de un manual de geografía, pero todo está vivificado por él" (OC III: 43–44)]. There is, of course, a main difference between the 1925 and the 1958 quotations—in the latter, Whitman "seems" to have been inspired by schoolbooks, but he manages to bring his material to life ("todo está vivificado por él"), and this is where Daneri fails.

The uses and misuses of enumerations are at the center of this problem. In the foreword to *El oro de los tigres*, Borges referrers to Whitman, "[whose] careful enumerations do not always rise above a kind of crude cataloguing" (SP 305) ["sus deliberadas enumeraciones [que] no siempre pasan de catálogos insensibles" (OC 1081)].[151] In other words, his enumerations sometimes manage to conjure up something larger than the mere sum of the items they list, but in other instances are little more, according to Borges, than mere inventories. But what makes these poetic enumerations fail or succeed? Borges gives two answers. In a few notes appended to *La cifra* (1981), he comments on "Aquel," one of the poems included in the book: "This poem, as almost all others, abuses chaotic enumerations. About this figure (so felicitously abundant in Walt

---

[150] Borges uses this expression to demolish "Le jaguar," a poem by Leconte de Lisle— in which, coincidentally, Leconte de Lisle offers, like Whitman, a description of the pampas (Bioy Casares 892).

[151] See also Bioy 1158.

Whitman) I can only say that it should *resemble* chaos and disorder but must be, intimately, a cosmos, an order." ["Esta composición, como casi todas las otras, abusa de la enumeración caótica. De esta figura, que con tanta felicidad prodigó Walt Whitman, sólo puedo decir que debe *parecer* un caos, un desorden, y ser íntimamente un cosmos y un orden" (OC III: 340; my emphasis)]. The semblance of chaos ruled by a secret order (in other words, an *apparent* disorder) is what distinguishes a successful "chaotic enumeration" from a mere mess. Daneri's grandiloquent and ridiculous poem, with its detailed descriptions of a few hectares in Queensland, a gas station in Veracruz, and some Turkish baths near Brighton (among many, many other things), is nothing more than a "pedantic farrago" (CF 279) ["fárrago pedantesco" (OC 621)], "a poem that seemed to draw out to infinity the possibilities of cacophony and chaos" (CF 280) ["un poema que parecía dilatar hasta lo infinito las posibilidades de la cacofonía y del caos" (OC 622)]. There is nothing illusory in Daneri's chaos—it is *truly* chaotic. In Whitman's successful poems, however, there is a subjacent order. And in this "secret order" Whitman and Poe converge: for both of them chaos is only apparent. There is meaning and sense underlying what seems a mere disorder. For Poe, the epiphany resides in the ultimate legibility of the world; for Whitman the epiphany resides in the ability to see that chaos is just a complex cosmos. Each in his own way, however, seems to aspire to the same orderly universality.

Borges's second answer to the question of successful chaotic enumerations is an elaboration of the first in subtler terms. In "El otro Whitman," Borges writes: "enumeration is one of the oldest poetical procedures [and] its essential merit does not reside in length, but in the delicate verbal attunement, the 'sympathies and differences' between words. Walt Whitman did not ignore this" ["la enumeración es uno de los procedimientos poéticos más antiguos [y] su mérito esencial no es la longitud, sino el delicado ajuste verbal, las 'simpatías y diferencias' de las palabras. No lo ignoró Walt Whitman" (OC 206)]. A poetic enumeration is not simply a juxtaposition of words: terms should illuminate each other, make each other vibrate, as if by harmonic sympathy. Daneri's hilariously awful (and seemingly endless) poem, needless to say, does not meet this requirement. Yet, his long, universal poem is related and indebted to Whitman—if *Leaves of Grass* begins with "Song of Myself," Daneri's opening section is titled "Augural Song, Prologurial Song, or simply Prologue-Song" (CF 276) ["Canto Augural, Canto Prologal o simplemente Canto-Prólogo" (OC 619)].[152] Daneri is a bad Whitman, a false Whitman in the same way his Aleph is also suspected to be a fake: "I believe that [Daneri's] Aleph was a fake Aleph" (CF 285) ["yo creo que el Aleph [de Daneri] era un falso Aleph" (OC 627)].

If Daneri is a bad Whitman, "Borges," the narrator, is a better Whitman. Comparing the enumerations in "The Aleph" and "Salut au Monde," Borges's constellation, made up of the surprising union of disparate (and often small, almost invisible things), makes Whitman seem as if he were, in effect, indulging in referential gluttony, obediently listing rivers, deserts, and volcanoes. As Borges wrote in 1925, "in Whitman breathed a miraculous thankfulness for the dense, palpable and colorful quality of things. But Walt's thankfulness was fulfilled with the enumeration of objects in an overcrowded heap that is the world" ["en Whitman alentó milagrosa gratitud por lo macizas y palpables y de colores tan variados que son las cosas. Pero la gratitud de Walt se satisfizo con la enumeración de los objetos cuyo hacinamiento es el mundo" (I 134)]. Of course, saying that Borges "out-Whitmans" Whitman himself implies accepting Borges's own parameters to begin with. And according to them, "Salut au Monde" does seem like a mere catalogue that just jumbles geographic accidents in a heap, hoping this *rudis indigestaque moles* will, somehow, conjure up an impression of the entire world. Borges's passage, on the other hand, accomplishes a rhetorical feat by producing a hyperbolic effect through litotes. The more partial, minute, and insignificant the things Borges enumerates (veins of metal, a tumor, the delicate bones of a hand, the shadow of a fern), the more vividly the impression of infinitude, endlessness, and totality is conveyed—much more so than by enumerating the oceans and the religions the world (although occasionally Whitman also has a few of those almost secret moments—as when he sees the mistletoe and the vervain).

---

[152] Hurley's translation reads "Canto" where I have opted for "Song." "Canto" is, of course, a good translation (and the immediate association it produces between Carlos Daneri and Ezra Pound surely would have delighted Borges). "Song," however, has a clear and loud Whitmanesque resonance that "Canto" does not.

"Salut au Monde" is not the only poem with Aleph-like enumerations in *Leaves of Grass*. Quite early on in "Song of Myself," there is a passage containing a long, heterogeneous list of objects and scenes. Among other things, the first person "hero" (that plural alter ego of Whitman's) sees a baby in its cradle, a suicide sprawling on the floor, the tires of carts, snowballs, and excited crowds (Whitman 33–35). There is a longer enumeration a few pages later that tries to capture the variety of the new nation: a contralto singing in an organ loft, a lunatic being taken to an asylum, a printer chewing tobacco, malformed limbs tied to the anatomist's table, a squaw selling moccasins, a critic squinting in a gallery, a child being baptized, a lady posing for a daguerreotype, the president holding a cabinet meeting, torches shining in the Chattahoochee nights, sleeping cities, sleeping fields—these are only some of the scenes enumerated (39–42). Compared with "Salut au Monde," this particular list seems closer to "Borges," the narrator of "The Aleph," than to Daneri, his archrival. And confirming Borges's notion that the first person in *Leaves of Grass* stands for a collective, choral hero, Whitman's extensive enumeration ends: "And these [the various people conjured up over the last three pages] one and all tend inward to me, and I tend outward to them,/And such as it is to be of these more or less I am" (42). This triggers a new, lengthy enumeration, where this first person defines himself as a plural subject (young and old; foolish and wise; maternal and paternal; a novice and an expert; southerner and northerner, at home on iceboats, at home in Texas; etc.). And here is where Borges and Whitman truly converge: for Whitman, the democrat, each individual is, in fact, the realization of this boundless vastness, an immensity where all things coexist in equal terms (and paradoxically enough, the exaltation of this democratic subject leads to its dissolution—to a limitless, undetermined, being who is not subjected to anything because it is everything). Every single person is a "Kosmos," "Who, constructing the house of himself or herself, not for a day but for all time, sees races, eras, dates, generations,/The past, the future, dwelling there, like space, inseparable together" (517). Each one of us, Whitman claims, is an Aleph. Thus, through radically different paths (one author sings an ode to democracy, the other is absorbed in seemingly abstract speculations), Borges and Whitman arrive at similar conclusions:

there is no difference between "the same and the other," to quote the title of Borges's book, because we are, as he said of Shakespeare, "everything and nothing." History and eternity once again come together: material processes and metaphysics lead to the same free, infinite subject.

AFTERWORD

El vaivén

In a 1967 interview published by *The Paris Review*, Borges recalls the different words for "knife" used in the slums during his youth. "One of the names . . . that has been quite lost—it's a pity—was *el vaivén*, the 'come and go.' In the word *come-and-go (making gesture)* you see the flash of the knife, the sudden flash" (140).[153] This flashing "back and forth" is an adequate metaphor for Borges's movements. Not only is there a constant *vaivén* between the historical and the eternal but one could also say that he stabs one with the other. Furthermore, the *come-and-go* also is a fitting image because it does not imply a point of departure or destination. In fact, in a true *vaivén*, if the swinging is kept up long enough, "to" and "fro" eventually become interchangeable until finally the distinction between "coming" and "going" is rendered irrelevant. And so it is with Borges, who never follows one single direction. He refuses to subordinate the eternal to the historical, and denies that transcendental issues are necessarily conditioned by contextual determinations. Reciprocally, he consistently avoids the idea that eternity trumps history. He rather prefers, as I have shown, to "come and go" from one into the other and illuminate the trajectory between them with a "sudden flash."

This chiasmic *vaivén* also illustrates Borges's traffic with the United States, not only because the term's origin refers to the

---

[153] I am grateful to Jason Fulford for having pointed this passage out to me and for having given my talk on Borges at *The Mushroom Collection* (Amsterdam, 9 December 2010) the felicitous title I now give this afterword.

history of infamy and violence so pervasive in both hemispheres but also because he never follows one single direction when connecting north and south. Borges did not receive passively the influence from the north, but he also intervened, as we shall see momentarily, in the literary tradition of the United States.

Poe and Whitman illustrate the *vaivén* of the historical and eternal quite clearly and even provide an adequate coda to "Political Theology," the first section of this book. As we have seen in references scattered throughout his entire work, Borges assigns a set of values to both writers—Poe is the decadent formalist and Whitman the civic-minded prophet. But Borges "comes and goes" from one end to the other, thus toppling the opposition he himself had established. Poe, the forerunner of symbolism and *l'art pour l'art*, provides Borges with the foundation of his more political fiction. The idea of an order superimposed onto the disorder of the world; the notion that reality might be administered; the suspicion that there is something ciphered in our everyday life—these are all thoughts that largely derive from the supposedly decadent Poe. On the other hand, Whitman, the singer of American democracy, whom Borges repeatedly defines as the founding father of social poetry, turns out to be a fundamental reference for the transcendental aspirations of Borges's literature. From *Leaves of Grass* he derives, for instance, the notion of an infinite subject (that also challenges authorial authority) or the attempt at representing the boundless universe. This same *vaivén* can be seen within Borges's own work. His political literature tends to flow toward metaphysics, and his philosophical fiction has a strong political undercurrent. And in each case, a "sudden flash" lights up these back-and-forth trajectories, illuminating aspects that would have remained in the dark in a unidirectional stream.

In this book I have only considered Borges's appropriation and manipulation of US literature. However, this is not a one-way street going north to south. It is hard to think of another Latin American writer who was so decisively influenced by North American literature and then became *himself* a crucial inspiration for that tradition. To trace Borges's impact in the United States would constitute a book-length project in itself, but at least I would like to point out the main lines along which the second part of this *vaivén* could be considered.

From the 1960s on, generations of North American writers have been deeply influenced by Borges. As David Foster Wallace wrote in the *New York Times* in 2004:

I was lucky enough to discover Borges as a child, but only because I happened to find *Labyrinths*, an early English-language collection of his most famous stories, on my father's bookshelves in 1974. I believed that the book was there only because of my parents' unusually fine taste and discernment—which verily they do possess—but what I didn't know was that by 1974 *Labyrinths* was also on tens of thousands of other homes' shelves in this country, that Borges had actually been a sensation on the order of Tolkien and Gibran among hip readers of the previous decade.

In the 1960s and early 1970s, Borges seems to have become omnipresent: in 1965, John Updike published a detailed article on Borges (and his scholars); in 1967, John Barth put him up as a model in his influential essay "The Literature of Exhaustion," and paid homage to him in his short stories (*Lost in the Funhouse* vi–vii; 1–2); in that same year, John Ashbery reviewed Borges's *Personal Anthology* for the *New York Times*; in 1969, William Gass wrote lucidly about his work in *The New York Review of Books*; in 1970, the *New Yorker* published his autobiography; on repeated occasions, Nabokov confessed that he was one of the few contemporary authors he read and liked (44; 80; 102; 184);[154] in 1973, Pynchon mentioned him in *Gravity's Rainbow*;[155] and before all of them, in 1964, Paul de Man hailed him as "A Modern Master."

---

[154] Borges, it should be said, did not reciprocate. He refused to comment on the censorship of *Lolita* claiming he had not read the book. He did, however, read the first pages of Nabokov's novel together with Bioy in 1959. Borges's reaction: "I would be frightened to read that book. It must really hurt a writer. One would believe it is impossible to write in any other way. You immediately find yourself monkeying for the reader, juggling, producing your top hat and your rabbit, becoming a busy Fregoli [a famous turn-of-the-century vaudeville performer, impersonator and quick-change]" ["Yo tendría miedo de leer ese libro. Ha de hacer mucho mal a un escritor. Uno advierte que es imposible escribir de otro modo. En seguida, estás haciendo monerías ante el lector, sos un malabarista, sacás tu galera y tu conejo, sos un atareado Fregoli" (Bioy 533)].

[155] Pynchon's may be the most Borgesian homage possible. He included in *Gravity's Rainbow* an apocryphal poem by Borges, dedicated to Graciela Imago Portales, an

In fact, deconstruction itself, by insisting that "there is nothing outside the text," seemed to be in synch with Borges, who imagined the universe to be a library. The rise of deconstruction (very much in spite of Borges himself, who loathed and scorned academic jargons, obscure neologisms, and the abuse of morphological licenses), offered a perfect launching platform for Borges's literature—or, rather, a *certain side* of Borges's literature: those self-referential, bibliocentric, erudite, palimpsests, and his texts that (yes) deconstructed literary tradition. Another crucial factor for Borges's surging popularity in the United States was the increasing importance of comparative literature departments—the American Comparative Literature Association, for instance, was founded in 1960. An author who could conjugate Confucius, Pascal, Schopenhauer, and Chesterton in one single sentence was the dream of any comparatist. In short, Borges became relevant in the United States not only because of his literary merits but also because there was a climate that was particularly receptive to his literature. This interest is still very much alive in the United States. In the late 1990s, Penguin published, in three vast volumes, Borges's *Collected Fiction*, his *Selected Poems*, and his *Selected Non-Fictions*, and in 2010, five more compilations of his texts.

This part of the *vaivén*, Borges's influence in the United States, deserves a book of its own. What was his impact on two of the most important native genres of the United States, detective fiction and science fiction? His ties with the former are quite clear, but his impact on the latter requires more consideration.[156] How did Borges change the flow of the triangulation between North America, Latin America, and Paris? For instance, his effect on the French scene, mainly the *nouveau roman*, and how this may have ricocheted in the United States could prove a productive line of research (likewise, it could be fruitful to examine how certain American authors bearing Borges's influence affected French literature). What is Borges's role in North American "postmodern" (a term I distrust and dislike but use for economy's sake) fiction, with its self-referentiality, its insistence

---

avatar of sorts of Beatriz Viterbo (the woman "Borges," the narrator of "The Aleph," is in love with). The two quoted verses read: "El laberinto de tu incertidumbre/Me trama con la disquietante luna" (Pynchon 383). The tone and the words chosen (every single noun, in fact—and the verb "tramar") are all Borgesian clichés.

[156] It is not irrelevant that William Gibson wrote the foreword to the new edition of *Labyrinths*.

on the unstable and quasifictional quality of reality, its pastiches, its intertextual obsession, its distortion of the boundaries between high and low culture, its vast paranoid plots, and its fixation with media?[157] These, of course, are all obviously (though, needless to say, not exclusively) Borgesian traits, and it would be valuable to map their presence in North American literature. By this, I do not mean one should highlight, again, the obvious connections between, say, Pynchon's Trystero organization and similar conspiracies in Borges, or stress, once more, how such texts as "Pierre Menard, Author of the *Quixote*," "Tlön, Uqbar, Orbis Tertius," or "Kafka and His Precursors" question basic categories employed in literary studies and aesthetics in general. This has already been sufficiently done, even by some of the authors who recognize Borges's influence, such as John Barth in his brilliant essay. Instead, the study proposed here should pay attention to those texts that have usually been neglected (and in some cases even remain untranslated) in the United States, many of which deal with seemingly "local" (i.e. Argentine) issues. But we have seen that "local" is an elusive and deceitful category in Borges, and that even some the writings that seem to fall into this category are informed both by philosophical concerns and influences from other traditions—among them, conspicuously, North American literature. Even though the influence of these overlooked texts certainly is mediated in the United States, it may prove to be quite significant, since, as I have shown, there is an indirect line from Borges' hoodlums to his metaphysical conspiracies so popular in North America.

If Borges's constant *vaivén* (between politics and metaphysics, between north and south, between the small and the vast, between the universal and the insular) proves something, it is that literature's relationship to borders of any kind is an arbitrary imposition. Nationalities, hemispheres, periods, schools, genres, and themes are artificial boundaries that may be useful for taxonomical purposes, but literature, as Borges repeatedly shows, should be read and written with a joyful disregard for these classifications.

---

[157] In Borges, this fixation was just reduced to one medium—the book. But Borges's bibliophilia takes other shapes and includes other media in his North American heirs. Consider, for instance, "the Entertainment" in David Foster Wallace's *Infinite Jest*, that video that the viewer literally cannot stop watching until he dies. "The Entertainment" is reminiscent not only of Borges's book-obsessed characters (many of whom are even doing life sentences in libraries) but also of "The Zahir," an object that, once seen, is impossible to forget; gradually its image takes over all thoughts, until the "viewer" goes insane and dies.

NOTE ON THE TRANSLATIONS

Despite Borges's popularity and relevance in the English-speaking world, many of his texts remain untranslated. Where no English reference is provided after a quoted passage, the translation is mine. If a certain syntactical vertigo is felt when reading the translations of his early texts, both in prose and in verse, it is because they intend to mimic the peculiar sentence structure and word choices of young Borges—part Latin, part seventeenth-century Spanish, part oral *criollo*, and completely baroque.

For convenience's sake, the three-volume Penguin edition has been used throughout this book, whenever possible. I have silently emended a few mistakes and curbed certain licenses ("matear," for instance, was translated as "to slaughter" instead of "to drink mate"; "traducir" as "reproduce"; "planeta" as "our own terraqueous orb"; "comprender" as "to understand," when the context clearly required "to include"; etc.). When the departure from the translation is drastic, I have added "edited" or "cf.," in case the reader wants to refer to the published English version. I have also ignored the italics that proliferate in *Collected Fictions* and are absent in Borges's originals.

ABBREVIATIONS OF BORGES'S TITLES

OI	*Other Inquisitions*
OP	*Obra poética 1923–1967*
P	*Prólogos*
S	*Siete conversaciones* (with F. Sorrentino)
SN	*Seven Nights*
PJLB	*Páginas de Jorge Luis Borges seleccionadas por el autor*
SNF	*Selected Non-Fictions*
SP	*Selected Poems*
TE	*El tamaño de mi esperanza*
TC	*Textos cautivos*
TR	*Textos recobrados* (3 vols)

WORKS CITED

Aristotle. *Metaphysics*. Trans. Hugh Tredennick. 2 vols. Cambridge: Loeb Classical Library, 1933. Print.

Asbury, Herbert. *The Gangs of New York: An Informal History of the Underworld*. New York: Vintage, 2008.

Ashbery, John. "A Game with Shifting Mirrors." *The New York Times*. 16 Apr. 1967, Books sec. Web.

Barrenechea, Ana María. *Borges, the Labyrinth Maker*. Ed. and trans. Robert Lima. New York: New York University Press, 1965. Print.

Barth, John. *Lost in the Funhouse*. New York: Anchor Books, 1988. Print.

— "The Literature of Exhaustion." *The Atlantic Monthly*. Aug. 1967: 29–34. Print.

Baudelaire, Charles. *Baudelaire on Poe. Critical Papers*. Ed. and trans. Louis Boe Hyslop and Francis Edward Hyslop, Jr. State College: Bald Eagle Press, 1952. Print.

Berkeley, George. *Principles of Human Knowledge. Three Dialogues*. Oxford: Oxford University Press, 1996. Print.

Bioy Casares, Adolfo. *Borges*. Ed. Daniel Martino. Buenos Aires: Destino, 2006. Print.

Boethius, Anicius Manlius Severinus. Trans. Hugh Fraser Stewart, Edward Kennard Rand, Standley Jim Tester. Cambridge: Loeb Classical Library, 1997. Print.

Borges, Jorge Luis. "Autobiographical Notes." *The New Yorker*. 19 Sept. 1970: 40–99. Print.

— *Borges en Sur*. Buenos Aires: Emecé, 1999. Print.

— *Borges, oral*. Buenos Aires: Emecé, 1979. Print.

— *Borges on Writing*. Ed. Norman Thomas di Giovanni, Daniel Halpern, and Frank MacShane. Hopewell: The Echo Press, 1994.

— *Collected Fictions*. Trans. Andrew Hurley. New York: Penguin, 1998. Print.

— *Conversations*. Ed. Richard Brugin. Jackson: University Press of Mississippi, 1998. Print.

— *Cuaderno San Martín*. Buenos Aires: Proa, 1929. Print.

— *Dreamtigers*. Trans. Mildred Boyer, Harold Morland. Intr. Miguel Enguídanos. Austin: Texas University Press, 2008. Print.

—*El idioma de los argentinos*. Madrid: Alianza, 2008 [1928]. Print.

—*El tamaño de mi esperanza*. Buenos Aires: Seix Barral, 1993 [1926]. Print.

—*Fervor de Buenos Aires*. Buenos Aires: [self-published], 1923.

—*Historia universal de la infamia*. Buenos Aires, Megáfono: 1935. Print.

—*Inquisiciones*. Buenos Aires: Seix Barral 1993 [1925]. Print.

—*Introducción a la literatura norteamericana*. Madrid: Alianza 2006 [1967]. Print.

—"Jorge Luis Borges. The Art of Fiction XXXIX." Interview by Ronald Christ. *The Paris Review* 40 (1967): 116–64. Print.

—"Journey Without an End." *Time Magazine*. 24 Mar. 1967, Books sec. Web.

—*Labyrinths*. Ed. and trans. Donald Yates, James Edward Irby. New York: New Directions, 2007. Print.

—*Leopoldo Lugones*. Buenos Aires: Emecé, 1998 [1955]. Print.

—*Luna de enfrente*. Buenos Aires: Proa, 1925. Print.

—*Obra poética 1923–1967*. Buenos Aires: Emecé, 1969. Print.

—*Obras completas*. Buenos Aires: Emecé, 1974. Print.

—*Obras completas*, vol. II (1975–1985). Buenos Aires: Emecé, 1994. Print.

—*Obras completas*, vol. IV (1975–1988). Buenos Aires: Emecé, 2009. Print.

—*Obras, reseñas y traducciones inéditas. Diario* Crítica *1933–1934*. Buenos Aires: Atlántida, 1999. Print.

—*Other Inquisitions*. Trans. Ruth L. C. Simms. New York: Washington Square Press, 1966.

—*Páginas de Jorge Luis Borges seleccionadas por el autor*. Buenos Aires: Celtia, 1983. Print.

—*Prólogos*. Buenos Aires: Torres Agüero, 1975. Print.

—*Selected Non-Fictions*. Ed. Eliot Weinberger. Trans. Esther Allen, Suzanne Jill Levine, and Eliot Weinberger. New York: Penguin, 1999. Print.

—*Selected Poems*. Ed. Alexander Coleman. Trans. Willis Barnstone et al. New York: Penguin, 1999. Print.

—*Seven Nights*. Trans. Eliot Weinberger. New York: New Directions, 2009. Print.

—*Textos cautivos. Ensayos y reseñas en* El Hogar. Ed. Enrique Sacerio-Garí and Emir Rodríguez Monegal. Barcelona: Tusquets, 1986. Print.

—*Textos recobrados (1956–1986)*. Buenos Aires: Emecé, 2007.

—*This Craft of Verse*. Cambridge: Harvard University Press, 2000. Print.

Borges, Jorge Luis, et al. *Obras completas en colaboración*. Buenos Aires: Emecé, 1979. Print.

Borges, Jorge Luis and Osvaldo Ferrari. *En Diálogo I*. Buenos Aires: Sudamericana, 1998. Print.

Borges, Jorge Luis and Esther Zemborain. *Introducción a la literatura norteamericana*. Madrid: Alianza, 2006. Print.

Borges, Jorge Luis and Fernando Sorrentino. *Siete conversaciones*. Buenos Aires: Casa Pardo, 1973. Print.

Brooks, Van Wyck. *The Flowering of New England*. Boston: E. P. Dutton, 1940. Print.

Darío, Rubén. *Los Raros*. Barcelona: Maucci, 1905. Print.

—*Poesías Completas. Edición del centenario (1867–1967)*. Ed. Alfonso Méndez Plancarte. Madrid: Aguilar, 1967. Print.

—*Textos socio-políticos*. Ed. Jorge Eduardo Arellano. Managua: Biblioteca Nacional, 1980. Print.

de Man, Paul. "A Modern Master." *The New York Review of Books*. 19 Nov. 1964. Web.

DeVoto, Bernard. *Mark Twain's America & Mark Twain at Work*. Boston: Houghton Mifflin, 1967. Print.

Descartes, René. *The Philosophical Writings of Descartes*, vol. II. Trans. John Cottingham, Robert Stoothoff, Dugald Murdoch. Cambridge: Cambridge University Press, 1999. Print.

Disch, Thomas. *The Dreams Our Stuff Is Made Of*. New York: Free Press, 2000. Print.

Faulkner, William. *Novels 1936–1940*. New York: Library of America, 1990. Print.

—*Las palmeras salvajes*. Trans. Jorge Luis Borges. Buenos Aires: Sudamericana, 1981. Print.

Foster Wallace, David. "Borges on the Couch." *The New York Times*. 7 Nov. 2004. Web.

—*Infinite Jest*. New York: Little, Brown, and Company, 1996. Print.

Foucault, Michel. *The Order of Things. An Archaeology of the Human Sciences*. New York: Vintage, 1994. Print.

Gass, William. "Imaginary Borges." *The New York Review of Books*. 20 Nov. 1969. Web.

Lafforgue, Jorge and Jorge B. Rivera. *Asesinos de papel. Ensayos sobre narrativa policial*. Buenos Aires: Colihue, 1996. Print.

Leibniz, Gottfried Wilhelm. *Monadology*. Trans. Nicholas Rescher. Pittsburgh: University of Pittsburgh Press, 1991. Print.

Ludmer, Josefina. "The Gaucho Genre." *The Cambridge History of Latin American Literature 1. Discovery to Modernismo*. Cambridge: Cambridge University Press, 2004. Print.

Lugones, Leopoldo. *La torre de Casandra*. Buenos Aires: Atlántida, 1919. Print.

—*Mi beligerancia*. Buenos Aires: Otero y García, 1917. Print.

Martí, José. *Obras Completas*, vol. II. Ed. Jorge Quintana. Caracas: Litho Tip, 1964. Print.

Melville, Herman. *Pierre; Israel Potter; The Piazza Tales; The Confidence Man;* etc. New York: Library of America, 1984. Print.

Molloy, Sylvia. *Las letras de Borges*. Rosario: Beatriz Viterbo, 2000. Print.

Nabokov, Vladimir. *Strong Opinions*. New York: Vintage, 1990. Print.

Noble Burns, Walter. *The Saga of Billy the Kid*. New York: Penguin, 1946. Print.

Parish, Helen Rand. *Bartolomé de las Casas: The Only Way*. New York: Paulist Press, 1992. Print.

Pauls, Alan. *El factor Borges*. Buenos Aires: Fondo de Cultura Económica, 2000. Print.

Peirce, Charles Sanders. *Writings of Charles S. Peirce. A Chronological Edition*. Ed. Christian J. W. Kloesel. 6 vols. Bloomington: Indiana University Press, 1993. Print.

Piglia, Ricardo. *El último lector*. Barcelona: Anagrama, 2006. Print.

—*Formas Breves*. Barcelona: Anagrama, 2000. Print.

Plato. *Cratylus, Parmenides, Greater Hippias, Lesser Hippias*. Trans. Harlod North Fowler. Cambridge: Loeb Classical Library, 1926. Print.

—*Republic. Books 6–10*. Trans. Paul Shorey. Cambridge: Loeb Classical Library, 1930. Print.

Poe, Edgar Allan. *Essays and Reviews*. New York: Library of America, 1984a. Print.

—*Poetry and Tales*. New York: Library of America, 1984b. Print.

Pynchon, Thomas. *Gravity's Rainbow*. New York: Viking, 1973. Print.

Rodó, José Enrique. *Ariel*. Ed. Ángel Rama. Caracas: Ayacucho, 1985. Print.

—*Ariel*. Trans. Frederic Jesup Stimson. Boston: Houghton Mifflin, 1922. Print.

Sarlo, Beatriz. *Borges, un escritor en las orillas*. Buenos Aires: Ariel, 1998. Print.

Schmitt, Carl. *Political Theology: Four Chapters on the Concept of Sovereignty*. Trans. George Schwab. Chicago: University of Chicago Press, 2006. Print.

Schopenhauer, Arthur. *The World as Will and Representation*, vol. II. Trans. Eric F. J. Payne. New York: Dover, 1966.

Todo Borges y . . . La vida, la muerte, las mujeres. Gente. 27 Jan. 1977. Buenos Aires, 1977.

Twain, Mark. *The Innocents Abroad. Roughing It*. New York: Library of America, 1984. Print.

Updike, John. "The Author as a Librarian." *The New Yorker*. 30 Oct. 1965: 223–46. Print.

Whitman, Walt. *Hojas de Hierba*. Trans. Jorge Luis. Borges. Buenos Aires: Juárez, 1969.

—*Poetry and Prose*. New York: Library of America, 1996. Print.

Williamson, Edwin. *Borges, a Life*. New York: Viking, 2004. Print.

ACKNOWLEDGMENTS

One of the greatest joys of writing this book was meeting Haaris Naqvi, a fantastic editor who has become a dear friend. Thank you, Haaris, for your support, your patience, and our many conversations.

Friends and colleagues read the manuscript at different stages and gave invaluable notes. My deepest gratitude to Ronald Briggs, Graciela Montaldo, Wendy Steiner, and (very especially) Paul Stasi, who all contributed to make this a better book.

I am indebted to the works and the words of my teachers, in particular Sylvia Molloy and Jorge Panesi.

Many thanks to Alexandra Levenberg at the Wylie Agency and Sarah Laskin at Penguin for their help with copyright-related issues.

I would also like to thank Emilio Weinschelbaum for his legal advice and Jason Fulford for his eye.

Dear Anne, dear Elsa . . .

INDEX

CPSIA information can be obtained
at www.ICGtesting.com
Printed in the USA
LVHW052325270319
612129LV00009B/101